With fond memories
of the ambience and
charm of "Clifford"
Green's View.

Keith Thebes

Oct. 1981

CLASS

with drawings by Timothy Jaques

CLASS

JILLY COOPER

Alfred A. Knopf   *New York*   1981

Copyright © 1981 by Jilly Cooper
Illustrations © 1979 by Timothy Jaques

All rights reserved under International and Pan-American Copyright Conventions. Published in the United States by Alfred A. Knopf, Inc., New York, Distributed by Random House, Inc., New York. Originally published in Great Britain by Eyre Methuen Ltd, London. Copyright © 1979, 1980 by Jilly Cooper.

Grateful acknowledgment is made to the following for permission to reprint from previously published material:

Chappell Music Company: Excerpt from "The Stately Homes of England" by Noël Coward. Copyright 1938 by Chappell & Co., Ltd. Copyright Renewed. International Copyright Secured. All Rights Reserved. Used by Permission.

Alfred A. Knopf, Inc.: Excerpt from *Cautionary Verses* by Hilaire Belloc. Published 1941 by Alfred A. Knopf, Inc. Used by permission.

John Murray (Publishers) Ltd.: Excerpt from *Collected Poems* by John Betjeman, John Murray (Publishers) Ltd., and Houghton Mifflin Co.

Taplinger Publishing Co., Inc.: Excerpt from an essay by John Mortimer in *My Oxford, My Cambridge,* ed. by Ann Thwaite and Ronald Hayman (Taplinger, 1979). Copyright © 1977 by Robson Books. Printed by permission.

Random House, Inc.: Excerpt from *The Pursuit of Love: A Novel,* by Nancy Mitford. Copyright 1945 and renewed 1973 by Nancy Mitford Rodd. Reprinted by permission of Random House, Inc.

Walker and Company, Inc.: Excerpt from *Call for the Dead* by John le Carré. Copyright © 1961 by Victor Gollancz Limited. Used with permission from the publisher, Walker and Company.

Library of Congress Cataloging in Publication Data

Cooper, Jilly.   Class: a view from middle England.

Bibliography: p.
1. Social classes—Great Britain. I. Title
HN400.S6c67   1981   305.5'0941   80–2718
ISBN 0–304–51414–9   AACR2

To Geoffrey Strachan, with love and gratitude

Contents

Contents

Acknowledgements

I am extremely grateful to the people who have helped me with this book. They include Andrew Batute, formerly manager of the French Revolution Restaurant in London, John Challis, formerly manager of Lloyds Bank, Sloane Square, Michael Davey, funeral director, Mathias of Putney, Brian Edgington, headmaster of Roehampton Church School, Brian Holley, divisional careers officer of ILEA (Putney), Heather Jenner, Auriol Murray, of Nannies (Kensington), Renate Olins, of the Marriage Guidance Council, Charles Plouviez, chairman of Everetts Advertising.

I also owe an eternal debt to my friends, who have entered into the spirit of things, and come up with numerous suggestions, some serious, some less so.

Five other people made it possible for me to complete the book. I would therefore particularly like to thank my agent, George Greenfield, who has always shown such enthusiasm for the project, Beryl Hill, who typed out the manuscript and who miraculously managed to decipher my appalling handwriting, and my resident major domo, Maxine Green, who retyped chunks of the manuscript when I couldn't read my own corrections and kept up my spirits throughout those dark, desperate weeks before the book was finally handed in. The lion's share of my gratitude, however, must go to my publisher, Geoffrey Strachan, who has been amazingly kind, patient and encouraging over a long long period, when he must have despaired that the manuscript would ever see the light of day, and finally to my husband, Leo, whose humour and powers of observation have been a constant source of inspiration, and who remained good-tempered, even when the whole house, including our bedroom, disappeared under a sea of papers and reference books.

Dramatis Personae

The people you will meet in this book are:

THE STOW-CRATS

HARRY STOW-CRAT, *a member of the aristocracy*

CAROLINE STOW-CRAT, *his wife*

GEORGIE STOW-CRAT, *his son*

FIONA STOW-CRAT, *his daughter*

and numerous other children, both regularly and irregularly conceived

SNIPE, *a black Labrador*

THE UPWARDS

GIDEON UPWARD, *a member of the upper middle classes*

SAMANTHA UPWARD, *his wife*

ZACHARIAS UPWARD, *his son*

THALIA UPWARD, *his daughter*

COLONEL UPWARD, *Gideon's father*

MRS. UPWARD, *Gideon's mother*

Dramatis Personae

THE DEFINITELY-DISGUSTINGS

MR. DEFINITELY-DISGUSTING, *a member of the working classes*

MRS. DEFINITELY-DISGUSTING, *his wife*

DIVE DEFINITELY-DISGUSTING, *his son*

SHARON DEFINITELY-DISGUSTING, *his daughter*

and numerous other children

THE NOUVEAU-RICHARDS

MR. NOUVEAU-RICHARDS, *a millionaire*

MRS. NOUVEAU-RICHARDS, *his wife*

JASON NOUVEAU-RICHARDS, *his son*

TRACEY-DIANE NOUVEAU-RICHARDS, *his daughter*

Introduction

About three years ago, when I rather tentatively suggested writing a book about the English class system, people drew away from me in horror.

"But that's all finished," they said nervously, "no one gives a hoot any more. Look at the young." They sounded as if I were intending to produce a standard work on coprophilia or child molesting. It was plain that since the egalitarian shake-up of the sixties and early seventies, class as a subject had become the ultimate obscenity.

Three years of research later, I can assure you that the class system is alive and well and living in people's minds in England. There may have been an enormous shift of wealth between rich and poor. Every day Jack may be getting nearer his master financially, but social stratification remains incredibly resistant to change. It takes more than jeans and a taste in pop music to make even the young all one class. In fact after a period of enforced egalitarianism in the sixties when pop culture and socialism were in the ascendant, a whole new generation have appeared, who want the boundaries re-defined. This perhaps explains the popularity of such books as *The English Gentleman* by Douglas Sutherland and the recently published *U and Non-U Revisited,* edited by Richard Buckle.

Added to this is the colossal success of all those television serials and plays about the higher classes: *Upstairs Downstairs, Flambards* and *Rebecca,* not to mention the royal sagas. The fact that they have all been set in the past—because nostalgia excuses everything, enabling people to click their tongues over the outdated inequalities, yet guiltily enjoy the sense of hierarchy—must mean a hankering after some kind of social pecking order.

What struck me, however, as soon as I started the book, was the enormity of the task I had taken on. It was like trying to catalogue the sea. For the whole system, despite its stratification, is constantly forming and re-forming like coral. "Even a small town like Swansea," said Wynford Vaughan Thomas, "has as many layers as an onion, and each one of them reduces you to tears." To me, the system seemed more like a huge striped rugger shirt that had run in the wash, with each layer blurring into the next one, and snobbery being the fiercest at the place where one stripe merged with another.

I found, too, that people were incredibly difficult to pin down into classes. John went to a more famous boarding school than Thomas, who has a better job than Charles, who's got smarter friends than Harry, who lives in an older house with a bigger garden than David, who's got an uncle who's an earl, but whose children go to a state school. Who is then the gentleman?

A social class can perhaps be rather cumbersomely described as a group of people with certain common traits: descent, education, accent, similarity of occupation, wealth, moral attitudes, friends, hobbies, accommodation; and with generally similar ideas, and forms of behaviour, who meet each other on equal terms, and regard themselves as belonging to one group. A single failure to conform would certainly not exclude you from membership. Your own class tend to be people you feel comfortable with—"one of our sort"—as you do when you are wearing old flat shoes, rather than teetering round on precarious five-inch heels. Aristocrats, for example, feel at home with aristocrats: "The nice thing about the House of Lords," explained one peer, "is that you can have incredibly snobbish conversations without feeling snobbish. Yesterday I admired a chap's wife's diamonds: he said they came from Napoleon's sword, and before then from Louis XIV."

When people consider they are not of the same class it becomes more complicated. "Who knows," wrote Montaigne, "when I play with my cat, whether I do not make her more sport than she makes me." In the same way, quite often you think you are being terribly democratic talking to some vulgar little man at a party, while he at the same time is thinking how decent he is wasting time on someone as socially insignificant as you.

Another charge has been levelled at me. What right, I am asked, have *I* to hold forth on the subject of the English class system? Most people who have tried in the past—Nancy Mitford or Christopher Sykes—have been members of the upper classes. The answer is no right at all; all I can claim is a passionate interest in the subject, and that, being ashamedly middle-class, I am more equidistant from the bottom and the top.

It is perhaps important to point out here the various definitions of class which have been in use in England over the past twenty-five years. Principally there is the Census: *Classification of Occupations,* which is published every ten years or so (the latest was in 1970), which classifies everyone by the occupation of the head of the household of which they are members, irrespective of all other circumstances. This arbitrary categorisation is used as "gospel" in most social surveys. Secondly there is "U and Non-U," a distinction invented by Professor Alan S. C. Ross in an essay first published in a learned Finnish periodical in 1954, which divided English people into "U" (upper class) and "Non-U" (non-upper class), mostly by the way they spoke and by the vocabulary they used. And finally comes the classification: "A, B, C1 and C2, D and E," which is used by the media and by advertising, but which is basically the same as that of the Census.

What follows is the idiosyncratic view of someone bred in Yorkshire who has lived most of her life in London. If it reveals an obsessive interest in the classes nearest to the one in which I put myself, showing envy of those just above me in the hierarchy, scorn of those just below, and a slightly romanticized fantasy of those most far from my own experience, this will surely only confirm what is most typical of attitudes to class. An interest in social mobility and an obsession with class are, after all, thoroughly middle-class characteristics.

It might therefore be appropriate here to digress a little to explain what my own origins are. My paternal grandfather was a wool merchant, but my paternal grandmother's family were a bit grander. They owned newspapers, and were distinguished Whig M.P.s for Leeds during the nineteenth century. My mother's side were mostly in the church, her father being Canon of Heaton near Bradford. Her mother was a beauty. Both sides had lived in the West Riding of Yorkshire for generations. They were very very strait-laced; to this day there has never been a divorce in the family.

My father went to Rugby, then to Cambridge, where he got a First in two years, and then into the army. After getting married, he found he wasn't making enough money, and joined Fords, and he and my mother moved somewhat reluctantly to Hornchurch, where I was born. At the beginning of the Second World War he was called up, and became one of the army's youngest brigadiers. After the war, we moved back to Yorkshire, living first in a large Victorian house. I was eight, and I think for the first time became aware of class distinction. Our next-door neighbour was a newly rich and very ostentatious wool manufacturer, of whose sybaritic existence my parents disapproved. One morning he asked me over to his house. I had a heavenly time, spending all morning playing the pianola, of which my mother also disapproved—too much pleasure for too little effort—and eating a whole eight-ounce bar of black-market milk chocolate, which, just after the war, seemed like stumbling on Aladdin's cave. When I got home I was sick. I was aware that it served me right both for slumming and for over-indulgence.

Soon after that we moved into the Hall at Ilkley, a splendid Georgian house with a long drive, seven acres of fields for my ponies, a swimming pool and tennis and squash courts. From then on we lived an elitist existence: tennis parties with cucumber sandwiches, large dances and fetes in the garden. I enjoyed playing little Miss Muck tremendously. I had a photograph of the house taken from the bottom of the drive on my dressing-table at school, and all my little school friends, and later my boy-friends, were very impressed when they came to stay.

My brother, however, still had doubts about our life-style: it was too bourgeois, too predictable and restricted, he thought. One wet afternoon, I remember him striding up and down the drawing-room, going on and on and on about our boring middle-class existence.

Suddenly my mother, who'd been trying to read a detective story, looked over her spectacles, and said with very gentle reproof: "Upper-middle-class, darling."

Occasionally we were taken down a peg by a socialist aunt who thought we'd all got too big for our boots. One day my mother was describing some people who lived near York as being a very "old" family.

"Whadja mean old?" snorted my aunt. "All families are old."

On another occasion when my mother was grumbling about her char not turning up, my aunt suddenly snapped: "And who are you to demand service?" Both became family catch-phrases.

There were very few eligible young men for me in Ilkley. The glamorous hard-drinking wool merchants' sons with their fast cars, teddy-bear coats and broad Yorkshire accents were as above me sexually as they were below me, I felt, socially. But when I was about eighteen, two Old Etonians came to live for a year in the district. They were learning farming before going back to run their estates. They were both very attractive and easy-going, and were consequently asked everywhere, every mum with a marriageable daughter competing for their attention. I was terribly disconcerted when, after a couple of visits to our house and one of them taking me out once, they became complete habitués of the house of a jumped-up steel merchant across the valley. Soon they were both fighting for the hand of his not particularly good-looking daughter. But she's so much commoner than me, I remember thinking in bewilderment, why don't they prefer my company and our house? I realise now that they far preferred the easy-going atmosphere of the steel merchant's house, with its lush hospitality, ever-flowing drink and poker sessions long into the night, to one glass of sherry and self-consciously intelligent conversation in ours. I had yet to learn, too, that people invariably dislike and shun the class just below them, and much prefer the class below that, or even the one below that.

I was further bewildered when, later in the year, I went to

Oxford to learn to type, and shared a room with an "Honourable" who said "handbag." This seemed like a blasphemy. Nancy Mitford's *The Pursuit of Love* had been my bible as a teenager. I knew peers' daughters, whom she immortalised as "Hon.'s," said "bag" rather than "handbag." At that time, aware, too, of a slowly emerging sexuality and away for once from parental and educational restraint, I evolved a new way of dressing: five-inch high-heeled shoes, tight straight skirts, very very tight cheap sweaters, and masses of make-up to cover a still rather bad skin. I looked just like a tart. People obviously took me for one too. For when the room-mate who was an Hon. introduced me to all her smart friends at the University, one young blood promptly betted another young blood a tenner he couldn't get me into bed by the end of the week. Before he had time to lay siege, the story was repeated back to me. I was shattered: shocked and horrified to my virginal middle-class core; I cried for twenty-four hours. My would-be seducer, who had a good heart, on hearing of my misery, turned up at my digs, apologised handsomely, and suggested, by way of making amends, rather than me, that he take me to the cinema. On the way there, he stopped at a sweet shop and bought a bar of chocolate. Breaking it, he gave me half, and started to eat the other half himself.

"But you can't eat sweets in the street," I gasped, almost more shocked than I had been by his intended seduction.

"I," he answered, with the centuries of disdain in his voice, "can do anything I like."

Hon.'s that talked about handbags, lords who ate chocolate in the streets like the working classes, aristocrats who preferred the jumped-up to the solidly middle-class: I was slowly learning that the class system was infinitely more complicated than I had ever dreamed.

It takes many years, writes Jonathan Gathorne-Hardy in *The Rise and Fall of the British Nanny,* for the outsider to master those complex, subtle distinctions, the nuances of accent, attitudes and behaviour that went, indeed which go, into that living, changing thing—English upper-class snobbery. He might have added that this is true of any class's snobbery.

The whole thing is relative. George IV said you could recognise the people who weren't gentlemen by the way they divide their coats when they sit down. The Queen Mother used to listen to B.B.C. radio's oldest daytime soap opera, now defunct, *Mrs. Dale's Diary*, to find out how life went on in a "middle-class" family. But most people who consider themselves middle-class, would regard Mrs. Dale's life-style as flagrantly "lower middle."

When I went on Yorkshire Television with Jean Rook of the *Daily Express* a few years ago, the interviewer began most embarrassingly by saying: "Now here you are, two columnists from Yorkshire, but from very different backgrounds. You're working-class, aren't you, Jean, and, Jilly, you're upper-class."

We both shrieked with horror.

"I'm middle, not upper," I muttered, going scarlet.

"I'm upper middle," said Miss Rook witheringly. "I know lots of duchesses."

Conversely when I go to very grand parties, my hostess invariably excuses my commonness and polyester cleavages by saying: "D'you know Jilly? She's rather famous."

Every court, I suppose, needs its jester.

But even in an egalitarian age, when it's no longer done to despise someone of a different class (although the chippy working classes don't make much effort not to), it's very difficult not to adjust your behaviour according to the company you are in.

Shopping in Harrods with a peer's daughter recently, I actually found myself buying a little white dress with blue snowdrops for a boy baby rather than a Baby-Gro, because I'd read the week before in *Harper's* that the upper classes thought Baby-Gros were common. Next day I was lunching in a restaurant with a working-class writer and I found myself, who never touch pudding, saying I'd love some because he had ordered pudding and I didn't want to appear snooty.

We pretend, too, that we are indifferent to social nuances, but nothing irritates people more than being misquoted in the newspapers using words which they consider vulgar. "Have a noggin," a

Duchess was alleged to have said in a recent interview. "That's a jolly nice perfume you've got on."

I heard also of a psychiatrist who was treating an aristocrat for depression. A month went by, and they seemed to be making little progress.

"I want you to be completely honest," said the psychiatrist at the next session, "and tell me exactly what's in your mind at the moment."

"I was thinking," said the aristocrat apologetically, "what a vulgar little man you were."

It was their final session. The psychiatrist was unable to go on, because he'd completely lost any feeling of ascendancy.

"And so," as John Coleman once wrote in the *Sunday Times*, "the old movements of social advance and recoil go on, just as much as they always did. It is the perpetual inaccuracy of imitation that makes up the English social comedy and tragedy."

But there is plenty of comedy. As a small boy at my son's last school pointed out in an essay, "All people should be gentlemen except ladies, but it puts a bit of variety into life if some are not."

I am very aware of the inadequacies of this book. The subject is so vast and so complex that I have only touched on a few aspects which seemed important to me. I have made many sweeping generalisations, which I hope people won't take too seriously, because other classes are not better or worse than one's own, they are merely different. I have also tried to show that there have certainly been changes in vocabulary and attitude in the past twenty-five years.

One need look no further for an example than Miss Barbara Cartland, being interviewed by Sandra Harris on the *Today* programme, and being asked whether she thought the class barriers had broken down.

"Of course they have," said Miss Cartland, "or I wouldn't be sitting here talking to someone like you."

Putney, May 1979

CLASS

Chapter 1

THE CLASSES

The aristocracy

According to sociologists, the aristocracy is such a tiny minority—about 0.2 per cent of the population—as to be statistically negligible. The ones that do not work or who run their own estates are not even listed in the Census. They are like the scattering of herbs and garlic on top of a bowl of dripping or, more poetically, like water lilies who float, beautiful and some would say useless, on the surface of a pond. Being a lord, of course, doesn't make you an aristocrat. Only about half the nobility are aristocracy, the rest being life peers. These are commoners elevated to the peerage so that they may sit in the House of Lords, but their titles die with them. And only about a third of the aristocracy are ennobled, the rest being families of younger sons or country squires, some of whom have had money and influence far longer and can trace their families back much farther than many a duke or earl.

A good example of this is Mrs. James, the aristocrat in Pamela Hansford Johnson's novel *The Unspeakable Skipton*. Mrs. James had an air of undefinable authority and spoke in a direct and barking shorthand:

"Feel sorry for poor Alf Dorset, son's marrying some girl who sings on the wireless." Unbound by convention, she made all her own rules, making a point of going everywhere out of season.

"That's why seasons are inevitably such a flop," says one of the other characters, "because if they're out of season they're wrong anyway, and if they're in season, Mrs. James had buzzed off to Gozo or somewhere extraordinary."

In fact so many of the aristocracy don't have titles that they regard *Burke's Peerage,* which covers the landed gentry as well, as a far more important source book than *Debrett's Peerage and Baronetage.* One peer told his secretary she must get an up-to-date copy of *Burke's* "so you'll know all the people I'm talking about." The point about the aristocracy is they all know each other.

Traditionally, as will be shown in later chapters, they didn't work for their living, and although many of them have jobs today, they find difficulty in applying the same dedication and materialism as the middle classes.

They used, of course, to be terribly rich. At the turn of the century, if you were asked to stay at Woburn, one chauffeur and a footman would take you as far as Hendon, where another chauffeur and a footman would be waiting to take you to Woburn. As a gentleman never travelled with his luggage, another two cars were needed to carry this. So it meant two chauffeurs and two footmen to get you and your luggage as far as Hendon, and two more chauffeurs and footmen to take you to Woburn. Eight men to transport one guest, in heaven knows how large a house party, down to the country. Then there was the Marquess of Hertford, who had a house in Wales he'd never been to, but where every night a huge dinner was cooked by a fleet of servants in case he *did* turn up.

The late Duke of Westminster's family in 1978 owned 300 acres in Belgravia and Oxford Street, 12,000 acres around Eaton, 14,000 acres in North Wales, 1,000 acres in Kent, 400 acres in Shropshire, 800 acres in North Wales and 1,000 acres in British Columbia, Hawaii and Australia. The heir, Earl Grosvenor, inherited sixteen million pounds on his twenty-first birthday. Hardly the bread line.

Today, as a result of death duties and capital transfer tax, however, most aristocrats are desperately broke, certainly by comparison with their grandfathers, and are reduced to renting off wings as apartments, selling paintings, turning their gardens into zoos and amusement parks and letting the public see over their houses.

Although they have considerable influence in the Tory party, the aristocracy no longer run the country as they did in the eighteenth and nineteenth centuries. But, despite the erosion of his privileges, the aristocrat's view of his responsibilities remains the same; responsibilities to the tenants, to the community (the good aristocrat always had a strong sense of public duty) and to the house he lives in, often so beautiful as to be a national monument, but to which the nation pays no contribution.

One of the characteristics of the aristocrat is the extreme sentiment he feels towards his house, and his inheritance. His wife is expected to feel the same. When the Marchioness of Tavistock recently expressed her boredom at running Woburn her father-in-law's sharp reaction was quoted in the *Daily Mail:* "If you marry some guy with a title, you have a duty and a responsibility to carry on what his ancestors did in the past. She was perfectly aware of what she was getting into. Trouble is she's an only child."

Because they believe in their inheritance, the upper classes set enormous store by keeping things in the family. They don't buy their houses like the middle classes, they inherit them. When the house gets too big for a grandfather and grandmother, they might move into a smaller house on the estate, to make way for their eldest son, but they leave all the furniture behind, as their ancestors have for generations. One definition of the middle classes is: the sort of people who have to buy their own silver.

Because the British aristocracy were so anxious to preserve their inheritance, they tended only to marry their own kind. The middle classes married for love. The upper classes married to preserve their rank. All twenty-six dukes are, as at present, related to one another. And as long as rank was protected, and money obtained in sufficient quantities to support this rank, infidelity after marriage, as Brian Masters points out in *The Dukes,* was taken for granted: "A painter," screamed the Duchess. "What painter? Sylvia Roehampton's daughter to marry a painter, but of course she won't. You marry Tony Wexford, and we'll see what can be done about the painter later."

As they weren't expected to be faithful, unlike the middle classes, they didn't feel guilty if they wandered, which explains the over-active libido of the aristocrat. He expected to exercise his *droit du seigneur* over his tenants but he also saw himself as a Knight Errant like Don Quixote, living in a world of romantic adventure. When your ancestors have been fighting battles and seducing women for thousands of years, one German nobleman told me recently, it's terribly difficult to settle down to one wife and an office job.

As a result of all this infidelity, a high proportion of the aristocracy is irregularly conceived, but, as they all know each other, they're still pretty dotty with inbreeding. When my uncle was Lord Spencer's agent, my aunt said she met all the local aristocracy, many of them as mad as hatters. When they talked about one of their friends "coming out," you never knew if they were doing the season or being discharged from a loony bin.

Colossal self-confidence is perhaps the hallmark of the aristocrat. Like the *chevalier* "without fear and without self-reproach" he goes through life unafraid, and doesn't question his own motives, or feel guilty about his actions. Not answerable to other people, the aristocrat is often unimaginative, spoilt, easily irritated and doesn't flinch from showing it. If he wants to eat his peas with his knife he does so.

"Dear Kate," said Henry V, "you and I cannot be confined within the weak list of a country's fashion; we are the makers of manners, Kate; and the liberty that follows our places stops the mouth of all find-faults."

Not caring a stuff what people think leads also to a rich vein of eccentricity: the Marquess of Londonderry throwing soup at a fly that was irritating him in a restaurant, and Sir Anthony Eden's father hurling a barometer out of the window into the pouring rain, yelling: "See for yourself, you bloody thing!"

Or there was the imperious peer who, when he missed a train, ordered the station-master to get him another one.

Professor A. S. C. Ross has said that above a certain level, all

"U" people are equal. With respect, I think few upper-class people would agree with him. The ancient aristocracy consider it's very vulgar to have been founded after the Tudors, which puts most of our present dukes beyond the pale. In fact, in the nineteenth century most of the aristocracy were so worried about the comparative youthfulness of their families that they all employed genealogists to try and trace their ancestors back to the Conqueror. When Oliver Lyttelton was made Viscount Chandos, his wife Lady Moira, who was the daughter of the tenth Duke of Leeds, was furious at becoming Lady Chandos, and having ostensibly to drop rank. Oliver Lyttelton was evidently so thrilled to be ennobled that he went round putting coronets on everything, including books of matches. Brian Masters tells a story of the Duchesses of Buccleugh and of Westminster sidling through a door together in their determination not to give precedence.

Between aristocrats and other classes there is certainly a barrier of rank. My mother and father used to live near Hampton Court Palace, where widows of distinguished men, some of them aristocrats, have apartments. My mother met a peer's widow at a drinks party, and they got on so well that my mother wrote to her next day asking her to dine. Back came a letter of acceptance, but with a P.S. "I hope you don't mind my pointing out, Elaine dear, that the palace should be the first to issue invitations."

It has been suggested that this obsession with rank probably had something to do with boredom. Without a career, the aristocrat had to fill his days. He was not a great intellectual: Jane Austen's Sir Walter Elliot, whose reading consisted of his own entry in *Burke's Peerage,* is fairly near the mark. He preferred more exciting entertainment, hence his addiction to blood sports and to gambling. I shall never forget watching an aristocrat and a television newsreader playing backgammon one evening. The newsreader's wife, who was ravishingly beautiful, and bored by the lack of attention, suddenly came in with no clothes on and danced round and round them. Neither of them took any notice.

The aristocrat, when he wants to, has very good manners. The

Scottish upper classes, in particular, have that shell-shocked look that probably comes from banging their heads on low beams leaping to their feet whenever a woman comes into the room. Aristocrats are also deeply male chauvinist, and, although you get left-wing extremists like Lord Weymouth who sends his children to a state school and has revolutionary ideas, on the whole they tend to be reactionary.

While writing this book I found there were very much two strands in the character of the aristocracy: first the wild, delinquent, arrogant, capricious, rather more glamorous element; and second the stuffy "county," public-spirited, but publicity-shy element, epitomised by the old baronet whose family were described as "old as the hills and infinitely more respectable."

Or, as a small boy, writing in my son's school magazine, pointed out: "Gentlemen are of two types: the nose-uppish and the secluded."

In order to write this book, I have dealt in archetypes. The aristocracy and upper classes are represented by the HON. HARRY STOW-CRAT. Son of the sixth Baron Egliston, educated at Eton, he served in the Coldstream. He now runs his diminishing estate, selling the odd Van Dyck to make ends meet, but does more or less what he pleases. He lives in a large decaying house in the North Riding of Yorkshire, and has a flat in Chelsea. He has a long-suffering wife, CAROLINE, who does a great deal for charity, an eldest son, GEORGIE, a daughter called FIONA, and several other children. He has numerous mistresses, but none to whom he is as devoted as to his black Labrador, SNIPE. He has had many moments of frustration and boredom in his life, but never any of self-doubt.

The middle classes

Would you come round the world next year in the *France* with
me? I got a letter from Gerry Wellesley on a cruise saying he'd
never met middle-class people before, and they are quite different from us. Isn't he awful.

Nancy Mitford

The middle classes are in fact *quite* different—being riddled with
self-doubt, which is hardly surprising after all the flak they've received over the years. The upper classes despised them for their
preoccupation with money, and because they suspected it was
middle-class malcontents rather than the rabble who had plotted
and set alight the French Revolution. "How beastly the bourgeois
is," mocked the working-class Lawrence, and in fact *épater le
bourgeois* has always been a favourite sport of both high and low.
Even their own ranks have attacked them: "The People in Between," wrote Hilaire Belloc, "Looked underdone and harassed,/
And out of place, and mean/And horribly embarrassed."

And they have even been blamed for the evils of the class
system. It is the middle classes, wrote one sociologist, with their
passion for order and reason, who have sought to impose a kind of
stratification on what is in fact an eternally malleable and bubbling
class system. Which is rubbish because, as we have already seen,
the aristocracy is just as obsessed with rank.

Occasionally they have their defenders. "I come from the middle classes," said Neville Chamberlain, "and I am proud of their
ability, the shrewdness, the industry and providence, the thrift by
which they are distinguished."

But even Chamberlain's finest hour, returning from Munich
proclaiming "Peace with Honour," was witheringly described by
some aristocrat at the time as "Retreat with Boasting."

In a way, the middle classes seem to suffer as the middle child
does. Everyone makes a huge fuss over the firstborn (just as all the

world loves a lord). And everyone adores and pets and coddles the baby (who is like the working classes, shored up by a great feather bed of the welfare state). But the child in the middle gets the most opprobrium, often left to fend for itself, and ganged up on by the other two. It is doubly significant that in the English Civil War, the rabble joined up with the King, against the Puritan middle classes. If Marx was the champion of the working classes, Calvin was the prophet of the middle classes. They believed implicitly in the Puritan Ethic, in the cultivation of such virtues as diligence, frugality, propriety and fidelity. Work to keep sin at bay, feel guilty if you slack. Shame is a bourgeois notion.

Although there is a world of difference between the top of the middle classes and the bottom, between the great merchant banker and the small shopkeeper, they are united in their desire to get on, not just to survive. Unlike the upper classes and the working classes, the middle classes thought careers were important. They started little businesses. They worked to pass exams after they'd left school. They believed in the law of the jungle and not the welfare state —if you got on in life, good luck to you.

For this reason they believed in the importance of education long before the other classes. They believed in deferred satisfaction. They saved in order to send their children to private schools or to buy their own houses. If the upper classes hand on the estates they have inherited to their children, the middle classes hand on the small businesses they have built up to theirs. To the working classes the most important criterion of middle-class membership, after money or income, is owning a small business or being self-employed.

At the moment they are under increasing pressure, as the working classes get richer and more powerful. One of the great divides between the middle and lower classes used to be that the former used his brain and the latter his hands. Today, however, the miner and the car worker with their free housing and free education have far more spending money than a newly qualified doctor or barrister, and certainly than a policeman or a major in the army. According to my ex-bank manager, the middle classes are having increasing difficulty making ends meet. In 1976, they rather than the working classes became the chief candidates for the pawnbroker, bringing in watches, wedding rings, golf clubs and binoculars.

Although they don't "know everyone" like the upper classes, the upper middles, and many of the middles, having been to boarding school, and probably their parents or even grandparents having been too, have a much wider-spread circle of friends than the working classes. They are also able to keep in touch with them by telephone or by their ability to write letters. Many of them have a spare room where friends can come and stay.

They therefore tend to know many more people outside the district where they live than the working classes, and don't need to depend on the street and their immediate neighbours for help or for their identity. They can afford to keep themselves to themselves. Aloofness, reserve and a certain self-righteousness are also middle-class qualities.

To illustrate the three main strands of the middle classes we again fall into archetypes, with SAMANTHA and GIDEON UPWARD As the upper-middle-class couple, HOWARD and EILEEN WEYBRIDGE as the middle middles and BRYAN and JEN TEALE as the lower middles.

Gideon and Samantha Upward: The merry-tocracy

The upper middle classes are the most intelligent and highly educated of all the classes, and therefore the silliest and the most receptive to every new trend: radical chic, health foods, ethnic clothes, bra-lessness, gifted children, French cooking. Gideon Upward gave his mother-in-law a garlic crusher for Christmas. The upper middles tend to read *The Guardian* at least as much as *The Times* and are proud of their liberal and enlightened attitudes. They are also the most role-reversed of the classes: Gideon does a great deal of cooking and housework. Samantha longs to be a good mother and have an Int'risting Job at the same time. To save petrol, she often rides round on a sit-up-and-beg bicycle, with wholemeal bread in the front basket and a bawling child in the back. Sometimes her long dirndl skirt catches in the pedals. She has a Second in history and a Fourth in life.

Gideon and Samantha both went to "good schools," Gideon probably to Winchester or to Sherborne. He might be an architect or work in the City. He wears a signet ring with a crest on the little finger of his left hand, in an attempt to proclaim near-aristocratic status, just as the middle middles would wear an old school tie, to show they'd been to boarding school; the lower middles would give their house a name instead of a number, to prove it wasn't public housing but bought; and the working class bring back plastic bulls from Majorca to show they've travelled.

Gideon and Samantha have two children called ZACHARIAS and THALIA, whom they might start off liberally sending to state school, while trying not to wince at the first "pardon," but would be more likely to send to a private school. They love their English setter, BLUCHER, and feel frightfully guilty loving it almost more than their children. Harry Stow-Crat would have no such scruples. Gideon plays tennis and rugger for a club, but he wouldn't use the club to make friends, and he and Samantha wouldn't touch a Country Club, as reeking of suburbia. They prefer to entertain in their own house, which is large and old, and being restored to its original state rather faster than they'd like. Samantha is into good works with a slightly self-interested motive: anti-pollution, conservation, the Parent Teachers Association.

As they can't be the most upper class in the land, Samantha is determined that they shall be the most "cultured." She and Gideon go to the theatre, the ballet and the movies, as they rather self-consciously call the cinema, and try and read at least two books a week.

In the past fifteen years, the upper middles have aimed for a standard of living they can't afford, taking on many of the pastimes of the upper classes. Gideon goes shooting quite often. They have two cars, which are falling to pieces and for which they have to pay a fortune every time they take their road test. They once had a country cottage, holidays abroad and a boat. Now they have two children at boarding school, and since the advent of the permissive society, Gideon has been playing at adultery almost like Harry Stow-Crat. As a result, he spends a fortune on lunches, and a fortune on guilt presents for Samantha afterwards. They are both so worried about trying to make ends meet, they're drinking themselves absolutely silly, which is why I call them the "merry-toc-racy."

Virginia Woolf wrote *The Years* about an upper-middle-class family called the Pargeters. "Parget" is an English dialect word meaning to smooth over the cracks in plastered surfaces. The Pargeters whitewash and gloss over the deep sexual and emotional fissures of life. In the same way Samantha doesn't particularly like her mother-in-law, or later, her daughter-in-law, or several of her neighbours; but she tries to get on with them, because she feels guilty about her dislike. If Samantha hired a gardener even for two hours, she wouldn't flaunt him as a status symbol, she'd keep quiet, because she feels it's more "creative" to do all the garden herself.

She and Gideon call each other "darling," rather than "dear." Gideon's parents, Colonel and Mrs. Upward, living on a fast-dwindling fixed income, are much more thrifty than Samantha and Gideon. As they're not drinking themselves silly, they don't smash everything and still have the same glasses and china as they did when they were first married.

Howard and Eileen Weybridge: The middle middles

Howard Weybridge lives in Surrey or some smart dormitory town. He works as an accountant, stockbroker, surveyor or higher technician. He probably went to a minor public school or a grammar school. He never misses the nine o'clock news and says "Cheerio." He wears paisley scarves with scarf rings and no bottoms to his spectacles. He calls his wife "Eileen, dear," and when you ask him how he is, says: "Very fit, thank you." He is very straight and very patriotic. His haw-haw voice is a synthetic approximation to the

uppers; he talks about "Ham-shar." His children join the young
*Con-*servatives and the tennis club to meet people. He buys a
modern house, and ages it up. It has a big garden with a perfect
lawn and lots of shrubs. He despises anyone who hasn't been to
"public school," and often goes into local government or politics
for social advancement. He is a first-generation pony buyer, and
would also use the pony club to meet the right sort of people. His
wife Eileen thinks the upper middles are terribly scruffy. They are
both keen golfers, and pull strings to get their road made private.
They are much smugger than the upper middles.

Howard Weybridge's father hasn't a bill in the world, and is on
the golf club committee, he found bridge to be one of the most
wonderful things in life, it's a very easy way of entertaining. He has
a sneaking liking for Enoch Powell. ("We should have stopped
Sambos coming here in the first place.")

Bryan and Jen Teale: The lower middles

The Teales are probably the most pushy, the most frugal and the
most respectable of all the classes, because they are so anxious to
escape from the working class. The successful ones iron out their
accents and become middle like Mr. Heath and Mrs. Thatcher, the
rest stay put, as bank and insurance clerks, door-to-door salesmen,
toast-masters, lower management, police sergeants and sergeant-
majors. In the old days, the lower middles rose with the small
business or the little shop, but the rise in rates, social security
benefits and postage has scuppered all that.

The lower middles never had any servants, but as they are
obsessed with cleanliness, and like everything nice, they buy a small
modern house and fill it with modern units which are easy to keep
clean. Jen and Bryan have two children, WAYNE and CHRISTINE, and
a very clean car.

As Jen and Bryan didn't go to boarding school, didn't make
friends outside the district and don't mix with the street, they have

very few friends, keeping themselves to themselves. They tend to be very inner-directed, doing everything together, decorating the house, furnishing the car and coaching and playing football with the children. Jen reads knitting patterns, *Woman's Own* and *Reader's Digest* condensed books. To avoid any working-class stigma, she puts up defensive barriers: privet hedges, net curtains, talks in a "refained" accent, raises her little finger when she drinks and runs with her hands turned out, as though she were drying her nail polish. Her aim is to be dainty and wear six pairs of knickers. The children are always being pulled up for some real or imagined coarseness of speech. The Teales don't entertain much, only Bryan's colleagues who might be useful, and occasionally Bryan's boss.

The working classes

One of the great class divides has always been "Them" and "Us." This, as a result of the egalitarian, working-class-is-beautiful revolution of the sixties and early seventies, has polarised into the Guilty and the Cross. On the one side are the middle and upper classes, feeling guilty and riddled with social concern although they often earn less money than the workers. On the other are the working classes, who have been totally brainwashed by television and magazine images of the good life, and feel cross because they aren't getting a big enough slice of the cake.

In a time of economic prosperity, everyone tends to do well, wages rise. The middle classes can afford perhaps a new boat, or central heating, the working-class man buys a new car and a fridge for the missus. Man's envy and rivalry is turned towards his immediate neighbour (keeping up with the Joneses) rather than towards the classes above and below. But in times of economic stress, when people suddenly can't get the things they want, and prices and the cost of living outstrip wages, they start turning their envy against other classes. Antagonism against a neighbour feathering his nest tends to be replaced by an awareness of class inequalities.

In a time of economic security, society therefore tends to look fairly cohesive, which is probably why in the early seventies a lot of people genuinely believed that class barriers had finally broken down. But as the decade advanced, the working-class people who'd bought their houses and were up to their necks in hire purchase suddenly found they couldn't keep up their payments. Their expectations had been raised, and their security was being threatened by the additional calamity of mass unemployment. This discontent, fanned by militancy, resulted in the rash of strikes in the winter of 1978.

For although the middle classes often imagine the working-class man earning huge sums on overtime, the rewards of his job are in fact much less. The manual worker doesn't have job satisfaction or a proper pension, he doesn't have fringe benefits, all the perks of cars, trips abroad, expense-account lunches and longer holidays. He has to clock in, and his earning span is much shorter. Once his physical strength goes, he can look forward to an old age of comparative poverty and deprivation. This all results in workers avoiding any kind of moral commitment to the management. We cheat the foreman, is the attitude, he cheats the manager, and the manager cheats the customer.

Richard Hoggart in *The Uses of Literacy* brilliantly summed up the workers' attitude to Them (i.e. the establishment and the management):

They are the people at the top, the highers up, the people who give you your dole, call you up, tell you to go to work, fine you, make you split up the family in the thirties (to avoid a reduction in the means test allowance), get yer in the end, aren't really to be trusted, talk posh, are all twisters really, never tell yer owt (e.g. about a relative in hospital), clap yer in the clink, will do y'down if they can, summons yer, are all in a click together, treat y'like muck.

Because they dislike the management, the working classes don't like people saving their money or getting on through hard work. They put a premium on pleasure now, drinking their wages, for example, or blowing the whole lot on a new colour telly. Traditionally the only legitimate way to make a lot of money was to win it. Hence the addiction to gambling, football pools, racing, bingo and the dogs.

Living from hand to mouth, they can't manage their money like the lower middles. When the army started paying guardsmen by cheque recently, my bank manager said they got into the most frightful muddles. If he wrote and told one of them he was overdrawn, say by £30, the guardsman promptly sent in a cheque for that amount.

Traditionally working-class virtues are friendliness, cooperation, warmth, spontaneity, a ready sense of humour and neighbourliness. "We're all in the same boat," is the attitude. That "love" is still the most common form of address really means something. They have been defined as people who belong to the same Christmas club, characteristically saving up not for something permanent, like the deposit on a house, but for a good blow-out. They have a great capacity for enjoyment.

Because they didn't have cars, or telephones, and couldn't afford train fares, and the men usually walked to work nearby, working-class life tended to centre on the street and the neighbourhood. "Everyone knowing your business," said one working-class man, "it's no good putting on airs because you earned more. The neighbours remember you as a boy, knew your Aunt Lil, who's no better than she should be, and took you down a peg. The network acts as a constant check."

Girls seldom moved away from their mothers when they married. Sons often came home for lunch every day, or lived at home, even after marriage. The working-class family is much closer and more possessive than most. They seldom invite friends into the house. "I've never had a stranger [meaning non-family] in here since the day I moved in," said one woman. "I don't hold with that sort of thing."

Being so dependent on the locality, the working classes are often lost and desperately lonely if the council suddenly moves them to housing estates, or shuts them up in little boxes, in some high-rise block. Working-class men have also lost much of the satisfaction that came from the old skills and crafts. Many of these have been taken away from them during the past twenty-five years and their traditional occupations destroyed by machines. In the old days the husband gained respect as a working man in the community.

Leaving school at sixteen, he feels inadequate because he is inarticulate. He is thought of as being so bloody-minded and lazy by the middle classes (because he can't express himself) that "Definitely, disgusting," in answer to any question put to him, is the only way he can show his disapproval.

Among their other rankings, the working classes divide themselves firmly into the Rough and the Respectable. The Rough get drunk fairly often, make a great deal of noise at night, often engage in prostitution, have public fights, neglect their children, swear in front of children and women and don't give a stuff about anything —just like the upper classes in fact. The Respectables chunter over such behaviour, and in Wales sing in Male Voice Choirs; they are pretty near the Teales. They also look down on people on the dole, the criminal classes and sometimes black people, whom they refer to as "soap-dodgers."

Mr. and Mrs. Definitely-Disgusting

Our archetypal working-class couple are MR. and MRS. DEFINITELY-DISGUSTING. They have two children, SHARON and DIVE, and live in a council house with walls so thin you can hear the budgie pecking its seed next door. Mr. Definitely-Disgusting is your manual worker, he might be a miner in the North, a car worker in the Midlands or a casual labourer in the South. He married young, and lived for a while with his wife's parents; after a year or two he went back to going to the pub, football and the dogs with the blokes. He detests his mother-in-law. But despite his propensity to foul language, he is extremely modest, always undressing with his back to Mrs. D.-D. and even peeing in a different way from the other classes, splaying out his fingers in a fan, so they conceal his member. He often does something slightly illegal, nicking a car or knocking off a telly. He is terrified of the police, who, being lower-middle, and the class just above, reserve their special venom for him. Mrs. Definitely-Disgusting wears her curlers and apron to the local shop, and spends a lot of the day with a cigarette hanging from her bottom lip gossiping and grumbling.

Mr. and Mrs. Nouveau-Richards

The other couple you will meet are the NOUVEAU-RICHARDSES, of working-class origin, who've made a colossal amount of money. Boasting and ostentation are their salient characteristics. At coffee mornings Mrs. Nouveau-Richards asks anyone if they've got "any idea whether gold plate will spoil in the dishwasher." She has a huge house, and lots of servants, whom she bullies unmercifully. She is very rude to waiters and very pushy with her children, TRACEY-DIANE and JASON, who have several hours of after-school coaching every day. Mr. Nouveau-Richards gets on the committee of every charity ball in London. The upper classes call him by his Christian name and appreciate his salty humour, but don't invite him to their houses. Jason goes to Stowe and Oxford, and ends up a member of the telly-stocracy, who are the real powers in the land, the people in communications who appear on television. They always talk about "my show."

Chapter 2

CHILDREN

At the beginning of the seventies, the small-is-beautiful brigade mounted a campaign to bring down the birthrate. Family Planning Association supporters brandished condoms outside the Commons, and sidled bossily up to women who'd just had babies at parties saying: "Two's yer ration." Middle-class lefties were rumoured to be concealing third babies in attics rather than display evidence of such social irresponsibility. Disapproving ads appeared in the cinema showing defeated slatterns in curlers trailing herds of whining children along the street. "Superdad or Scrounger?" howled the *Daily Mirror* when a man on social security proudly produced his twenty-first child.

In the face of economic gloom, a rocketing dole queue and mothers wanting to get back to work, people probably thought twice about bringing more children into the world. Whatever the cause, the campaign worked. The birthrate in the U.K. dropped by 30 per cent. The working classes in particular, having discovered the Pill, curbed production dramatically and at the last count were only producing 2.16 children per family while the upper middles were down to 1.7. The higher you go up the social scale, in fact, the smaller the family, although the aristocracy tend to run unpatriotically riot, probably because, as Evelyn Waugh pointed out: "Impotence and sodomy are socially O.K., but birth control is flagrantly middle-class." One can't imagine an aristocrat having a vasectomy.

With the working classes on the Pill, the middle classes, particularly the wholemeal-bread brigade, started panicking about long-term effects, and switched to the coil or sterilisation. The respectable working class still favour the sheath, described by Mrs. Definitely-Disgusting as "my hubby always using something."

The birth

Caroline Stow-Crat gives up work with relief the moment she gets pregnant. The office is relieved too, they're fed up with the endless telephone calls, the Thursday-to-Tuesday weekends and falling over the Labrador every time they go to the filing cabinet. Samantha Upward tends to work till the last possible minute, ticking away like a time bomb, and terrifying all the men in the office.

Our Queen was born by Caesarian, feet first. When Prince Charles was born, the Duke of Edinburgh was playing squash. Today he would probably have been squashed into the maternity ward of St. Mary's, Paddington. The trend now for the higher socio-economic classes is to have epidurals, which makes the whole thing less harrowing, and for the husband, albeit very reluctantly, to be present at the birth. "They do rather get in the way," said my G.P. "It's best if they stand at the head of the bed to give their wife moral support, but they keep creeping down the bed to have a look" (probably the first they've had in months).

When the wife of Superdad-or-Scrounger produced their twenty-first child, four of the children were allowed to watch. Perhaps the television had broken down. "It was very exciting," said the eight-year-old afterwards.

The upper classes are not wild about newborn babies. Nancy Mitford once described one as a "howling orange in a black wig." But they are delighted to have their double-barrelled names carried on by sons.

A few years ago *Harper's* published a brilliant piece on the "Sloane Ranger," the girl who has a flat in Kensington and parents in the country, who lives in headscarves and went to a "good" girls' boarding school. She epitomizes the strand where the more traditional upper middles merge into the lower rungs of the upper classes. The Sloane Ranger husband is very proud whatever sex child he has. If he has a boy he goes straight off to his club and writes two letters, one to "my housemaster at Eton, one to Mrs. Ingham at Eaton House." Then he opens a bottle of champagne.

Harry Stow-Crat, who certainly wasn't present at the birth, doesn't bother to write letters to anyone, perfectly confident he can get his son in anywhere. He might ring up his mother and his old nanny, have a large whisky and soda, then go off and see his mistress.

Poor Gideon Upward is having a horrid time. He now knows exactly why it's called a "con-finement"—he's being conned rotten forking out for a private room, and it's not very *fine* the way Samantha, who insisted on natural childbirth, disapproving of epidurals, is now yelling her head off. Still he's delighted when little Zacharias (Samantha went right through the Bible to find a name no one else had used) appears. It's so nice to have a boy first so he can take little 0.7 to dances when they grow up.

While Samantha was in hospital, Gideon was planning to have a crack at his secretary, but ever-thoughtful Samantha has arranged for married friends to ask him out every night. Gideon gets drunk out of frustration, and the prospect of his mother-in-law coming to stay next week, and makes sodden passes at the wives while their role-reversed husbands are doing the washing up. The passes are tactfully forgotten about afterwards.

Mr. Definitely-Disgusting finds it difficult to visit his wife in hospital because of shift work and National Health visiting hours. When he does, the conversations are usually monosyllabic and inhibited by groans from the labour ward next door.

Aristocrats often get married just before the birth to legitimise the child in case it's a boy. I attended one such wedding where the bride was actually in the last stages of labour. The hospital had thoughtfully provided an altar with a brass cross and two plastic orchids in a mauve vase. The bridegroom hadn't bothered to brush his hair but looked so impossibly handsome that the screaming queen of a hospital chaplain got thoroughly over-excited; and spent so long holding his hand he almost forgot to join it to that of the bride, who was manfully carrying on with: "To have . . . *(groan)* . . . and to hold, from this . . . *(groan)."*

The announcement

If you are very grand *The Times* reports the birth on the social pages free of charge. The rest of the upper classes put it in the birth column as briefly as possible.

"To Caroline, wife of Harry Stow-Crat—a son."

Harry wouldn't have bothered, but Caroline thinks Mummy's friends would like to know. The Upwards' announcement might include the name of the baby, "Zacharias Daniel," and a "née Garland-Watson" to remind people of Samantha's former up-market connections. Jen and Bryan Teale might include the name of the hospital and mention earlier children: "a brother for Christine and Wayne." Less smart but more reactionary members of the middle classes use the *Daily Telegraph.* The left-wing middles, conveniently combining parsimony with a flouting of convention, don't bother, which explains why *The Guardian* seldom has any birth announcements.

Mrs. Definitely-Disgusting, who gets her children's names from the *TV Times,* tends to put the announcement of Sharon Esther, a sister for Dive Darren, in the local paper, with a special thanks to the midwifery department of the hospital. It is a working-class characteristic to be touchingly grateful for any kind of hospital care, enjoying the rare treat of a rest and three free meals a day cooked by someone else.

Sometimes the Teales, who like a dainty word for every thing, and the Definitely-Disgustings, who have difficulty in expressing themselves, will send out cards to friends and relations, entitled "Baby's Announcement," with a picture of a stork on the front. Inside they fill in: "My name is Sharon Esther, I weigh 10 lbs., my happy mum and dad are . . ."

Receiving one of these cards, Auntie might send off a nylon quilted pram set in canary yellow with the words: "A gift for baby from . . ." printed on the box. Other alternatives might be a fluffy brushed nylon stuffed rabbit or a teddy bear, referred to by everyone from the lower middle classes downwards as a "cuddly toy."

The upper and upper middle classes, particularly the slightly retarded Sloane Ranger belt, have a tendency to add "y" or "ie" onto everything. In the twenties they did it with names: "Bertie," "Diney," "Jakey," "Piggy." Today they have "choccy cake," "presies"; "cheesy things," which children like so much better, don't you agree; "Araby," which the private wards are getting awfully; and their "gyny," whom they always fall in love with. The Queen's gynaecologist is called Mr. Pinker, the colour he goes, perhaps, when he examines the royal person.

The upper classes don't mix socially with their doctors, but Caroline Stow-Crat makes an exception by asking her "gyny" to come to her first dinner party after the birth. Fantasising about one's "gyny" is the only thing that makes those agonising postnatal screwings possible. (Samantha Upward knows Gideon must not be denied sex longer than six weeks after the birth.) The crush on the "gyny" usually lasts about six months.

On return from hospital, the upper classes often get their old nanny out of mothballs to come and help with the baby. She usually leaves after a few days in high dudgeon because things are being done the wrong way. With the middle classes, Granny often forks out for a maternity nurse for a month, or else the wife's mother comes to stay, and husbands have to remember to put on a dressing-gown when they go to the loo in the middle of the night. The working classes are often living with, or near, their parents anyway, or haven't got a spare room for anyone to stay in. The middle-class career mother, avid to get back to work, is praying that the new *au pair,* who isn't being very good about waking up in the night, is going to work out all right.

Clothes: The wages of synthetic fibres is social death

The upper classes, as was pointed out in the introduction, think Baby-Gros are common. Consequently, Caroline Stow-Crat prefers to dress babies of both sexes in long white dresses in wool or cotton, which probably explains little Lord Fondle-Roy and the strong strain of sexual ambiguity about the aristocracy. "Leggings and cardigans nubbly from being knitted by old Nannies," says *Harper's,* are also all right. So is the matinee jacket, which always sounds like some moulting musquash cape worn by old ladies to afternoon performances of *The Mousetrap.* Anything nylon, polyester or made from any kind of synthetic fibre is definitely out.

Convenience, however, is a great leveller. Ironing long smocked dresses and washing eight nappy liners a day was fine in the old days when there was Nanny to do it. Today when there aren't many servants, and upper-class mothers often have to cook dinner for returning husbands, they may resort to Baby-Gros and disposable nappies when no one is looking, their babies only going into regulation white dresses for tea parties or when grandparents come to stay.

Little Zacharias Upward lives in Baby-Gros, in whatever colour *Vogue* is promoting for grown-ups. He only goes into pink and yellow nubbly cardigans knitted by Samantha's mother's Mrs. G. when the family go and stay with Samantha's mother, and Mrs. G. comes in to wash up on Saturday night.

The Nouveau-Richardses, having denuded the Toddler's Layette at Harrods, have also acquired the biggest, shiniest Silver Cross pram for Tracey-Diane. They have furnished it like their car, with nodding Snoopies, hanging dolls, parasols and frilled canopies to keep off the sun. Tracey-Diane rises from a foam of nylon frills and lace like Venus from the waves.

Samantha Upward, conscious how important it is for children to be brought up with animals, nevertheless invests in a cat net. She also knows how jealous husbands get with new babies around and is paying particular attention to Gideon. In Harry Stow-Crat's house, the only member of the family who suffers from post-natal depression is Snipe the Labrador. One maternity nurse said half her day in upper-class houses was spent boosting the dogs' morale.

Breast-feeding is also coming back into fashion. In the old days the upper classes had their babies suckled by wet nurses or fed from bottles at once. Jonathan Gathorne-Hardy, in *The Rise and Fall of the British Nanny,* quotes one nanny as saying her mistress was "remarkable, in fact as far as breast-feeding goes she was well nigh incredible." It turned out she'd fed the baby for one month. Today, as a backlash against working mothers abandoning their babies to the bottle and rushing back to the office, Caroline Stow-Crat and certainly Samantha Upward are tending to breast-feed for several months.

Breast-feeding in public is indulged in by left-wing trendies, and surprisingly by Jen Teale, who (probably thinking it's uninhibited upper-class behaviour) will even whip out a tit in the middle of a christening, sending uncles, grandfathers and male godparents fainting into the garden. Mrs. Definitely-Disgusting feeds Dive whenever he's hungry. The left-wing middle-class mother, too, feeds her baby on demand, and it's been demanding ever since.

Old-fashioned nannies, who came from the working classes, tended to get their children on the pot and out of nappies very early —quite understandable, as they had no washing machines in those days. Geoffrey Gorer in his book *Exploring English Character* suggests that the obsessive desire for privacy of the upper-class male is the result of being watched over on the pot. "Immersed in clubs, behind ramparts of newspapers, silent in the corner of first-class carriages, at last he is free of Nanny."

Caroline Stow-Crat talks about "toilet trining" with a cockney accent to excuse the use of the word "toilet."

It is very Jen Teale to use the word "diapers." (Caroline says "nappies.")

Let us now digress slightly onto nomenclature. While the upper classes, spurning euphemisms, will tend to say someone is "pregnant," the middle classes describe it as "expecting a baby" or "starting a family." The working-class mother, however, will say: "Three months after I had Dive, I fell for Sharon," which doesn't mean that due to post-natal gloom she developed lesbian tendencies, merely that she got pregnant again.

Upper- and middle-class children call their parents "Mummy" and "Daddy," although the boy might call his father "Dad" as he gets older, or refer to him as "my father." The lower middles and working classes call them "Mum" and "Dad." Socially aspirant lower middles also call their mothers "Mummy." Trendy lefties and women who are reluctant to grow old insist their children call them by their Christian names. Jen and Bryan Teale call each other "Mummy" and "Daddy."

A lot of confusion is caused by the word "nanny." To the upper and middle classes it means someone who looks after children for money, although Samantha Upward would prefer to call her "my girl" or "the *au pair.*" To the working classes "Nanny," "Nana" or "Nan" is one's grandmother, who, as all the mothers are rushing back to work, probably also looks after the children—but is not paid for it. To the upper classes "Nana" means a large dog in *Peter Pan.*

The upper classes call their aunts "Aunt Mary," the middle classes "Auntie Mary." Lower-middle and working-class children are often expected to call any friend of their parents "Auntie" or "Uncle." Two working-class expressions that seem to be creeping upwards are: "Baby needs changing," as though you were fed up with her already, and "I've potted Sharon," as though she were a shiny red billiard ball. Confusion is also caused by the term "putting down." The upper classes "put down" sick or senile dogs. Jen Teale tends to "put them to sleep" or "send them to the Happy Hunting Ground." The middle classes "put down" children for schools, but when the working classes say: "I've put Sharon down," it means they've put her to bed. When they say: "I mind children," it doesn't mean they dislike them, but that they look after them.

The sociologist refers to the child as "the Third Estate of the nuclear family." The lower middles and working classes call him a "kiddy," the middle classes a "kid." The upper middles and uppers talk about "the children." But upper-class people, trying to be democratic, have started to call them "kids." This unnerves Samantha Upward.

It is also an aristocratic trait to refer to members of one's family by name, assuming automatically that other people will know who they mean. Caroline Stow-Crat would say: "Harry's shooting, can I bring Fiona and Georgie?" (i.e. the children). She would also say "the baby," rather than "my baby" or "Baby" or the American-influenced "my little girl," which is very Jen Teale. Harry, on the other hand, if asking a friend how his son was getting on, might easily say: "How's your boy?"

One of the first events in the baby's life is a trip to the clinic. On rainy days the place is deserted, because the Mrs. Definitely-Disgustings, who always dress up to wheel their prams to the clinic, don't like getting their best clothes wet. You can tell the middle-class mothers because they are much more scruffy and have smaller prams (to fit into the Volvo). On a recent visit I made to a clinic in Putney, there were naturally no upper-class mothers, because they don't live South of the River and they never go to clinics. Several working-class mothers in miniskirts, leather coats and high-heeled shoes with very done-up babies were capping each other's crawling and teething stories. Two left-wing middle-class mothers with eager, unpainted faces, ragged hair and dirndl skirts were talking about an anti-aircraft-noise meeting that night. Behind them a pretty Samantha Upward appeared to be carrying on a very enunciated conversation with another upper-middle-class mum, to which no one could help listening. Suddenly I realised she was addressing a non-stop monologue to her own six-month-old baby, having obviously read somewhere that the more you talk to your baby, the sooner it talks back. The ratlet race had begun.

The christening

The next *big event* in a child's life is the christening. The Queen was christened in a private chapel at Buckingham Palace at five weeks, baptised with water from the Jordan, and was dressed in christening robes of cream Brussels lace, worn by every baby in the royal family since Victoria's children.

The aristocracy tend to be christened in their own thirteenth-century churches, wearing slightly yellowing christening robes embroidered with the family crest. *The Times* will report it on the social page. A London christening takes place at the Guards Chapel or the Crypt at the House of Commons, with lunch at Boodles afterwards.

Sloane Ranger christenings tend to have Earl Grey tea, not enough champagne, and if they're short of cash, the top layer of their wedding cake re-iced. Christening presents include silver mugs with at least four initials to take in the double barrels, and premium bonds, but not napkin rings or building society shares, which are very middle-class.

As the trendy upper middles are fast reaching a state when they can't open their mouths without a glass in their hands, their christenings are tending to get later and later, with champagne, chicken drumsticks and leprous quiche at 5:30.

The suburbs and Jen and Bryan Teale tend to go in for multiple christenings with each couple looking beadily at everyone else's baby, and thinking how much more "well spoken" their own godparent is when she names this child. The vicar looks in at all the parties afterwards, and has difficulty not shlurring his wordsh at Evenshong.

The left-wing middles, combining parsimony with agnostic puritanism, don't have their "kids" christened.

Mr. Definitely-Disgusting goes out minicabbing to pay for the party and a new costume for Mrs. Definitely-Disgusting, who makes all the food, which includes pork pie, apple pie with pastry leaves, sponge cakes and fruit punch. The godparents probably keep the local pub.

Social climbers choose famous or successful godparents who might advance their careers or improve their status. They've dropped all their childhood friends. Sloane Rangers' mothers advise them not to ask that awfully nice girl from next door in

Fulham, because you probably won't see her after you move to the country. Jean Cocteau once acted as a godparent, then promptly forgot about the child. Some while later he met the father, who reproached him for neglecting his duties. Mortified, Cocteau at once sent his godson a large teddy bear.

"Was he pleased?" he asked next time he met the father.

"Not awfully," came the reply. "He's a colonel now."

The ratlet race

The christening over, the ratlet race starts in earnest. The battle is particularly vicious among the middle classes, where if you can't boast an "int'risting" career, you justify your existence by rearing a little genius. This is another part of the backlash against women going out to work. Newspapers and women's magazines are constantly stressing the importance of the child being mentally stimulated during the first five years of its life. Journalists recant on women's lib principles and expound the joys of motherhood. This is very easy for lady journalists, who can always write at home *and* see their babies when they want to. Society is teeming with women having nervous breakdowns because they feel so inadequate about only being a wife and mother.

At plonk-and-pâté-tasting-of-old-socks parties beloved by the upper middle classes, you can hear the battle raging. Samantha Upward, who, in spite of having a degree, believes in staying at home to creatively raise little Zacharias, is talking to a career mum.

SAMANTHA *(who knows one is never regarded as a cabbage if one's interested in other people):* How's the job?

CAREER MUM: Oh, exhausting. I had to lunch Jackie Stewart on Monday, look after Graham Greene all week, then we had a press party for Isherwood last night. *(Fifteen-love to Career Mum.)*

SAMANTHA: And how's Damian?

CAREER MUM: All right, I think. How's the baby? *(Not being round much she doesn't even know Zacharias's name.)*

SAMANTHA: Oh, he's just finished *Alice in Wonderland,* simply couldn't put it down, I do recommend flash cards, and he can already beat Gideon at chess. We're a bit worried he's a Gifted Child, but you can't really tell at two. *(Fifteen-thirty to Samantha.)*

Harry Stow-Crat doesn't believe in wives working, or husbands, for that matter. It would interfere with the shooting and fishing. After all, someone's got to provide luncheon.

The upper classes have "nurseries" upstairs. The upper middles call them "playrooms," and tend to have them downstairs so the children won't miss any cultural pearls dropped by their parents. In the kitchen, a cork board groans with Zacharias's first scrawlings. Jen Teale, who is determined that little Wayne shall get on in life, has settled for the lounge, with model soldiers on the mantelpiece and children's posters on the wall. The garden will be filled with a playhouse and social climbing frames.

Dive Definitely-Disgusting will have no room set aside for him, and often sleeps in the same room, or even bed, as all his brothers and sisters. The reason they go to bed so late is that Mrs. Definitely-Disgusting has to ensure one child is soundly asleep before she can put the next one to bed, and so on. The cot will often be bought with cigarette coupons.

The upper classes send their children to bed early, at six-thirty, so they'll be out of the way before their father comes back from shooting or the city. The role-reversed upper middle classes, who believe contact with the father is essential, tend to keep them up slightly later, so they'll have half an hour with Daddy before going to sleep. Gideon Upward, knackered after a hard day, is corrected by little Zacharias every time he tries to skip a page of Paddington Bear and longs for a little bit of upper-class peace downstairs with a large gin and tonic.

Sleeping alone, the middle-class child is often frightened of the dark, but his parents can afford to leave a light on all night outside his room. The middle classes have always given a lot of parental authority to the father. The upper and working classes tended to leave disciplining to the mother, nanny or grandmother. But with shorter working hours and less shift work the working-class father is tending to be at home more, take more interest in his children and no longer be ashamed to be seen pushing the pram. "Vic takes Baby up the park on the weekend, while I get the dinner on," says Mrs. Definitely-Disgusting.

Equally, as the upper classes get poorer and can't afford servants, the fathers are forced to pay more attention to the children.

"I used to shove the baby into his arms," said one maternity nurse, "and walk out of the room. He'd hold it like a rattlesnake, but by the time I left, he was pushing the pram and changing nappies." One upper-class husband, she said, refused to push the pram, but he'd walk behind his wife when she was pushing it, pushing her.

By the time the middle-class child is a year old, say the statisticians, he will be less likely to have a tantrum than the working-class child, have had a much better diet and be off the bottle (as though he'd been on an alcoholic binge for the first twelve months). Baby Georgie Stow-Crat will have had a grille put in the back of the estate car to stop him bothering Snipe the Labrador, and had his first children's party, which he won't remember, but which was a great show-off occasion for his nanny. Wayne Teale will now be referred to as a "toddler" or a "tiny tot." Samantha Upward will now be out on the culture beat, hawking little Zacharias round museums and art galleries to stop herself becoming a cabbage.

Children's clothes

Little Georgie Stow-Crat will be out of long dresses now and into romper suits with Peter Pan collars, or short trousers which he will wear until he's half-way through prep school. Occasionally in Hyde Park on cold days one sees the camp sight of little upper-class boys wearing tights under their shorts. He might occasionally be allowed to wear jeans like the middle classes but never ones that fit, in case their tightness stops him carrying on the line. Upper-class little girls are smock-marked.

The middle classes dress their children like small adults—in the hope that they'll grow brighter and more adult earlier. In the same way that the upper classes force boy babies into little dresses, the middle classes force little girls into jeans. Jen Teale's daughter Christine wears her dresses slightly too short, to display hen's bum knickers.

All little girls, in fact, are lower-middle by inclination. If allowed, they would permanently dress like Christine Teale in frilly party dresses with matching pochettes or peasant blouses with elasticated waists and sleeves, their hair in bunches, sticking out above the ears. Or like Tracey-Diane Nouveau-Richards in earrings, painted toenails, huge nylon bows in the hair, pink plastic butterfly slides and white sling-back or even high-heeled shoes. The Teales and the Nouveau-Richardses encourage such prissiness by saying: "Always try to be a little lady" or "Isn't Tracey-Diane a little flirt." Mrs. Nouveau-Richards, who believes in getting her pound of flesh from the nanny, insists that all Tracey's clothes be "hand-washed," as she calls it. Mrs. Definitely-Disgusting dresses her children in polyester and acrylic in very bright colours; shocking pink, mauve, royal blue and turquoise being the most popular. They also wear very shiny tee-shirts and mock-suede coats with nylon fur collars. The upper classes used only to allow their children to wear anoraks on the ski slopes, but have now given in.

Hair is also a class indicator. Upper-class little boys have their curls brushed flat and cut in the shape of a pudding basin. The middle classes have their hair tapered. Upper-class little girls wear their fringes either on the eyebrows like Shetland ponies or drawn off their foreheads (pronounced "forrids") with a small velvet bow at the side or the crown of their head. They sometimes wear Alice bands, but sewn and with proper velvet, not made out of stretch material. Jen Teale cuts Christine's fringe half-way down the forehead, so there is no danger she won't be able to see out. She cuts

Wayne's hair short at the back so that half an inch or two of neck shows. The working classes no longer Brylcreem their kiddies' hair into tight curls—too much like "the darkies"—but they do brush Baby's hair upwards like a Sioux Indian's.

Until recently, it was much easier to tell a child's background from its clothes than its mother's. But since the entire nation's youth is now clad in spin-offs from whatever film is fashionable and Mary Quant (who staged the great sixties revolution, making duchesses interchangeable with shopgirls) has gone into children's clothes, all children will soon look alike.

The regime

Upper-class mothers believe in fresh air and walks to feed the ducks in the afternoon. Ducks in Kensington Gardens ought to be members of Weight Watchers, so stuffed are they with bread (but never sliced, because the upper classes think it's common). Ducks that live near the Round Pond in Hampstead get wholewheat crusts. As soon as Georgie Stow-Crat can walk he's put on a pony. From Monday to Friday upper-class London children have to make do with the rocking horse at Harrods.

Conventional upper-class children have cake, sandwiches and perhaps as a treat an ice at four o'clock—what the working classes would describe as "afternoon tea." Middle-class children have "high tea" about six consisting of baked beans, beefburgers or fish fingers and yoghurt. The working classes tend to have the same, but if any of the food is cooked, the meal is called a "dinner"—i.e. "Karen has a dinner at lunchtime and a dinner in the evening." The working classes might also say: "I gave Baby juice and cereal at three." The upper classes would specify "*orange* juice," and "cornflakes" or "Weetabix."

Upper-class children tend to have other children over to tea at four as a social occasion. Middle-class children come over to play at any time. When the middle classes send their children to state schools, they ask their working-class school-mates home to tea and then feel hurt because they never get asked back. It never occurs to Zacharias Upward that Dive Definitely-Disgusting might feel ashamed of the smallness of his house or flat and the fact that he doesn't have a nursery.

The working classes tend to cram their children with sweets. Samantha Upward, having read about nutrition, tends to restrict Zacharias's sweet-eating, although career mums, conscious of being away too much, bombard their children with guilt presents every time they're late home. Little Zacharias, who is only allowed two sweets after lunch and is fed up with museums, wishes Samantha would get a part-time job, so he could get guilt presents too.

Upper-class children are taught nursery rhymes by their nannies and know them all by the time they're eighteen months, which gives them a vocabulary of about 500 words. Traditionally a lot of nursery rhymes chronicle the activities of their forbears anyway. Little Jack Horner pulling out a plum and presumably putting it in his mouth, for example, refers to the fat pickings culled by the Horner family during the dissolution of the monasteries.

Sharon Definitely-Disgusting only knows television jingles. In a recent quiz at a state school, none of the eleven-year-olds could say what Little Miss Muffet sat on.

Staying with Granny

Working-class children, as has been said before, often live with or near their grandmothers, and the working-class Nan is much the best with children, because she's had the most practice. Since Georgie Stow-Crat's grandparents often live in the country, they have more room and servants to take the children off the mother's hands. Zacharias Upward's grandparents live on their nerves and ever-dwindling fixed incomes. They move into smaller and smaller houses, but hang on to all the ornaments, which are double-parked on every piece of furniture. The place looks like an antique shop. All the china is moved up a shelf when grandchildren come and stay, but eventually they break the place up, because they're fed up with not being allowed to touch anything and with playing the same old brought-out game of bagatelle. A terrible family row develops because one ball bearing disappears. Both daughters and daughters-in-law feel on trial all the time; the tension is transmitted to the children. If they're let out into the garden, footballs snap the regalia lilies. Mealtimes are a nightmare because the middle classes are obsessively hot on table manners.

"Why do all my grandchildren eat as though they're gardening?" said one middle-class granny recently.

Children invariably let the side down saying: "Why can't we have baked beans in front of the telly like we do at home."

Upper-middle-class grannies invariably had nannies to bring up their own children, and cannot understand why their grandchildren should be so exhausting or so much more badly behaved than they remember their own children were. They forget they only saw them when they were presented newly washed for an hour after tea.

Samantha drives her mother-in-law crackers. Every time little Zacharias interrupts, she stops whatever adult conversation she is having to answer his question.

The middle classes tend to reason.

The working classes tend to clout.

The working classes have pacifiers.

Middle-class children are more likely to suck their thumbs.

Growing up

Sexual modesty is also a good index of social class. The majority of the working classes never see their parents naked, which must be quite an achievement, as they often sleep in the same room—rather like undressing on the beach.

Social Class I (which according to the Census includes scientists, doctors and structural engineers) are much more likely to let their children see them with no clothes on. Pretty horrifying really, and enough to put one off sex for life, having a hairy scientist streaking round the house.

The upper middles are less likely to worry about masturbation, and more likely to tell their children the facts of life. They are aided in this by Althea, of Dinosaur Books fame, who has written a very explicit children's book about having a baby. Known locally as the "rude" book, it is a great favourite to read aloud when Granny comes to stay.

To Jen Teale, the word "rude" means slightly smutty. To the upper classes it means "impertinent." Similarly the uppers use "cheeky" to mean impertinent, to Jen Teale it means a bit risqué, or near the knuckle.

The working classes don't explain, so you get their children coming into the public library asking: "I want a book about life."

"Whose life?" says the librarian. "Biographies over there."

"Facts a life, miss."

Georgie Stow-Crat doesn't need to be told about sex because he's seen plenty of farm animals copulating and procreating. As a result, upper-class men often take their wives from behind.

My husband heard about sex for the first time when he was walking in a prep school crocodile along the beach.

"I say, chaps," said a boy called the Hon. James Stewart, "I know how babies are made."

Whereupon they all gathered round saying: "Go on, Stewart, tell us."

"The man lies on top of the woman," said Stewart portentously, "and is excused into her."

The middle classes will start taking their children to the dentist almost before they've got teeth, the working classes tend only to go when their teeth ache. "You can tell what class a person is the moment he opens his mouth," said John Braine, "by the state of his teeth." That's why Sharon Definitely-Disgusting claps her hands over her mouth whenever she laughs.

The upper classes give their children 10p. from the fairies when a tooth comes out. Inflation and indulgence have pushed the middle classes up to 50p. Among the upper-middle merry-tocracy the fairies often get drunk and forget to put the money under the pillow and have to compensate with twice as much the next day. When the local fun-fair arrives every year, children have been known to tug teeth out with forceps untimely for more money to spend on the fruit machines.

People are gradually realising that illiteracy in schools today is nothing to do with the teaching, but simply because children have been turned into a race of zombies watching television. Soon the middle classes will start banning television altogether, and illicit watch-easys will be set up in darkened dives round the country. Samantha Upward tries not to let little Zacharias read comics or watch more than an hour's television a day. Upper-class children go into the kitchen and read the housekeeper's children's comics. Samantha reads out loud to Zacharias in a clear voice, altering words she thinks are common.

The Queen evidently read very early because in the evenings her mother used to read her books "about animals and horses and they would recite gay poetry." (Marlowe and Oscar Wilde perhaps.) Lower-class children can't read but they can write SOD and FUK in aerosol on bus shelters.

By the age of two, little Georgie Stow-Crat will be looking out on life with a clear blue gaze, frightened of no one, totally self-confident. He will also have a frightful accent from playing in the stables but no one is in the least bit worried. Working-class children always hold their noses in the country.

The lower-middle-class child will already be shell-shocked with instructions. Don't tread in Doggie's duty. Put your hand over your mouth when you cough. Don't turn your fork over to eat peas. It's rude to whisper. It's rude to shout. Talk in a low, clear voice like Mrs. Thatcher. Class is beginning to creep in. Middle-class children twig that they can bully the cleaning-woman's children, but the cleaning-woman's children can't beat them up in return. They also know that there are certain children in the road their mother prefers them playing with to others. Samantha has great difficulty explaining to little Zacharias why he may sprinkle his pepper but not his salt.

I once heard my son regaling his friends:

"Mummy says 'pardon' is a much worse word than 'fuck.'"

Jen Teale's children will be constantly pulled up for some real or imagined coarseness of speech or enunciation. It's so important to be "well-spoken."

Middle-class children put cherry stones on the side of their plate with their spoon and chant: "Tinker, tailor, soldier, sailor, rich man, poor man, beggerman, thief." The upper classes put them on the side of their plate, concealing the journey from mouth to plate with a curled fist, and saying: "Army, Navy, Law, Divinity, Independent, Medicine, Trade."

The working classes only eat cherries out of tins of fruit salad, with the stones removed already.

Children's parties are a sophisticated form of torture. The upper classes tend to give parties just for nannies and children, mid-week, and ending at six so as not to involve the husbands. No drink is offered to collecting parents.

Nanny Stow-Crat couldn't stop Fiona inviting Tracey Nouveau-Richards as they sit next to each other at nursery school, but Caroline says she's not having those ghastly parents in the house: "They never know when to leave and once through the door, they might make a habit of dropping in."

Samantha Upward, being very democratic, encourages Zacharias to invite all his little state school friends who run absolutely wild all over the newly planted perennials that were once going to make an herbaceous border. They refuse to play party games and drive the conjuror into hysterics by explaining in loud voices how every trick is done.

Mr. Nouveau-Richards, who feels that only the best is good enough for my Tracey-Diane, employs a caterer, a comedian gives each child a doll's house as a going-away present, and shows the premiere of *Star Wars II* after the interval. All the surrounding middle-class mums would like to refuse, but daren't because they'd get such flak from their children.

The upper-middle merry-tocracy mix drink, nannies and mothers, thereby making the children's party a much more jolly occasion. Parties in Putney are rather like singles bars with separated fathers turning up to collect children and meeting pretty divorced mothers and getting nose to nose over the Soave and the hassle of bringing up children on one's own.

Chapter 3

THE NANNY

The daughters of tradespeople, however well educated, must
necessarily be underbred, and as such unfit to be the inmates
of our dwellings or guardians of our children's minds, and
persons.

Charlotte Brontë

Anyone studying the English class system will have noticed certain
similarities between the extreme upper and lower classes: their
toughness, their xenophobia, their indifference to public opinion,
their passion for racing and gambling and their fondness for plain
speaking and plain untampered food. Jonathan Gathorne-Hardy,
in *The Rise and Fall of the British Nanny,* says the reason is that
the ruling classes for the last two hundred years have been brought
up almost entirely by working-class nannies, their parents abdicat-
ing all responsibility.

"With maternity nurses, nannies, prep school and public
school," admitted one mother, "it's almost as though we put them
in care."

Certainly one of the reasons the aristocracy has always notched
up so many marriages was that they never had any boring middle-
class worries about how it might affect the children. Nanny would
always be there to look after them and provide continuity.

Working for the great, nannies took on their own snobbisms,
not unlike suburban crones working in Knightsbridge dress shops
for £50 a week who make you feel bitterly ashamed of your scuffed
heels and the fact you can't afford £500 for a little black dress.

There was a group of nannies who ruled Hyde Park.

"Are you a titled mummy's nanny," said one gorgon when a newly employed nanny tried to sit down beside her.

The new nanny shook her head.

"Well, I'm afraid," said the gorgon, "this bench is reserved for titled mummies' nannies."

Until a few years ago, Nanny was a fixture in the upper-class house, taking on the surname of the family, and often staying with them until she died, when an announcement would appear in *The Times*, stating the family's gratitude at her length of service. When her charges grew up, there were always grandchildren. Sometimes she regained her ascendancy when the master became senile, and needed looking after, or when Miss Caroline became an alcoholic. One friend of mine spends £6,000 a year keeping a large house in Sussex going simply as a base for his old nanny and her dog. Another nanny, when her children grew up, took over the care of the three family dogs, keeping them in baskets upstairs, and giving them the same nursery routine of brushing, walks, mealtimes and early beds. While yet another old nanny keeps an eye on visiting dogs. When a friend's golden retriever had been cavorting in the loch for an hour, she sidled up and said: "I think Porridge has been in for long enough."

Today, alas, the old-fashioned nanny whose life was her children, who welcomed the role of surrogate mother, imposed on her by her employers, delighting in the challenge of coping with everything, never taking a holiday, is virtually an extinct breed.

"You'll be lucky if you get a girl to stay six months," said Nannies of Kensington. "They just don't want to get involved for too long." A few years ago Mrs. Walters of Knightsbridge Nannies, who provided "treasures" for half the crowned heads of Europe, said her telephone was permanently jammed with cries of "Help me, Help me" from harassed society women left in the lurch by their nannies and faced with the appalling prospect of having to forego a game of bridge or a trip to Fortnums. It also suits the agencies to foster this myth of unavailability. The more often a nanny moves around, the more often they get their cut.

By the end of the seventies, however, the position had changed slightly. The rocketing cost of living has made the nanny's job much more attractive. If she lives in, she gets all her bills paid: rent, telephone, rates, electricity, gas and food, and £25–£35 tax-free pocket money on top of that, which makes her far better off than a secretary on £5,500 a year. The only way you distinguish the nannies from the mothers picking children up from school is that the nannies are younger and better dressed.

On the other hand the more women go out to work, the more they are dependent on others to look after their children. If the nanny is working for a divorced or separated woman, or even in a household where the woman is the chief breadwinner, her power is absolute. If she walks out, her employer will have to jeopardize her job staying at home and looking after the children, or fork out for a temporary at £50 a week.

Before the war, the upper and middle classes tended to be undomesticated (my grandmother once went into the kitchen, saw a dishcloth and fled, never to return) and were therefore neurotically dependent on servants. Today any career woman or working mother who has to rely on a recalcitrant daily woman (someone once said they were called "dailys" because they leave after one day) or a capricious nanny in order to go out to work will understand this neurosis.

One sees this absolute power developing so often. A plump little lower-middle-class girl arrives from the country with rosy cheeks and a Yorkshire accent. She starts off doing absolutely everything for £10 a week, but gradually she makes herself indispensable. She also starts aping the mannerisms of her employers and goes to a West End hairdresser, her accent disappears as do the inches off her hips. Next she meets a boy-friend and, terrified of losing her because she's become such a treasure, her employers let the boy-friend move in. Soon there's a broad-shouldered denim-jacketed back watching television every time the parents come in from an evening out, which is soon followed by additional aggro because he's having fry-ups in the morning, drinking the house Carafino and using the bath.

The employers are by now frightened of using the car in case the nanny is intending to take it home for the weekend, and start fighting as to which one of them is going to ask her to baby-sit, if they occasionally want to go out, standing outside her door, saying, "No, you do it. No, *you* do it."

By now the boy-friend starts shop-stewarding around, telling the nanny she oughtn't to be working those hours: "Girls in our office only do nine to five, and you never get a lunch hour." More and more concessions are made, anything to avoid the hassle of working in a new girl.

Usually a row blows up about once a month, whereupon the nanny sits in the kitchen muttering to next door's nanny and ringing ads in the *Evening Standard,* or *The Times.* While her employer doesn't feel up to going to work and sits nervously writing an ad for *The Lady,* or ringing up agencies on the upstairs telephone: "Tell anyone who might be interested to ring my husband at the office, or she can ring here at weekends." Usually she and the nanny get bored of rowing by the evening, and make it up over a litre bottle of Soave. By the time the husband comes home all wound up to read the riot act, wife and nanny are plastered but fondly tearful over an empty bottle.

A few years ago middle-class husbands used traditionally to knock off the *au pair.* Today, far more often you find husbands getting jealous of the mutually sycophantic, love-hate relationship that exists between the wife and the nanny, particularly since the advent of the permissive society, when nanny often covers up for the wife's sexual peccadilloes and therefore has even more power over her.

Samantha Upward only works part time and doesn't feel this justifies a nanny, so she gets foreign *au pairs* to help Zacharias with his French and says: "Go and do your Devoir, darling," when he gets home from school. Gideon hopes every time for someone like Brigitte Bardot, but Samantha has so much middle-class guilt about employing anyone, and spends so much time scurrying round doing all the work, that the various Claudines and Marie Josés soon become au pear-shapes.

No such scruples overcome Mrs. Nouveau-Richards, who, as a first-generation employer, is determined to get several pounds of flesh off the nannies. She expects them to work six days a week for only £12, to wear uniform, to keep the children upstairs and to call her "Mrs. Nouveau-Richards." One nanny told us that her newly rich employer allowed her to call her by her Christian name only if they went out together in the evening, never during the day. She also allowed the nanny to use the front stairs, but the other servants had to use the back stairs.

One of the professional nanny's least enviable tasks is helping with the playgroup. The rich send their children to nursery schools, where trained nursery nannies take them over for three hours a day, and teach them the rudiments of reading, writing and making castles out of the insides of lavatory-paper rolls. The less rich have to make do with playgroups, where different mothers take it in turns in threes to supervise the children. Here the lower-middle Jen Teales are *far* more bossy than the upper-middle mums, and if a working mother sends her nanny or her *au pair* instead of herself, the Jen Teales, probably feeling themselves perilously close to the status of the nanny, refuse to talk to her, except for making her do all the dirty work. When my own nanny used to do it, she was the only adult who wasn't offered a cup of coffee.

Many people who didn't have nannies themselves regard them as a status symbol. One *nouveau riche* family who employed a girl insisted she wear a uniform, but gave her a nervous breakdown by never allowing her near the baby. And although many permanent nannies today act as managing director for the whole household, for some reason they feel they will be looked down on socially if they admit what their job is. I had one girl who instead of saying she was a nanny used to tell her boy-friends that she was on the dole and only staying with me. Another girl was just getting her employers and the children off for a weekend when some man rang up. "Hang on," her employers heard her saying, "I'm just saying goodbye to some friends."

On another occasion when a commercial was being made in her boss's house, she asked him to carry his newly ironed shirts upstairs because she didn't want the film crew to realise she was a nanny. If asked what she does she says she's a P.A.

The nanny-employer relationship is interesting because it is one of the few occasions when the classes meet head-on, not just during the day, as people do in the office, but at all times, and the nanny has to adjust to a completely different life-style.

Nannies divide households into "upstairs" and "downstairs" families. The upstairs families keep the children upstairs, and allow the nanny complete, if lonely, autonomy. Downstairs families are usually middle-class, where the nanny and the mother muddle along, both looking after the children in uneasy complicity. Nannies in the past have tried to impose gracious living on our household: mauve bath crystals, white plastic flower vases filled with plastic flowers, plastic punch bowls with eight little matching cups and a glass ladle, short back and sides for both children, an acrylic white cardigan edged with pink tulips which my daughter thought was absolute heaven, as she did a pair of wedge-heeled walking shoes. Nothing could illustrate my innate middle-classness more than the fact that I was too wet to put my foot down and insist they should either be taken back or not used.

Caroline Stow-Crat wouldn't have had any such problem. On the other hand she would never correct her nanny in front of anyone else like a woman with her nanny and child who passed me and my dog in the street.

"Look at the lovely doggie," said the nanny to the child.

"That is a dog, not a doggie," said her employer in chilling tones.

Chapter 4

EDUCATION

After three years at a private day school, the upper classes pack their children off to prep school at eight because they're too stupid to do the homework any more, because they can't cope with the complications of getting them to school and because even though they're not at all afraid of the school staff, they have no desire to mix with them socially at the string of fund-raising events laid on by day schools. Even at eight, little Georgie Stow-Crat misses home less than a middle-class child because his affection is divided between his mother and the nanny. He misses Snipe the Labrador most of all and calls Caroline Stow-Crat "sir" in the holidays. Any boisterousness or subversive tendencies are ironed out of him at school, and everyone, particularly his grandmother, says how much he is improved. No one, on the other hand, can explain why the housekeeper's cat has been strangled.

Samantha Upward, trying to be enlightened, starts Zacharias off at a state primary, which she refers to as "the village school," but even with his head start little Zacharias doesn't do as well as expected, and develops a frightful accent, which makes his grandmother wince. After a lot of heart-searching and Gideon Upward having to give up smoking and drink wine instead of whisky, Zacharias is sent to the local day prep school at eight, only to find that all the other upper middles by now have been sent off to boarding school, and the place is crawling with pushy lower middles and Nouveau-Richards. Against such competition Zacharias does less and less well. He's called "Zacharine" and beaten up in the playground by Jason Nouveau-Richards and his gang and is eventually sent off to a cramming boarding school at eleven, because the headmaster has suggested the horrible possibility that he might not pass Common Entrance (required to get to a public school), and because Gideon and Samantha can't get him to do two hours' homework a night against a background of television.

Left-wing intellectuals pack their children off to the local comprehensive, rejoicing in the spare cash, and the first glottal stop. Actually their children are bright enough to waltz through any system; if not, they have them coached. Six years later the parents shriek like hell when they have to fork out for university.

The middle classes, of course, always work the system. They have cars to take their children to the better state schools, and they deliberately buy houses in the right area. The Oxford local papers, for example, advertise houses with swimming pools, four bedrooms and location in the catchment area for a fashionable state school.

Often a group of middle-class parents picks on a school and enforces its own standards, until it's so over-subscribed the head can pick and choose. There is a primary school in Berkshire known as "the Trojan horse of the state system," where the headmaster only takes children whose parents have been to boarding school or a university, or whose mothers are extremely pretty. The result is scholarships to all the top public schools, and speech days full of headscarves and Labradors. The only difference between this and the local day prep school is that the mothers picking up their children from the state school are better dressed because they have more cash to spend.

"Hooray, now we can afford a Volvo," said one mother when she heard her child had got a place.

Meanwhile Jen Teale is tearing her hair because she can't get Wayne or Christine in, and has to fork out for a day prep. Having forked out, she is extremely pushy. She always goes along to open day to see what she's paying for, and says she's "very satisfied" because little Wayne is bound to get qualifications later, and that's all that matters. Wayne has also brought home some very nice boys, which could never have happened at the local primary, where the hazard of him chumming up with the local dustman's son was always a thunderous possibility. In conversation with friends who have children at state schools she often mentions Wayne's French, or asks them if they've got a Latin dictionary.

The Nouveau-Richardses dispatch little Jason to a day prep, and then to one of the top boarding schools, paying extortionate fees to buy a little upper-middle-class child on credit (alias the never-never).

The Tory press recently turned up a docker, a warehouseman and a gasmeter reader who were sending their children to private schools while a vast number of middle-class parents couldn't afford it any more. How ironic, the report went on, if the working classes commandeered private education, as it moved further and further out of the reach of the middle classes. I think this is improbable. Traditionally the financial situation of working-class parents makes them accept the state system as normal. And the middle classes receive different and longer education, and are educationally more successful. The chances of the child of an unskilled worker being a poor reader at seven are six times greater than in the case of the upper-middle-class child, who arrives at school tuned in to educational demands and who, when he gets home, has someone to help him with his homework, and somewhere quiet to do it.

While half the children in the Census Social Class I (the upper middles) reach higher education, either at university or polytechnic, only one in a thousand of Class V (unskilled workers) stays on at school after sixteen. Leaving school young is deeply embedded in working-class sections of the community, where parents keep their children at home to babysit or do housework, or, if money is short, send them out to work.

The middle-class child is realistic about prospects and sees success in terms of steady progress and cumulative success, while the working-class child sees it in terms of a quiet life or sudden fame as a pop star or a footballer. Those who leave school early often regret that they can't get a particular job because they haven't got any qualifications, or that lack of education makes the job difficult.

Parental involvement

The National Foundation for Educational Research, who ought to be collectively shot, is convinced that the greater the parental involvement, the more Able (Abel as opposed to Cain) the child will be. Parental involvement is the main hobby of the non-working mother; it's an extension of justifying your existence by creative child-rearing. The frightfully lower-middle expression a "caring and concerned parent" is bandied around a great deal by both the press and the teaching profession. If a child isn't doing well at school, you ring up the parents and rocket them that the home back-up isn't "caring" enough, and do spot checks by asking the children to write essays entitled "My Mummy" or "My Daddy." If Zacharias Upward writes: "My Daddy drinks whicksy all day, and my mother looks like a princess, but never comes to kiss me good night," Samantha and Gideon get a black mark. You also rate as a bad parent if you don't visit the school enough—but if you visit and criticise rather than help with the jumble sale, you are marked down as "overzealous."

"The middle classes can be a frightful bore," said one school-master. "The ideal pupil would be an industrious middle-class child with working-class parents who kept out of your hair." The worst parents are evidently middle-class intellectuals, who can't accept that their child is average and the child gets so pressurized it just cops out.

A daunting idea put forward by all schools today is that parents should educate themselves in order to help their children. Samantha Upward is taking an Open University course in absolutely everything in an attempt to push Zacharias. Jen Teale has gone back to part-time teaching, to catch up on the latest techniques.

Parents are advised to join the Parent-Teachers Association and bully for their own maths workshops. In the same way that Communists monopolise union meetings, so the middle classes, even in a comprehensive school, tend to take over the P.T.A., leading to a serious distortion of influence. (Mrs. Definitely-Disgusting doesn't speak the same language as the staff, and is often frightened of them.) With massive condescension, one schoolmaster suggested starting a school playgroup, or a building project, or even a car mechanics club to attract the working classes into the P.T.A.

Not only are the middle classes being taxed out of existence and struggling to pay the fees, they are also made to feel guilty if they're not pouring money into the school kitty and taking afternoons off to be present at school events. If they asked one to sponsor a walk to save-the-parents it would make more sense.

The schools themselves never let up—coffee mornings, knit-ins, jumble sales, P.T.A. dances. These are usually organized by the Friends of the School, a posse of busybodies in tweed skirts who call the headmistress by her Christian name, and haven't enough to do in the afternoons. The good parent has to be there on Saturday afternoon manning a stall. It's not enough to send a cheque for £5 on the Monday after.

The Nouveau-Richardses go to everything because you meet such a nice class of parent there. Samantha Upward goes to everything because she feels it helps Zacharias. Her social life is entirely taken up with school events, from biology workshops and concerts to P.T.A. dances, and, as she insists on Gideon coming as well to create an impression of solidarity, they have to spend a bomb on baby-sitters.

The Stow-Crats never go to anything. Mrs. Definitely-Disgusting arrives at the door, hears the Hampstead middle-class whine and goes home again. The upper middles often feel it their duty to patronize events of this kind, have several drinks at home first and refuse to dance.

About once a week, a note with a perforated section about forthcoming events arrives full of lower-middle-class words like "refreshments," "pleasant" and "enjoyable." "If you can be of service as a helper," it concludes rather wildly, "please tear off your slip and send it to one of the committee."

At Christmas there's a nativity play, which at state schools is often held in the morning. This means lots of working-class fathers on shift work, and Gideon Upward looking at his watch and wondering how late he dare be at the office. The Virgin Mary's parents are invariably divorced and acrimonious. They turn up and sit glaring from opposite ends of a school bench, but in the end are forced to sit next to one another through lack of space. No one can hear the kiddies tunelessly chanting "'Ark the 'erald" or "Once in Royal Divid" because of all the baby brothers and sisters squawking their heads off.

At fee-paying schools, there are no babies, because the parents pay someone to look after them for the afternoon. The following announcement was once sent out by my son's old day prep school: "We hope you will all come to our informal Carol Service on December 15. This year we shall be having kindergarten boys for the first time. I'm sure we shall all enjoy them."

School meals

When my son first went to a primary school five years ago, faced with the utter impossibility of having the right dinner money every day, I asked if I could pay by cheque for the whole term. The school was extremely shocked; it was good for discipline, they said, for the children to bring the right money each day, and was I too insensitive to realise that it was beyond most working-class budgets to fork out all at once for a whole term? Now I notice that most state schools allow parents to pay by cheque. Private schools call it "lunch" and put it on the bill. State school dinners are supervised by someone grandiosely called a "dinner lady."

The "milk run"

The routine of taking children to school by car on a rota shared among parents, often known as the "milk run," causes more aggravation than any other part of the day school curriculum, particularly when mothers are trying to shunt three children to three different schools all coming out at different times. Where the children are concerned it's one of the last bastions of snobbery—the bigger and shinier the car you're picked up in, the better. On the whole, mothers dress more scruffily the higher-class they are. Caroline Stow-Crat turns up in jeans in a filthy Range-Rover, and is admonished by Georgie, who thinks she ought to wear smarter trousers and clean the car more often. Why can't she be more like Mrs. Nouveau-Richards, who is always dressed up to the nines and takes the "show-*fur*" and the Rolls?

Jen Teale, who is terrified her children may miss a second of school that's being paid for, gets quite hysterical when Samantha's French *au pair* oversleeps and picks up the Teale children ten minutes late.

Caroline Stow-Crat is always getting stuck in someone else's house at weekends and ringing up at midnight saying she's snowed up and can Samantha do the milk run. Samantha is furious, but doesn't say so. "A lady never lets herself go." Nor can she get any sympathy out of Mrs. Nouveau-Richards, who is only too glad to put her "show-*fur*" at Caroline's disposal at any time. Jen Teale, who cleans the Volkswagen herself, thinks Caroline's Range-Rover is much too draughty, and she's fed up with having Snipe's hairs all over little Wayne's newly brushed blazer.

On Wednesday the milk run to the doctored state primary, where the music's so good, is like the bus of the London Symphony Orchestra with all the children's instruments sticking out of the window.

Georgie Stow-Crat complicates matters on Samantha's milk run by telling everyone that he's being allowed to stay up till midnight tonight, because his mother is giving a party for eighty people—to which none of the milk run mothers have been asked.

A friend's child went to a pre-school open day at one of the most fashionable London high schools. All the little new girls were told: "At the end of the afternoon, you stand in the hall, and the moment you see your mummy's car coming up the drive, you can tell your form mistress, and go and meet Mummy." It was automatically assumed that all the parents had cars.

In state schools, many of the children walk or go by bus. When Samantha suggested Zacharias might go by bus, so she could take a little part-time job, Zacharias refused; he didn't want his cap knocked off by "comprehensile" boys.

The most relentless upstaging goes on between children on the school runs.

"My mother went to Princess Anne's wedding," said one child.

After a long pause, the second child replied: "My parents were asked, but they didn't want to go."

The attitude towards chauffeurs is interesting too. One working-class boy, whose father had made good, made the chauffeur drop him off a quarter of a mile from his primary school, and walked the rest of the way, so the other boys wouldn't mob him.

But two teenagers at a private day school had different ideas. The younger sister hated the chauffeur wearing his cap because the other girls would think it so snobbish. The older girl, on the other hand, hated him not wearing his cap: "It would be so awful if anyone thought he was Daddy."

Accent

Primary Mary, teacher wary,
How does your accent grow?
With cockney vowels, and Mummy's scowls
And glottal stops all in a row.

An English upper-class accent is often called a "public school accent." But as Jonathan Gathorne-Hardy has pointed out in his book *The Public School Phenomenon,* accent became a distinguishing characteristic socially with the emergence of the court and the capital of London long before the founding of the public schools. This dialect of London, Cambridge and Oxford was originally South East Midlands but as it became the social speech of a class, it developed apart from the regional variety. William the

Conqueror spoke Norman French but by the sixteenth century London English (hence the King's English) was regarded as the only language for a literary man or a gentleman, and remained so throughout the seventeenth and eighteenth centuries. The public schools merely intensified this.

In the nineteen-sixties during the hippy egalitarian revolution against materialism and never-having-it-so-good, the upper and middle classes identified profoundly with the new culture and became devotees of long hair and pop music. Working-class became beautiful and everyone from Princess Anne downwards spat the plums out of their mouths, embraced the flat "a" and talked with a working-class accent. Even today you can invariably age twenty-two- to thirty-year-olds by their voices. Prince Charles preceded the revolution and speaks his mother's English, Prince Andrew came after it. Nicholas Monson, one of the new wave of right-wing writers, said that during that period he got very embarrassed with being at Eton and having a smart background, so by listening carefully to the housemaid he began to talk with a modulated regional accent.

"After Eton," he went on, "I put off trucking to Katmandu and discovering Zen. Instead I went to Kingston Polytechnic. As I was mixing with 'real' people, I put on sweaty T-shirts and dirty jeans, let my hair collapse in rat-tails over my shoulders and affected an accent that owed its origins to Liverpool, California and the East End of London . . . I was uncomfortable with this voice, so I said little, but nodded vigorously and tried to look tough . . . We also sneered at a certain lecturer . . . who wore a pinstriped suit and talked posh. It was at such an airing of bigotry . . . I realised, to my acute embarrassment, that I was guilty of the same crime as before. I was a snob."

It must have been about this time in the seventies that many other people were undergoing the same realisation. The prosperity ran out, and the working class, the simple life and dropping out became less attractive—because there were no jobs to drop back into when you'd had enough. Upper- and middle-class schoolchildren became more conventional again—more right-wing—and shed a good deal of their working-class accent. As my niece said: "It simply isn't cool to talk like a yobbo any more."

The result is a different kind of speech, much more clipped, "awf'ly" and "frightf'ly," "ya" or "yp" instead of "yer" or "yeah." Georgie Stow-Crat might say "funtustic," and "whole" to rhyme with "doll," but he wouldn't say "amizing" like the cockney child. He is often bilingual and will lapse into mid-Atlantic or disc-jockey when he's with his friends. And when he wants to irritate Caroline in the holidays, he cultivates a glottal stop and asks her to pass the "bu-er." To the middle classes, although they won't admit it, a fee-paying school means "no more ghastly accent." Or, as a head-master said euphemistically, "We try to get rid of accents, they're a lazy way of speaking."

Alas for the Nouveau-Richardses, the effect often isn't lasting. When I lived in Yorkshire, the rich manufacturers sent their sons to Roogby to iron out their accents, but a few years after they left, they were speaking broad Yorkshire again.

"It's extraordinary," said a don at Radley, "how bucolic some of the old boys sound when they come back after a few years."

Quite often you get marked class discrepancies in a family because a father made his pile while his children were growing up and was able to send only the younger children to boarding school —or alternatively went bankrupt in the middle and was forced to send the youngest child to a comprehensive.

The left-wing trendies who send their children off to the local state school go into ecstasies at the first flat "a." She has not failed us, she has not failed us. Accent makes the heart grow fonder.

The Jen Teales often regard moving from place to place as an advantage. Not only does Bryan up his salary, but there is more likelihood of Wayne and Christine being well-spoken and not picking up a regional accent.

Class consciousness

A gentleman has good table manners and should not make wild gestures when speaking at banquets, so that he sweeps a bowl of semolina into his neighbour's lap.

Kings House School, Richmond, magazine

There is no worse snob than the prep school boy, but he is usually a possession snob, status being dependent on the size of his parents' car, how many rooms his house has, whether they have a swimming pool, where he went on holidays and the intricacies of his digital watch.

The dawnings of true class consciousness vary. A duke's daughter said she was aware of her position for the first time when she was four; she was playing in the garden and a particularly oily butler said: "Would my lady like some luncheon?" She was very clever, however. And she said that at school her intellect was much more of an embarrassment than her title. Rather like my niece the other day asking my nephew what subjects he was planning to take for A levels.

"Maths I and II, and Physics," came the reply.

My niece gave a gasp of horror:

"Oh Henry, what *will* you talk about at dinner parties?"

My daughter, at seven, is unaware of class, except in so far as she'll suddenly lapse into a Liverpool accent to make her friends laugh. My son, at ten, is beginning to come out with remarks like, "How many Lords do we know?" And when my husband told him to undo the top button of his shirt he said,

"Well Ken doesn't."

"Ken," snapped my husband, "is not a gentleman."

"Of course he is," said my son. "He's a millionaire."

Most snobbery, in fact, is instilled by the parents. For a brief period an earl's son was sent to my son's previous day school, and it was horrifying the way the mothers urged their sons to ask him to tea and birthday parties. He must have seen *Star Wars* about fifteen times.

There is a beautiful story of a very aristocratic child, going away to prep school for the first time, who got hauled up before the headmaster because he insisted on calling his form-master "Mr. Brown" instead of "sir."

"I suppose," said the headmaster with infinite sarcasm, "you expected Mr. Brown to call *you* 'sir.'"

"Yes, I did," said the boy simply.

I spoke to a girl who had just left a London fee-paying school in the city.

"No one ever talked about class," she said, "but one day a friend whispered, 'You and I are upper-middle, but the rest of the class are incredibly lower-middle.' Most of them come from small suburbs, their parents have scraped the money together to send them. One girl's father is a chartered accountant from a grammar school. Another girl's father is the head of a primary school, he won't let her out in the evening, she has to work. If you ask her where she lives, she always says 'the back of beyond,' actually it's somewhere like East Ham. One girl lives in public housing. Her father's a postman, but she wants to be an accountant and go to the London School of Economics. Because they tend to be alderman class, they're very job-conscious and materialistic. They have no desire to do good for other people, only themselves. They're very impressed by the professions, probably because they regard it as a step up. We went round the class; 17 out of 25 wanted to do law, solicitors rather than barristers, because it's more secure, and probably in local government. I was the only one who wanted to do English.

"The rest all dress very neatly—white shirts that stay tucked in, and clean shoes and skirts. They think I'm incredibly scruffy. They buy a lot of cheap shoes, but never any books.

"Their idea of social success is to be asked to a tennis club or cricket club dance. They talk a lot about losing their virginity but are more interested in whether it will ruin the relationship than the moral aspect. And they endlessly discuss the pill, but there again, because they might put on weight. They're all terribly competitive, but the main battleground, apart from the academic, is the rush to drive. They're obsessed with provisional licenses and three-point turns. One girl's father gave her a car when she passed her A levels."

These girls, as can be seen, are the same class as Bryan and Jen Teale.

Warfare

I am conscious, moreover, of a marked distaste for those who have not benefited from a public school education. This distaste is based on no superficial prejudice, it is founded on experience. People who have not endured the restrictive shaping of an English public school are apt in after life to be egocentric, formless and inconsiderate. These are irritating faults. They are inclined also to show off. This objectionable form of vanity is in its turn destructive of the more creative forms of intelligence.

Harold Nicolson

Whenever people attack the English class system they start slinging mud at the public schools. I say "English" specifically because there aren't any famous public schools in Wales and because education in Scotland is far more democratic. In *The Public School Phenomenon* Jonathan Gathorne-Hardy makes the interesting point that the expression "working class" was only used pejoratively for the first time in the 1830s, when the Industrial Revolution was spewing forth Nouveau-Richardses in unprecedented droves. "There is a natural tendency," he writes, "for those who have just made money to join the company, and ape the manners of those who have always had it, and despise those they have left behind. In the nineteenth century this was hugely reinforced by the fact that the newly rich appeared at a time when the land-owning upper classes still held political power."

The easiest way for the Nouveau-Richardses to join the upper

classes was via a public school. Obviously you could never become
a gentleman if you remained jammed up against a lot of common
tradesmen. The upper classes, as Gathorne-Hardy goes on, had
evolved distinct ways of speaking, dressing, holding their knives
and forks, writing letters and so on. And boarding schools, where
everyone was in view of everyone else, and away from the coarsen-
ing influences of home, were a particularly good way of elaborating
and enforcing these aspects of behaviour.

In the nineteenth century, the difference between the old
landed gentry and the manufacturing classes was that the first
inherited their money, the second earned it. And, paradoxically,
although the ambitious merchant or industrialist exalted work,
once his son went to a boarding school and then on to Oxford or
Cambridge, and mixed with the upper classes and espoused coun-
try-house life (probably the most seductive of all life-styles), he had
to value idleness as the supreme mark of status. The point of the
aristocrat, as we have seen, is that he does not need to work for his
living. This is *crucial* to the understanding of English class attitudes. It underpins the idealisation of the amateur, it explains why
money went on the houses, horses and beautiful things, rather than
back into the business. It explains the horror of trade, and why the
English, unlike the French, Americans and Germans, have always
regarded "intellectual" as a dirty word.

The public schools were not required to educate: they taught
strength of character, leadership and self-reliance. This, in turn,
explains why until a few years ago the upper and upper middle
classes took little interest in education. "The English gentleman,"
wrote Douglas Sutherland as recently as the middle seventies, "regards any child who comes more than half-way up the class with
extreme suspicion."

Things have been changing during the last twenty-five years,
however. Capital transfer tax has made it harder to leave much
money. The only inheritance one could be sure of giving one's child
was a good education. When the Russians come a good engineering
or physics degree might save him from the salt mines.

In the nick of time, most public schools have subordinated their earlier aim of building "character" and acting as a gentleman factory to the achievement of academic excellence. The Old Boy Network is a thing of the past.

This obsession with education has spread down the classes, because, according to the Census, you can't be in Social Class I unless you've got a degree (nuns for some reason being the only exception). To the working classes barristers, doctors and dentists are upper class. To them an "educated" voice means an upper-class voice. A good education therefore means climbing the social scale. It gives the bright child the chance to leap from Class V to Class I, and enables the middle-class child to stay put.

Education, as a result, has become a complete rat-race—with nine-year-old day-school children working ten hours a day; with teenagers being offered holidays in Bermuda if they pass A levels; and whole families, including the cat, going on tranquillisers before O levels.

In 1978, 67 per cent of middle-class children interviewed said they would rather work for an exam than go to a party and one working-class family knifed their father collectively because he pushed them so hard to go to a university. Even the upper classes are infected and in August the beaches and the grouse moors echo with Caroline Stow-Crat and her friends upstaging each other over how many A levels Fiona got.

Consequently the crammers are overflowing, coaches are having a field-day teaching new maths in the holidays, and the paediatricians are making a fortune testing middle-class children because they aren't coming top of the class. They've even evolved a new category called "Gifted Children," who are the new educationally deprived, according to the *Daily Mail*, because they're not being sufficiently stretched. One can't think how Beethoven and Shakespeare managed in the old days. The Great Train Robbers are all supposed to have been gifted children.

We now see that the aim to produce "extra-bright" children is common to all classes. The pressure on the middle classes to stand firm against competition from below not only kept the private and direct-grant schools full, in spite of increased fees, but has also been a factor in people having smaller families.

In the middle seventies the products of public schools, which took about a sixth of the school-going population, were still bagging the top jobs: 80 per cent of judges, 67 per cent of bishops, 80 per cent of directors of clearing banks, 68 per cent of directors of major industries.

In *The New Anatomy of Britain* (written in 1972) Anthony Sampson doubted whether the public schools could maintain a dominant position in the eighties. The middle classes would no longer be able to afford them; the great lower-middle-class movement, the growth of the grammar schools, was acting as a bridge between the lower classes and the corridors of power. Getting into a grammar school was the crucial step for upward mobility, since this facilitated entry into the middle classes and the professions. University re-inforced the upward climb. In 1975, however, with the abolition of the grammar schools, the bridge was smashed. With this scrapping of the grammar schools, the old social schism was intensified. The comprehensive schools and fee-paying schools glare at each other across the abyss—Us against Them again—the result is well and truly a class war.

Traditionally the public schools look down on the grammar schools, and equally the boarders at public schools look down on the day boys because they pay less for their education. Etonians look down on everyone, and the smartest Catholic school, Ampleforth, looks down on Eton. The big London public schools tended to be superior academically, but it wasn't smart to be academic, and most of the St. Pauls and Westminster intake lived in and around London, and no gentleman lived in London. And so it goes on. The great public schools, Eton, Harrow, Winchester, Rugby and Marlborough, look down on the minor public schools. And the boarding prep looks down on the day prep, who looks down on state school boys, who, in return for such contumely, beat prep school boys up on the way home. Finally the good comprehensives despise the "sink" schools, where the brighter children despise the dumber ones, and the dumber ones actually refer, according to one schoolmistress, to the bright ones as "snobs."

The seventies also ushered in another great movement: the fight-back of the middle classes; they were soon selling their houses, giving up drink and holidays, the fathers taking highly paid jobs with the Arabs, grandparents digging into capital and flogging the silver—all to keep their children at boarding school, or, as my daughter calls it, "balding school." (You go bald worrying about paying the fees.)

The independent schools themselves are also showing a strong will to survive. Godolphin and Latymer, one of the London direct-grant schools, rather than become a mini-comprehensive, accepted the challenge of independence. Their plight appealed to the middle classes; legacies and covenants poured in; old ladies sent postal orders. "Old Dolphins" ran Christmas bazaars, girls organized mammoth sponsored skip-ins. Parents coughed up. Industry helped with £1,000-a-year bursaries.

Meanwhile, headmasters have taken up fund-raising with a vengeance, producing glossy brochures with photographs of scaffolding with the word *Erection* printed underneath, and whizzing round the country giving appeal parties, which, after all, is far more fun than teaching. Suddenly it became all-important for them to become financial wizards. The Headmaster of Millfield, for example, is the consultant to a firm of brokers in the City. Radley got their half million for a new complex devoted to industry in under a year. My son's old prep school raised £42,000 in a few months.

But how long can they all survive? At first sight the fee-paying schools seem to be booming, and all appear to be heavily oversubscribed. In fact, as John Rae, Headmaster of Westminster, pointed out recently in *The Sunday Telegraph,* more and more public schools are losing boarders, the extent of the loss being concealed by the recruitment of girls and foreign pupils. There are well over 7,000 girls in boys' schools now, stripping, as it's delightfully put, the girls' schools of their sixth form, and making it increasingly difficult for them to hang on to their staff. Recently a leading girls' school refused a reference to any girl who deserted to a boys' school.

Apart from general fund-raising, the schools are devising all sorts of schemes such as enabling parents to pay on the never-never and establishing recruitment agencies in Hong Kong and the Middle East, which conjures up a marvellous picture of masters in lovat green tweed coats and baggy trousers sidling up to rich Arabs muttering, "Not-at-all-feelthy public schools."

The public and private school holidays are also getting longer and longer: nine weeks in the summer, compared with six weeks in the state schools and four-and-a-half weeks at Christmas and Easter (compared with the state schools' two-and-a-half weeks) and the children allowed home nearly every weekend, which means food and train fares, particularly if they bring school friends with them. One father said having teenagers home for the weekend was like entertaining mediaeval barons. The massive increase in rail fares also means that parents are tending to send their children to schools much nearer home, so in a way public schools are becoming more local.

In the future, according to John Rae, it looks as though the middle and upper classes will shop around. Some will try state schools up to thirteen, then use the independent schools to try and get their children through A levels; alternatively state schools up to sixteen, then a sixth-form college. Others will send them to a good prep school and hope that the discipline will carry them through comprehensive school. The direct-grant schools have places at eleven and so cream boys off the prep schools. Public schools, suspecting that parents can't afford to fork out from eight to eighteen, may lower the entrance age to eleven, juggling to catch a new market of parents who sent their children to a state primary. Whereupon the prep schools, feeling the draft, may extend the curriculum through to O levels, thus knocking the small public schools. A glorious free-for-all is envisaged with parents getting more and more muddled and obsessive.

Except for the inner cities, Mr. Rae feels, the comprehensive schools are likely to improve to a point when the middle classes opt out of the private system, and when they do it's likely to be in droves.

"We must abolish the private schools," writes C. E. Daunt, a schoolmaster who had moved over to the state system, "for they more than any single institution perpetuate the hoary social curse of our uniquely divisive and persistent English class system." On the other hand in the next chapter he lists the obvious advantages of boarding schools: "the education, the widening of horizons, the stimulus of new activities, friendships, a relief from the tensions commonly built up in the nuclear family during adolescence, and above all the development of autonomy."

One of the saddest passages in a book called *The Hothouse Society*, which consists of interviews with schoolchildren, comes from an East End boy in a state boarding school in East Anglia: "I leave in four weeks time, and have been very happy here. Just you try living in Bethnal Green, instead of watching it on T.V. or reading those sociological books about it by people who live in Hampstead. I'll never live in a lovely house like this again, the grounds, the birds, the trees, the space here all helped me, and the people, they're kind and interested."

In fact, if you examine the rigours of public-school life, it's amazing people feel any envy at all. It seems that beautiful, glass-wall, modern buildings are for children of unskilled workers and are free; while mediaeval ruins with ancient, ink-stained desks all jumbled up on top of each other are for sons of managing directors and peers of the realm.

Boarding schools in the old days were far worse than Borstal: Marlborough used to toss people in blankets over the stairs until one boy missed and fell to his death; in another school new boys had to crawl along boiling hot radiators, singing "Clementine" and have their faces slapped at the end.

But although schools are now less spartan than they used to be, the younger boys still suffer. Take another extract from *The Hothouse Society:* "My teddy helps me when I cry," said a seven-year-old prep-school boy. "It is from home. He's old but I like him. I miss my mother tucking me up. I worry because when I'm eight in the big boys' dormitory they take teddies away."

In fact, Mrs. Definitely-Disgusting, who charges round to schools threatening to duff up a form master if he so much as lays a finger on one of her children, would never put up with weeping on Waterloo Station as her darling was towed away to a one-sex borstal with all the risks of beating and buggery behind the squash courts.

But one can't believe that the abolitionists lose a wink of sleep over teddyless small boys, or the flogging and the buggery. What irritates them is that these products of what seems like a cross between the Weimar Republic and a concentration camp somehow make people who haven't been there feel inferior.

The difference, too, is that the public schools select while the comprehensive schools are meant to take everyone. The grammar schools accepted the able minority and discarded the incompetent. Comprehensive schools are supposed to encourage a wide standard of excellence and protect the incompetent—a sort of Non-Utopia. "You realise X can't read, and you respect him for it," said one state school master pompously, which is all very well as long as you go on respecting the boy who can. The Labour Government wanted to introduce F levels which will be far less demanding than A levels, in order that more children will leave school with qualifications.

The situation has now been reached that the more "disadvantaged" a school is (a euphemism for the more problem pupils it has) the more money it gets from the Government. As a result our local state school, which has an impeccable reputation and no hooligans, gets its subsidies slashed every year, and has to rely more and more on contributions from parents. Equally, all comprehensive schools have three bands like a deb dance: 25 per cent in band one for bright children, 50 per cent for average children, and 25 per cent for below average, so you often find a bright child can't go to the school she wants because band one is over-subscribed.

There is also the belief that fee-paying schools push you harder: "I'm sending Darren to a fee-paying school," said a Mr. Nouveau-Richards from Cheam, "because they teach you to *com*-pete."

"Independent schools have a different attitude to work," said a girl at Godolphin and Latymer. "My friends at comprehensive school don't care if they work or not. Someone like me who is basically lazy needs the push of a school like Godolphin and Latymer."

A comprehensive school mistress told me that she would beg, borrow and steal to send her daughter to an independent school over the next ten years until the dust settles. The most pessimistic say it will take 75 years to sort the mess out.

Eton

"Our chaps often get scholarships to Winchester and Bryanston," said a Surrey prep-school master, "but not Eton. We don't aim that high."

On the same note, Simon Raven, an Old Carthusian, tells a horrible story about a Jewish boy who was a brilliant cricketer who'd played regularly in the eleven, but who was dropped when the team went to Eton. Where boarding schools are concerned Eton is the *crème de la crème*.

As the lower middles drop Latin into the conversation, the middle classes drop Eton. One parvenu always boasts that his wife had a second cousin there. Girls will casually mention a brother who went.

Eton is also a very large school, which means there are a lot of Old Etonians about. They have long had a tradition of political dominance, stemming from the days when power lay in the hands of the landowning aristocracy, who automatically sent their sons to Eton. They still hold considerable sway in the Tory Party. Six were members of Mrs. Thatcher's first Cabinet. The only branch outside London of Coutt's Bank stands in the High Street at Windsor.

Eton is also a prime example of self-perpetuating selectivity. Seventy per cent of the boys are sons of Old Etonians.

It is very vulgar to wear an Old Etonian tie except with a morning coat. Frank Harris, who started as an American cowboy, when later living in France used to get his biographer Hesketh Pearson to send him out six at a time. All gentlemen go to Eton, but not necessarily all Etonians are gentlemen. There is also a belief

that Eton is secure enough to assimilate all types, that the Nouveau-Richardses will be less pilloried there than at other schools,
that intellectuals and eccentrics are more tolerated. Recently, however, a boy who said he supported Labour had his study covered
in red paint.

To muddle *les autres,* Etonians often refer to the school as
"Slough Comprehensive." Like most public schools, they have a
private language. They call masters "beaks," the matron the
"dame," terms "halves," and use quaint expressions like "Lower
Boy Pulling" or one's brother having been in "Pop," which means
he was one of the elite, not a fizzy-drinks manufacturer. In the
school list, Hon.'s are called "Mr.," while those without any title
are listed just by their Christian names and surnames.

Eton's activities are closely reported by the *Daily Mail,* which
regularly quotes the *Eton Chronicle,* as though it were gospel for
upper-class behaviour.

The press also regard Harrow as very up-market.

"Harrow boys may all come from the upper classes," a
housemaster's wife is quoted as saying a few years ago, "but they
are not rich, some of the boys even do their own laundry, and we've
even got two punk rockers" (rather like token blacks).

One is reminded of the Winchester headmaster, chided in the
nineteenth century by the authorities for only taking rich boys, who
somewhat irreverently replied: "The boys are not rich, in fact most
of them are extremely poor, it's their parents who are rich."

Sports day

The upper classes, regarding the word "sports" as vulgar, call sports
day things like "the Fourth of June" or "Gaudy." At Eton it is
rather like a race meeting without the horses, but the deficiency
is more than made up by the braying voices. Everyone knows
everyone, so the din is tremendous. As picnics of megalomaniac
lavishness are unpacked, a dog bowl is always laid on the long grass.
The place, in fact, is stiff with Snipe Stow-Crat and other dogs,

barking with delight to see their young masters again. The year I went other pets included a parrot, a white rat, a hamster and several guinea pigs.

The horseplay among the young was unbelievable; one old boy charged about carrying a bearskin aloft, and was finally brought down by a rugger tackle. In the tea tent a lot of the boys and their girl-friends were openly necking and yelling at each other.

"Wouldn't see behaviour like this at a comprehensive school," said one grandmother.

"Everything's gone to the dogs," said her friend. "They've even got tea bags instead of proper tea now."

The captain of the cricket eleven, who'd made a lot of runs, came in. No one took any notice of him, so he went out again. Someone let off a stink bomb, and we all went off to watch the procession of boats.

The crews wore boating jackets (evidently the word "blazer" is common), white flannels and straw boaters fantastically garlanded with flowers: roses, peonies, trailing laburnum, lupins, syringa. It's probably part of the gilt-edged security of being a member of the upper classes that none of them appeared at all self-conscious.

In the middle-class sector, sports day used to be a great hassle, but now that parents are far more interested in academic than athletic achievement, they are very relaxed occasions. At prep schools, a lot of little boys run round a daisied lawn for "silver" cups. Every time the starting pistol goes off, all the Labradors look up, expecting a large duck to fall out of the sky, rather like Chekhov with fairy cakes. There are a lot of masters in lovat green tweed jackets and baggy grey flannels swaying from one leg to another. At state school sports days, the masters wear off-the-peg suits, or tee-shirts and track suits. At state schools, the children all wave back at their parents. At prep schools, they insist you turn up and then ignore you; it is the beginning of middle-class inhibition.

What is amazing at middle-class sports days, which are usually held during the week, is the number of fathers present. Are they all "concerned and caring parents," or just malingering or on the dole?

The pattern is always the same. Harassed working mothers talking about *au pairs*, and non-working mothers having grisly heartburn that Simpkins minor might not make Oxbridge. There's always a sprinkling of bra-less earth mothers, with compost and wholemeal flour under their fingernails, wearing long skirts because they've been caught on a hot day with unshaven legs, who wobble in the mothers' race. Perhaps that's why all the fathers go.

At comprehensive schools, masters have great difficulty making any of the children turn up at sports day. In 1978 one headmaster suspended the whole sixth form a week before A levels, because none of them had bothered to put in an appearance. They said they preferred working for their exams.

Vocabulary

Both the upper and upper middle classes consider it is very vulgar to use the word "teacher." In ordinary adult conversation the upper classes say "schoolmaster" or "schoolmistress." At school they will say "master" or "mistress." Jen Teale resists the word "mistress," because it has sexual connotations, and says "schoolteacher."

It is all right to describe someone as a "good teacher" if you mean he is good at teaching, but very common if you mean he is a morally irreproachable schoolmaster.

"Teacher" without an article (e.g. "Teacher says . . .") is even worse.

"Youngster" is another very lower-class word. So are "lad" and "lass"; e.g. "I've got two fine lads at College." Harry Stow-Crat would say "Georgie is up at Oxford." "Youth" and "teenager" (perhaps because it's American) are somehow more O.K. Other unacceptable expressions include "plimsolls" for "gym shoes"; "P.E." for "gym"; and "bathing costume" or "swimsuit" for "bathing dress" or "swimming suit." "Scholar" should not be used as a synonym for "pupil"; it means a child who's won a scholarship.

Here is an example of lower-middle-class journalism. It is a report on Prince Andrew's girl-friend:

A scholar at exclusive Gordonstoun School, Scotland, she penned an excited note to her Gran on Palace notepaper. Among the Xmas cards gathered on the mantelpiece above a coal fire was a card from Prince Andrew.

"We are not particularly wealthy," enthused her Gran. "At the moment she is studying for an examination, she's very keen on sports."

There are at least nineteen expressions here which Caroline Stow-Crat would regard as socially dubious.

Journalists invariably use the words "exclusive" and "select" as a euphemism for "rich" or "upper-class."

It is very bad form to ask someone where they went to school. The expression "public school" is also very lower-middle in the sentence "Wayne is going to public school next term." Among the upper classes it would be assumed a child was going to one anyway.

Girls' schools

Be good, sweet maid, and let who will be clever.

Animosity against the public schools is aimed far more at boys' schools than girls', because it is still the men, rather than the girls, who are bagging the top jobs, because girls' schools are far less snobbish and because among the upper echelons it matters far less where girls went to school, a lot of people still believing it's nice for a girl to stay at home.

The upper and middle classes traditionally spend far less on their daughters' education than on their sons'. A feeling still persists that it doesn't matter so much for girls, as long as they learn

French and nice manners, get a few O levels and make some jolly nice "gairl" friends.

A classic example of this was the diplomat quoted in *Harper's* who sent his secretary to find a boarding school for his daughter, adding that if she had been a boy, "I'd have had to do it myself."

Girls at boarding schools are seldom taught any domestic science beyond making cod in cheese sauce and rhubarb crumble, nor do they ever learn how to clean a room. This is a hangover from the old days when it was assumed they would always have servants when they grew up.

Comprehensive schools have home economics sections, often grander than those of any finishing school, but the girls get so good at housework that this often leads to conflict at home.

Some girls' schools pretend the class barriers are breaking down, but the old prejudices remain. Gathorne-Hardy quotes one headmistress as saying she would love her girls to go to dances with neighbouring boys' schools, but alas there were none in the area. Actually there were several comprehensives: what she meant was no public schools.

English vice

You can't expect a boy to be vicious till he's been to a good school.

Saki

If, when you're looking round for a suitable boy's boarding school, you tell someone you've decided on X, they promptly say, "Oh, they're just a bunch of queers there," so you say, "Well, Y's my second choice," to which they reply, "Oh, they're a bunch of queers there too." So you say, "Well, what about Z? All the masters are married, and they've just introduced girls." "Oh," comes the reply, "that's just a blind. They're still just a bunch of queers."

Perhaps that's why the Labour Party never bothered to abolish the public schools. If they're only producing queers, they're less likely to marry and produce lots of upper- and middle-class children. Certainly in no other country do boys spend the years from eight to eighteen away from home locked up in single-sex schools. In the debating society of one of the most famous schools recently, a master rather rashly asked one of the more glamorously decadent of the senior boys how widespread homosexuality was.

"Well," drawled the boy, echoing Mrs. Patrick Campbell, "at least we don't do it in the passages."

The deliberate segregation and mutual dependence of English public school life has led, Gathorne-Hardy suggests, not only to the Old Boy Network, but also to a strong strain of homosexuality (and I would add misogyny) in upper- and upper-middle-class men. It is interesting too that only in England—home of *le vice anglais*—does the word "stroke" mean both a caress and the lash of the cane. The fact, too, that prostitutes say a high proportion of their clients who want to be beaten, or to watch beatings, come from the upper and upper middle classes must be something to do with older boys being allowed to cane younger boys, and also be present at beatings to see the cane doesn't go higher than the head.

In the old days the only glimpse schoolboys got of naked women were from smuggled-in copies of *Health and Efficiency* or of black ladies in *National Geographic.* Now instead of sporting prints on the study walls, they have posters of near-nude Bardots and Jacqueline Bissetts. The latter, with her small-breasted androgynous figure, is a significant choice, because as John Mortimer, an old Harrovian, points out in *My Oxford:*

When emerging from the chrysalis of schoolboy homosexuality, the girls we preferred were notably boyish. Veronica Lake rather than Betty Grable, and Katharine Hepburn in *Philadelphia Story,* described by Frank Hauser as the natural bridge into the heterosexual world.

The only women we saw at school were elderly and fierce matrons. We were waited on at table by footmen in blue tailed coats, and settled down for the night by a butler called George. Our homosexuality was therefore dictated by necessity rather than choice. We were like a generation of diners condemned to cold cuts of beef because the steak and kidney was off.

One of the great panics of upper and middle-class mothers is that their sons may turn out homosexual. Samantha Upward feels a major hurdle has been cleared when Zacharias surreptitiously spends some pocket money on the *Daily Star,* and equally surreptitiously tears out the coloured page with the nude, and pins it over the poster of John Travolta above his bed. Mrs. Nouveau-Richards, however, who is too working-class to be on the lookout for homosexuality, is enchanted that Jason has a photograph of his school friend, little Lord X, by his bed in the holidays.

The latest generation of public school children, reacting presumably against their parents' idiocies during the permissive age, are much calmer and straighter than their predecessors. The drug problem which haunted the sixties is supposed to have been cured by inflation and fashion, although a Harrovian was recently caught buying cocaine by mail order. Drink has now taken its place. Every public school boy worth his salt has a bottle of Southern Comfort hidden under the floor boards, and gout has become the fashionable disease among teenagers. The punishment does not necessarily fit the crime, however. Thirteen-year-old Viscount Linley, son of Princess Margaret, was recently caught drinking whisky at Bedales with a couple of mates, and made to weed the garden for a couple of hours, but thirty less august children were suspended for holding a midnight party. No one gets sacked for homosexuality any more —they wouldn't have any boys left.

Chapter 5

UNIVERSITY

I'm afraid the fellows in Putney rather wish they had
The social ease and manners of a varsity undergrad.
For though they're awfully decent and up to a lark as a rule
You want to have the varsity touch after a public school.

John Betjeman

The expression "an Oxford accent" (like "a public school accent") was once used synonymously for an upper-class English accent. And certainly among the lower and lower middle classes, going to a university gives one social cachet.

I remember a Jen Teale in one office in which I worked who fell for one of the more degenerate copywriters, saying she knew that her mother would approve of him because he was "a graduate and nicely spoken." Mr. Definitely-Disgusting thinks his sons have "gone up in the world, because they've both got letters after their names." Howard Weybridge and the more entrenched right wing of the middle classes, however, might disapprove of undergraduates. To him "intellectual" means wishy-washy lefty—and why should young layabouts looking exactly like trainee Old Testament prophets spend three years at some fun palace at the taxpayer's expense? The words "hotbed of communism" are often on their lips. Like the Leicester businessman who said that most of the people he knew were Conservative—"But I've got a brother who's a Socialist, one of the things he picked up at Oxford."

Mrs. Nouveau-Richards is frightfully excited about Oxford and gets everything wrong. She tells all her friends Jason is going to

"New." Harry Stow-Crat didn't go to a university, he'd acquired quite enough character at Eton by the time he was eighteen, but his great-great-grandfather, being a nobleman, was allowed to graduate after two years, and Georgie Stow-Crat—now the upper classes are beginning to take education seriously—worked hard at Eton and managed to scrape a place at "The House" (Christchurch College, Oxford). In John Betjeman's time, the House was the home of the aristocracy and this is certainly true today. Writes Sir John:

Christchurch undergraduates gave the impression of dropping in at Oxford on the way to a seat in the House of Lords . . . They hunted, fished and shot, but I never heard of any of them playing football or hockey or even cricket, although cricket was played on the grounds of country houses within motoring distance of Oxford, and men from the House might have been called in to swell a village team.

The House was also the mecca of the socially ambitious in the fifties, when I was at an Oxford typing school. I had one or two boy-friends at Christchurch, and went to several parties there. I'd never encountered people so noisy, wild and totally self-assured. They always seemed to be drinking champagne, whizzing up to London in fast cars to go to nightclubs or breaking up the rooms of luckless grammar school boys. One of them was sent down for shooting a don through the foot with a twelve-bore. All of them ran up the most frightful debts.

Fortunately for them, they were surrounded by a galaxy of witty Nouveau-Richardses who were always ready to pick up the bill. None of them appeared to do any work or go to any lectures. I was totally intoxicated by their sophistication and their ancient names: Mowbray, Bathurst, Ashton, Stormonth Darling. But for me it was a time of great insecurity. Not only did I feel intellectually inferior because I wasn't an undergraduate, but also socially inferior because I was middle-class. It was the first time I'd met the upper classes *en masse*.

If school, with its private and state sectors, is the great divider, university should be the great bringer-together. For many undergraduates it's the first time they meet people of different classes. My thrill at Oxford was that I met the aristocracy, but for Angus Wilson the thrill was rubbing shoulders with the working classes:

There had, of course, been my London sexual encounters, many of them with cockney working-class young men, but the glory of Merton was I found myself meeting for the first time working-class men who came from the Midlands and the North.

This and the earlier extract by John Betjeman comes from *My Oxford*. Recently published together with *My Cambridge*, this is a book in which very successful people each wrote a chapter describing their experiences as undergraduates. What is remarkable —apart from the high standard of writing—is what incredibly class-conscious documents they all are. One feels that the authors wrote with an honesty about their origins they would never have displayed if they hadn't been so successful.

Eleanor Bron, for example, found herself mixing with an upper-middle-class intellectual elite, which made her unable to communicate with her own family (working-class Jewish) when she went home: "I was too clever, like Alice I had grown and couldn't fit in the door any more."

Alan Coren arrived at Oxford at the beginning of the "flat-A working-class-is-beautiful era": "This was in the post-Angry days, when people referred to themselves as 'one,' blushed and started referring to themselves as 'you,' and tall willowy lads with inbred conks and hyphens stood before mirrors abbreviating their drawl, dropping aitches, and justifying a family that went back to the 14th century by saying they were all solidly behind Wat Tyler."

Piers Paul Reid, upper-middle-class and second-generation intellectual, arrived a few years later at Cambridge when the egalitarian movement had reached its height, and the middle classes actively sought out working-class company. One of his friends recounted with delighted frisson that there was actually a miner's son with rooms in the same building. Alas, in Piers Paul Reid's college, "There was only *one* boy who lived in a council flat. But he could grasp logic and metaphysics, and at the same time amass a variety of scholarships and grants by the judicious exploitation of his background. He avoided paying bills and was treated leniently because colleges were as eager to cultivate those proletarian seedlings as were American colleagues to cultivate black students."

Having ferociously despised Etonians at the Pitt Club, Piers Paul Reid then reluctantly discovered that they were rather nice. Finally he went to a May Ball at St. Johns, "where there were girls in long dresses, and men in hired white tie and tails, not Etonians, instead bright guys from the grammar schools, and minor public schools, intoxicated by the mirage of success"—Jen Teales, in fact, trying to maintain some standard of gracious living in the face of rampant egalitarianism.

By 1968 the working-class-is-beautiful movement was coming to a head with student power joining forces with militant workers (a far cry from the undergraduates who rallied in 1926 to break the General Strike). But from then on things began to change, the austerity years arrived, and instead of power, undergraduates started worrying about survival, about fast-diminishing grants and getting a job when one went down. The possibility of actually joining the working classes on the dole queue suddenly made them seem less attractive. People no longer wanted to get a job helping people or burned to do something in the Third World. Instead they wanted to amass a fortune in the Middle East.

"Apart from medics and Indians," said one Oxford undergraduate, "all anyone wants to do when they leave here is to make a fast buck." According to the *Sunday Telegraph,* in recent years the main scramble has been into those twin middle-class fields of indispensability: law and accountancy. The proportion has doubled in the last two years. Soon, no doubt, the market will be flooded, and there'll be hundreds of out-of-work accountants working as waiters (at least they'll be better at adding up the bill than out-of-work actresses).

"A few years ago," confirmed a don, "I spent my time convincing people that Marx hadn't said the last word on everything. Now I spend the same amount of time persuading them everything he said wasn't complete rubbish."

The universities in fact have become bourgeois. How then have the classes re-aligned?

"One does generally mix with people of one's own type [i.e. class]," said an upper-middle-class undergraduate from Oriel, "though this is by no means a conscious or rigid principle—but it does seem that many comprehensive and grammar school types are not very interesting people, or at least seem to have less in common with one because of their background."

"At teacher training college," said a working-class boy, "we found our own level, and stuck together. Particularly in evidence was a stuck-up group we called 'the semis' [lower middle, Jen Teale again], who got engaged in the first year. All they talked about was houses and cars."

"You don't notice people's backgrounds," said an Old Harrovian now at Reading, "until someone almost beats you up for asking his name. Yobbos are less tolerant of having the piss taken out of them, and tend to over-react, which public school boys don't understand. When they get a bit of confidence, yobbos who've been up for three or four years take a delight in mimicking one's accent, which can get very offensive.

"I went out with a grammar school girl," he went on, "and I shared a flat with a boy from a comprehensive school. Apart from his talking about 'lounge,' 'settee' and 'toilet,' we got on very well, although communal eating was a problem. He wanted to eat early, I wanted to eat late.

"One thing I did learn was that if I got drunk, I broke up public school boys' rooms, and they always broke up mine. It's much easier to break up rooms of those who don't mind so much about possessions and who you know will take it well. Public school boys don't seem to mind so much about their possessions or other people's whereas yobbos do seem to care."

Today at university the classes seem principally to be re-aligning into the upper- and middle-class guilty; the lower-middle materialistic; and the working-class cross. And although the middle and upper classes are no longer assiduously courting the working classes, a terrible inverted snobbery has now developed. The young, reports Ann Thwaite in the introduction to *My Oxford*, "tend to avoid Oxford and Cambridge for egalitarian reasons, opting for Sussex, York or East Anglia, as somehow being more mysteriously like real life."

Then there was the don at a university redbrick who said he would never dare write a book about the middle classes, because he couldn't possibly justify it to his students.

Nicholas Monson, the journalist, wrote about overhearing two sociology students having a passionate row over which of them was more working-class.

One said his father was a miner in Darlington, while the other countered victoriously that, although his father had worked as an insurance clerk, his grandfather had gone on the Jarrow march. The first refused to concede his superior origins because his opponent's origins had been particularly diluted by the capitalist occupation of his petty bourgeois father.

"They clearly needed the assistance of a recognized authority," added Mr. Monson drily. "Perhaps next year we might see the first edition of *Burke's Peasantry.*"

Even upper middle classes at Oxford are worried about their image at the moment. They were perfectly beastly to Princess Anne, priestess of the flat "a," when she visited the Union recently. Gay libbers, women's libbers and general lefties jostled her and shouted four-letter words outside; inside there was intense heckling and a ghastly audience participation exercise in which everyone had to turn to the person on their right and "say in your poshest voice 'Hullo dahling.'"

Then *The Cherwell* also runs a competition for the pushiest freshman: "He who hacks most people in the most disgusting way in his first term." A hack is someone who solicits, pesters, toadies, and generally social climbs, in order to cunningly gain an advantage over others, by boring the pants off people in the Union bar, and then relying on their vote. Rather like Eton running an Upper-Class Twit of the Year contest.

Oxford, in some way, is more a target for egalitarianism than Cambridge. As Eleanor Bron pointed out, "At Oxford all acquire a veneer of upper-middle-classiness, while at Cambridge, home of scientists and fact rather than opinions, they simmer down to a vague middle and lower-middleness." Oxford's trouble is that, despite efforts to the contrary, they get more and more elitist. "In the old days considerable gifts of spirit and intellect were needed to counter severe economic disadvantage," said J. I. M. Stewart, "but now most people are hard up, no college is noticeably cluttered up with hopelessly thick or incorrigibly idle youths from privileged homes."

Ironically, although they may no longer be idle and over-privileged, 50 per cent are still from fee-paying schools because Oxford can't get enough candidates from the state system.

"Chaps from comprehensives simply aren't up to it," said one don. "You look for promise not achievement, then you say, 'Dash it, would they ever pass prelims if we let them in?' and so in the end you say, 'No, go somewhere else where they'll feed you compulsive lectures.'"

An interesting statistic is that English women graduates as a whole tend to be grander socially than men. Most of them come from Social Class I in the Census, which means they are daughters of all those upper-middle-class lawyers, doctors, engineers and accountants. This is probably because the upper middles are the least male chauvinist of all the classes, and therefore, unlike the aristocracy and the lower middle and working classes, wouldn't be so resistant to women educating themselves.

The exception to the upper-class rule is, of course, the Pakenham family, who were all expected to get a First. Evidently when Lady Antonia Fraser broke the terrible news to Lord Longford, her father, that she'd only got a Second, there was a long pause; then he said with characteristic charity: "Never mind, darling, I expect you'll get married."

According to the Old Harrovian at Reading University, "A lot of girls go to university to find a husband, although they would be livid to be told that. I fancied a girl who'd been to grammar school. Very clever—three As at A level—who I started to go out with, but she would only allow me to kiss her, saying if I wanted more I'd have to promise more. Well, I ran away like a coward, and in my absence a creepy sort of chap stepped in and having promised all, i.e. an engagement which he'll never keep, is enjoying her favours."

The undergraduate at Oriel said that, in almost every case, people take sexual partners from the same class. "If they're socially mis-matched there's usually not enough common ground to keep a conversation going."

"Nice girls," wrote Antonia Fraser about Oxford in the fifties, "never accepted invitations from unknown undergraduates in the libraries, and lived in mortal fear of being seen out with men in college scarves and blazers with badges on," and adds, with commendable hindsight now that her husband is the far from patrician Harold Pinter, "no doubt missing the company of almost every interesting man in Oxford."

Social style

At Oxbridge wearing college scarves and blazers is traditionally considered vulgar. But Dive Definitely-Disgusting is so proud of getting to a university he wants to advertise the fact by wearing college scarves, and blazers with badges, at the same time dissociating himself from the plebs in the street, showing that he's "ge-own," not "te-own."

In the conventional late seventies, sales of college scarves went up sevenfold in Oxford, and sales of blazers with badges fourfold. This may have been because the "campus look" was fashionable; because in a time of uncertainty people search for identity; or because they were all being bought by Zacharias Upwards trying desperately to look like yobbos.

Georgie Stow-Crat imports crumpet (i.e. girls) from London, spends about three hours a week reading geography (a traditionally thick Yock-Yock's subject) and runs the college beagles.

Jason Nouveau-Richards gave his college scarf and blazer with a badge to a jumble sale after one acid comment from Georgie, and now wears cavalary twill trousers, a tweed coat and fine green check shirt, and looks more straight than Georgie, all of whose gambling debts he paid off. Mrs. Nouveau-Richards has learned that "Magdelene" should be pronounced "Maudlin" and the High Street is known as "the High" but she makes Jason wince by talking about the "varsity" and "freshers" and "undergrads," which is almost as common a word as "students."

Zacharias Upward wishes Georgie would ask him to his parties. With seven men to one girl, he never even gets a fumble. Where Stow-Crats rush in, Upwards fear to tread.

When Samantha and Gideon take their daughter Thalia back to Sussex, Samantha in her ethnic and Gideon in his jeans, it looks as though Birnam Wood has arrived at Dunsinane, the car is so thick with potted plants for her room. Samantha was certain she would be miles the youngest and trendiest mother, and was disappointed to find the entire campus swarming with identical middle-aged Bolivian peasant ladies.

Dive Definitely-Disgusting feels horribly disorientated and homesick his first year. He's never been away from home before, and this is his introduction to "adollt" life, and his college doesn't even look "ollde." Mrs. Definitely-Disgusting has had a telephone installed for the first time since her latest baby, Joanne, was taken on by a modelling agency, so Dive rings her every night, holding the telephone miles away because Mrs. D.-D. talks so loudly. Dive is reading maths or science. Used to being a big fish in a small comprehensive pool, he finds no one takes much notice of him here, they all seem to be in clicks. No wonder he eats in hall every night, and sticks to his rooms. He doesn't meet any girls and in desperation imports his steady girl-friend from home, but is so broke on his grant he has to smuggle marmalade rolls out for her from hall. Mrs. Definitely-Disgusting doesn't quite appreciate the glory of having a son at Oxford, until she sees him on *University Challenge* on television.

Games, it seems, are the one great social mixing ground. Social divisions are genuinely forgotten and genuine friends are made between people of different classes. The smart set would never bother to know anyone who didn't go to a public school if it weren't for rowing or cricket.

Rowing used to be elitist, but although Old Etonians have gained 640 Blues since the Oxford-Cambridge boat race began (schools such as Radley and Shrewsbury failing to get within 500 of the score), times are changing. Over the past ten years, Eton still leads with 22 Blues, but Hampton Grammar is now third.

In 1978 there were three undergraduates in the Oxford boat who formerly would have been dismissed as "colonials," four grammar school boys and three public school boys. "The class thing is going fast," said one of the crew. "Last year there was a touch of class feeling, a sort of 'them' and 'us' in the boat, but not this year. Perhaps it's something to do with the whole sport opening up. All along the river are clubs who want good rowers, and don't care where they went to school."

In the national eight, there are now more dockers and lightermen than people who went to a university.

Chapter 6

OCCUPATIONS

Oh let us love our occupations,
Bless the squire and his relations.
Live upon our daily rations,
And always know our proper stations.

According to the sociologists, the two most important factors affecting upward mobility are your job and marriage. But this may be partly due to the fact that the Census, upon which most government and sociological statistics are based, judges a person's class entirely by the occupation of the "head of the household" in which they live. In all societies, there is a division of labour and consequently a hierarchy of prestige, but such arbitrary distinctions as the Census makes lead to a gross over-simplification of the complexities of the class system. Photographers, for example, are rated Class III, which puts Patrick Lichfield and Anthony Armstrong-Jones in the same social bracket as David Bailey and Terry Donavon. Brewers, including presumably the Guinesses and the Cobbolds, are even lower, in Class IV. Athletes all rate Class III, which puts Princess Anne on a level with Georgie Best. While the Marquess of Anglesey as a writer (Class II) is rated lower than all the dentists, chemists and opticians in Class I. The deb, working as a waitress (Class IV) and having *nostalgie de la boue* fantasies about lorry drivers, is actually bettering herself because they're rated Class III. Peers of the realm don't get a rating at all, unless they have a profession, and are lumped together with the disabled, undergraduates, ex-convicts and the chronically sick, which should mean that Lady Chatterley, as a peer's wife, pulled herself up like mad when she embarked on an affair with a (Class III) gamekeeper.

PERCENTAGE OF ECONOMICALLY ACTIVE
AND RETIRED PEOPLE IN EACH SOCIAL CLASS
IN GREAT BRITAIN DEVISED FROM CENSUS, 1971

SOCIAL CLASS I—Professional—4%

Accountants, chemists, university dons,
lawyers, vets, opticians, ornithologists,
scientists, vicars, engineers, architects,
dentists.

SOCIAL CLASS II—Intermediate occupations—18%

Airline pilots, chiropodists, farmers, members of parliament, schoolmasters, police
inspectors, artists, nurses, publicans,
journalists, sculptors, diplomats, chicken
sexers, actors, company directors.

SOCIAL CLASS III (N)—Skilled occupations—Non-Manual—21%

Sales reps, secretaries, shop girls, bank
clerks, photographers, restaurateurs,
policemen, cashiers, models, undertakers.

SOCIAL CLASS III (M)—Skilled occupations—Manual—28%

Bus drivers, cooks, miners, guards in
trains, upholsterers, butchers, all athletes
including horseback riders and footballers,
plumbers, shoemakers, printers, brewers.

SOCIAL CLASS IV—Partly skilled—21%

Farm labourers, barmen, bus conductors,
fishermen, postmen, telephonists, milk-
men, gardeners, hawkers, ambulance men,
barmaids, brewers, waiters and waitresses.

SOCIAL CLASS V—Unskilled—8%

Office cleaners, porters, builders' labourers,
messenger boys, lorry drivers' mates,
stevedores, window cleaners, chimney
sweeps, ticket collectors, charwomen.

Cabinet ministers, M.P.s and diplomats are only graded Class
II, which figures. Once upon a time diplomats used to be all Old
Etonians with Firsts, now they're parvenus like Peter Jay, and all
the British embassies, according to a recent observer, ring with flat
"a"s and regional accents.

When you marry, according to the Census, you automatically
take on the class of your husband, which means that the day a
duke's daughter (even if she's qualified as a Class I barrister) marries a chimney sweep she is promptly assessed with him as
Class V.

What one does, on the other hand, can be used as a class
indicator. One thinks of solicitors as being middle-class, and lorry
drivers working-class—but then again I know of a peer of impeccable and ancient lineage whose daughter has been a long-distance
lorry driver for the last five years. Repeatedly, however, one is
struck by the relativity of the whole system. The aristocrat regards
barristers and solicitors as "middle-class." The Census rates them
as "Class I" and to the working class, equally, they seem not
middle- but upper-class. A solicitor told me that lower-class women
invariably put on a hat when they come and see him, and in *Family
and Class in a London Suburb* Michael Young quotes a man in
Woodford Green saying: "We have a very dear friend who's a
practising barrister, and it amazed us that people might want to
know us because we knew him and called him by his Christian
name."

The other day I met a woman at a party who said her daughter
had just got engaged to a dustman. Uncertain of her political
affiliations, I was wondering whether to compose my features into
a "How splendid!" or a "How awful!" expression, when she went
on complacently: "But it's quite all right, because his father's a
general." (But then again, a general who'd started his career in the
cavalry would probably be a very different class from one who had
begun in the Royal Corps of Transport.)

One poll conducted among the working classes showed that
being a footballer was regarded as the most prestigious career,
followed by that of a chauffeur. My daily woman was grumbling

one day that her daughter didn't speak to her any more since she'd married into the professional classes. What did her son-in-law do, I asked.

"Oh," said my daily woman, "he's an undertaker."

One notices too that occupations that have a slightly comical image acquire new, more euphemistic and therefore more Jen Teale titles: "dental surgeon" instead of "dentist"; "rodent operative" for "rat catcher"; "public health inspector" for "sanitary inspector"; and, worst of all, "refuse collector" (presumably because they refuse to collect) for "dustman."

The position of the doctor is also ambiguous. The working classes think of him as upper-class. He has even usurped the lord as the most popular hero in romantic fiction. But a publisher I know was driving down the village street with a very grand old woman when he saw a man on the pavement waving at her.

"Some friend's trying to attract your attention," he said.

"That's not a friend," snorted the old lady, "he's a doctor."

I recently heard a very upper-class girl say she must go home to Lancashire, because "I've got to help Mummy with a horror party for the doctor, the dentist, the solicitor and the agent." Medicine, except in the private sector, is fast dropping caste, along with teaching, nursing and the army, because they are all dependent on state pay and are generally too ethical to go on strike, and getting broker and broker and more and more demoralized as the system breaks down.

Doctors, too, used to get invited to a lot of smartish parties, but now that your G.P. won't come and see you any more, and you can't welcome him in a glamorous nightie in the privacy of your home, people tend not to know them socially. Certain doctors are also to blame for this loss of status. A friend who hadn't been to her doctor for over a year was greeted with the words, "Not you again."

The upper-class attitude to farmers is curious, too. Many aristocrats have land run by farm managers, with whom they enjoy talking shop and whom they far prefer to businessmen or people in the professions who don't know their place—"more genuine" is the phrase used. Harry Stow-Crat also has to suck up to neighbouring farmers in case he should want to hunt, shoot or fish over their land. Upper-class young often go and work on farms as apprentices, before going home to manage their own estates, and say "How sooper the farm blokes are," although they don't drink in the same pubs as them.

The preference of the upper classes for the working class because they are far enough away socially is exquisitely summed up by Jane Austen's Emma (who I suppose could be described as "landed gentry"):

A young farmer whether on horseback or on foot is the very last sort of person to raise my curiosity. The Yeomanry are precisely the order of people with whom I feel I can have nothing to do. A degree or two lower and a creditable appearance might interest me, I might hope to be useful to their families in some way. But a farmer can need none of my help and is therefore in one sense above my notice, as in every other sense he is below it.

Emma, believing her young friend Harriet to be the illegitimate daughter of a *gentleman,* firmly discourages her from marrying this particular young farmer as being far beneath her. When, however, Emma discovers Harriet is only the daughter of a rich *tradesman,* she changes her mind, and finds the farmer a perfectly suitable match.

Which brings us to the upper-class horror of trade. A gentleman doesn't have to earn his living, as has been pointed out in Chapter 4. "The acceptance of high living and leisure," wrote Evelyn Waugh, "as part of the natural order, is a prerequisite of the aristocratic qualities and achievement. The aristocrat who goes into business and sticks to it and makes good is soon indistinguishable from his neighbour in Sunningdale. You should not have said that aristocrats can't make money in commerce, but that when they do they become middle-class."

In fact, if one looks back on most of the great families, they started off in trade. Many of them got rich lending money to both sides in the Wars of the Roses, and then bought land. (William Greville, the flower of the wool merchants, who died in Chipping Campden in the fifteenth century, was the forbear of the famous and ancient family of Greville.) But once their pile was made, the life of leisure was espoused and their origins rejected, which explains the parlous state of British industry today.

Trade seems less despised if one is flogging works of art, and somehow shipping and oil seem to be more respectable.

"Wouldn't it be heaven if Hamish got a job in Shell at £600 a year," wrote Nancy Mitford in the thirties, and the Onassis and Niarchos families seem to have been accepted totally by the English and French aristocracy, if not by the Greeks, which is often the case. One's social deficiencies always seem more glaring to one's fellow countrymen than they do abroad. Onassis and Niarchos have been brilliantly described as "parachutists," people who drop out of nowhere into a new class.

Social advancement is also dependent on access. Businessmen tend not to meet the upper classes. But members of the "professions"—architects, doctors, dentists, estate agents, solicitors—encounter all classes, and so do West End tailors, interior decorators, dressmakers and journalists, while chauffeurs, nannies and masters at boarding schools have long-term access. All these people not only see the upper classes at close range and have the opportunity to observe them and ape their manners, but also, if they have charm and a certain deference, often get "taken up." When Michael Fish was invited to some frightfully smart house, the keeper was overheard saying to the butler: "Things have come to a pretty pass when they ask the shirtmaker to stay."

In Germany and America the businessman is of a far higher caste, and at the same time more democratic. In America, even though the men on the shop floor call the managing director by his Christian name, no one looks down on him socially. Advertising is also much smarter in America because ad men get paid such vast sums of money.

"Advertising is still not considered a fit occupation for a gentleman," David Ogilvy, the celebrated English advertising tycoon, observed recently. "If I were top of another profession, such as law, I would be in the House of Lords today. If I were an actor or even a jockey I would have been knighted, as it is I get the C.B.E. When the Queen heard what I did, her expression was a mixture of amazement and amusement."

On the other hand, the laid-back, lotus-eating entrepreneurial atmosphere of advertising must be very well suited to the upper classes.

"What do you do?"

"Nothing."

"In which agency?"

Jobs for nobs

Lord Finchley tried to mend the Electric Light
Himself. It struck him dead: And serve him right!
It is the business of the wealthy man
To give employment to the artisan.

Hilaire Belloc

Nobility of birth commonly abateth industry, said Bacon, but during the twentieth century, the gospel of work has been spreading to the upper classes. What career, then, is open to Georgie Stow-Crat? He has obviously got to start making a living, since the money won't last much longer—two more generations at a pinch. He's unlikely to go into any of the professions (Lord Colwyn as a trumpeter and a dentist being a rare exception), because he lacks the application to train for six years and he'd find the people too stuffy. One aristocrat who actually managed to pass his bar finals left the legal profession after a year: "I couldn't stand the other barristers, they were so pompous and middle-class, and only interested in shop.'

Georgie wouldn't like the bar because he couldn't take Snipe into court. He might temporarily become a stockbroker, like the Marquess of Tavistock, or dabble in accountancy, like Lord Gree-

nock. This would help him to run his estate later and learn the
rudiments of tax evasion. Others take up "head-hunting" or go into
property, where they do very well because they know all the right
people and get hot tips about whose land is coming onto the
market. Georgie might also run a restaurant or add kudos to a smart
nightclub, acting as bait to rich upper-class friends and even richer
nouveaus.

Some aristocrats try photography because it gives them the
chance to get at pretty girls, others flatten their "a"s and go into
the pop music business or produce films. They are very good as
front men in P.R. because they know the right people, but they are
better at charming the press and clients than dealing with all the
follow-up work.

A lot of them are going into Sotheby's, or Christie's, or smart
art galleries, because being surrounded with beautiful things at
home, they're supposed to know something about furniture and
pictures. They don't, of course. One Christie's valuer told me that
only once, in all the houses he'd visited, was he made to dine in
the kitchen with the servants, although in another house there was
an old nanny in residence who wouldn't let him watch television
after 8:30.

Then there are the whore lords, who get their names onto as
many firms' writing paper as possible. Kind hearts may mean more
than coronets, but a lord on the board means business and im-
presses customers, particularly Americans.

Georgie is most likely to go and farm his own land. If he were
a younger son he might go into the army. Cirencester Agricultural
College takes heirs to prepare them for the duties of managing
their estates, and in 1979 boasted three sons of earls, three sons of
viscounts, two barons' sons, a peer and, much to the joy of the
popular press, a bewildered-looking Mark Phillips. Sandhurst takes
more second and subsequent sons for training in the martial arts.
All that shooting is such good practice for the grouse moors later.

There is also a strong correlation between the aristocracy and
the arts. Genius, being unbridled, is certainly patrician. In the old

days Sir Philip Sidney said look in your heart and write but don't get paid for it. No one worries about that today. Lord Kilbracken and Lord Oaksey are journalists, the Marquess of Anglesey is writing a four-volume history of the British cavalry. Dukes and earls burst joyously into print publishing their memoirs, or extolling the merits of their ancient houses. Lord Weymouth paints murals and writes thrillers.

In the same way, there's nothing unsmart about science as long as it's not applied. It is perfectly all right for his lordship to potter around in the West Wing letting off stink bombs and making hot-air balloons. It should be pointed out that, in the arts and among academics, social snobbery is invariably suspended in favour of intellectual snobbery. This works both ways between the two cultures.

"When I find myself among scientists," said Auden, with unusual silliness, "I feel like a shabby curate who has strayed by mistake into a drawing-room full of dukes."

Or as John Betjeman, gently taking the mickey out of donnish attitudes, put it: "Objectively our common room/ Is like a small Athenian state./ Except for Lewis, he's all right,/ But do you think he's quite first rate?"

That tentative, fusty "quite first rate" seems to sum up the whole world of academic snobbism. The egghead is mightier than the strawberry leaf.

"Scientists," said one sociologist pompously, "tend to have a classless image, which can be embraced by working-class students without involving a denial of biological self," which means they have very short hair and are all so common they have to go abroad to achieve any status, or hide themselves in laboratories engaged in what they call *"ree-*search."

Most academics get on together talking shop, but all hell breaks out when their wives meet and are expected to get on.

"It was dreadful," said one sociologist's wife after a dinner party. "All the walls of the lounge were papered in different colours."

You may be a giant among bio-chemists but a pygmy at the
local P.T.A.

Compute, compete, and commute

To the middle classes, wrote Ralf Dahrendorf, the career is the
supreme reality. Fear of failing is almost as strong as the urge to
succeed, the fittest survive and escape to another rung up the
ladder, the unsuccessful are ostracised. The historical origin of the
middle classes lies in trade. They can be traced back to the bourgeoisie in the chartered towns, where they grouped together, to
demand their rights and govern the towns, terrifying the aristocracy in much the same way as the unions scare the middle classes
today. (Samantha Upward's mother thinks T.U.C. stands for "Terribly Unkind Communists.")

The middle classes didn't become really powerful until the
Industrial Revolution, when the development of industry brought
the need for new types of work: insurance, banking, accounting,
engineering and science. Many of the people who entered these
professions were successful craftsmen or farmers who had left the
land. The penalty of failure was to sink back into the working-class
ranks, so a gulf grew between the classes. As the big towns developed, the ranks of the middle classes swelled. Eventually they
moved out of the towns and made suburbs and dormitory towns,
and this seclusion enabled them to copy the way of life of the upper
classes. Their children, as has been pointed out in Chapter 4, were
sent to the new boarding schools, and developed refinements of
dress and speech, and, like all newly risen classes, walked through
life gingerly as though they were treading on eggs. Their distinctive
characteristic was that their work was non-manual and, like the
working class, they had numerous rankings between themselves.
They included manufacturers above the grade of foreman, most
farmers, the majority of civil servants, professional people, businessmen and shopkeepers who owned their own shops, as well as independent craftsmen. It seems ludicrous to lump the small shop-

keeper with the great banker, but all were united by their dedication, persistence and desire to get on.

Ever since the Middle Ages the "professions" have considered themselves superior to bankers and businessmen, and as the middle class emerged they became almost a class of their own; medicine, law and the church were more suitable occupations for a gentleman: they did not dull the brain like manual work, nor corrupt the soul like commerce, they did not advertise. Some sort of qualification was needed, so they formed professional associations and became members of closely knit and protective groups. The smartness of the various professions is subject to change. Architects are considered smart today because there is something creative about their work. There would never be any stigma attached to a young man going into the church, because the upper classes have to believe in God. Indeed, a country parish was traditionally the destiny of younger sons of the aristocracy with small private incomes. Medicine, as we have pointed out, is on the way down, except in the private sector. Dentists, on the other hand, are on the up. They tend to make much more money than doctors, because they've escaped the clutches of the National Health, and because the desire for perfectly capped teeth has spread from America. Vets are also on the way up, aided by a little touch of Herriot in the night, because they make so much money and because the profession is getting so popular.

Schoolmasters could be described as middle-class, but again there is a vast difference socially between the headmaster of one of the great public schools or fashionable prep schools and the junior master in an urban "sink" school. On the whole, schoolmasters within the private sector feel guilty about not being part of the comprehensive sector but look down on state teachers socially. On the other hand, they make exceptions. I was talking about the headmaster of a fashionable state primary school the other day.

"Oh yes," said the head of my son's former prep school, "he's obviously a coming man, *I've met him at a dinner party.*"

Engineering has always been an unsmart profession, partly because no one knows what it involves. Harry Stow-Crat thinks it is something to do with driving a train. But once again things are changing. For the last few years, engineering has been far away the most popular career for public school leavers. According to the Public Schools Appointments Board, law and accountancy are both down, probably due to the difficulty newly qualified lawyers and accountants are having in finding work. Medicine and teaching are also down, and the civil service has halved since 1967. Industry, on the other hand, is up, along with farming, forestry, geology and biology.

Amongst the great variety of middle-class occupations there are three main strands which are particularly in evidence: The "burgesses," the "spiralists" and the lower middle class. The terms "burgess" and "spiralist" were coined by W. Watson in his article "Social Mobility and Social Class in Industrial Communities" (1964). The *burgess* tends to stay put in the neighbourhood where he was brought up or started work, and establish prestige in the community. The burgess is often the country solicitor, accountant or local businessman who takes an interest in the community and often gets into local government to further his business interests.

In *Middle Class Families* Colin Bell quotes a burgess describing his life. He is a typical Howard Weybridge. The Weybridge expressions are italicised.

My *people* have always been *comfortably off*. After going into the *forces*, I went into *Dad's* business. We have several *representatives*, who have come up from the shop floor. . . . I am a very keen member of *Rotary* [on a par with Teacher and Doctor]. I belong to many clubs and associations because I think it's a good thing other Swansea *folk* see me at the right *functions*, and realise we are not just tradesmen. I also belong to several *social clubs* as a duty so that I meet the important Swansea people.

This is typical middle-class behaviour, the careerist socialising, the pomposity of expression, the desire to be a power in the community, a big fish in a small pool, and the joining of clubs, which would all be unthinkable to the working or upper classes.

The second category in Watson's brilliant description, the *spiralist*, moves from job to job, and place to place, upping his salary and his status as he goes. Colin Bell quotes a chemist from a working-class background who is far more upper-class and direct in his language than the burgess.

I went to a grammar school and then to a university, very red-brick and provincial, I worked like hell and got a first, then did a Ph.D. in chemistry to avoid going out in the world. Meantime I got married and had several children, after that I moved from firm to firm, upping my salary every time, then I was promoted to Holland [where class and accent didn't matter].

He then left the research side, because if he didn't, he realised, he wouldn't get on, and went into the middle-class admin. side, which was far more cutthroat, but which counted more. Now as the head of a large industrial plant he had to decide whether to move to the head office in London to up his salary or to change jobs. His only friends were people he worked with, his wife's only friends were their wives. The only way to get on, he felt, was to move. He hoped it didn't interfere too much with the children's education. "If I get a couple of notches further up," he concluded, "I'll send them to boarding school. Not that I really approve of it, but it will make moving about easier."

Here you have a man, sometimes working-class, sometimes lower-middle in origins, who is prepared to sacrifice friends, children and principles to his career—in fact, he's happy to leave his family and the friends of his childhood, because they might be a social embarrassment. Later the spiralists often jettison their wives and trade them in for a Mark II model that goes with a new life-style.

Interesting, too, that this particular spiralist showed working-class shyness by taking a Ph.D. and cocooning himself against the world a bit longer; made a typically working-class early marriage to combat the loneliness; but then made a deliberate decision to move over to the middle-class admin. side because it would further his career.

In a survey of managers' wives, it was shown that they all wanted their daughters to marry a *burgess* in the professions. All believed that this would provide more effortless security than a marriage to someone in industry, higher status and enough money so one didn't have to keep on moving. They could not see how many young barristers have to tramp the streets for months after qualifying before they get any work. Nor could they appreciate the status props that go with the spiralist's job: the houses, the company cars, trips for the wife, gardeners and chauffeurs, the source of which can all be concealed from the neighbours.

The salient characteristic of the spiralist, whether he is from the working classes or the lower middles, is his adaptability and his total ruthlessness. He is the cog in the wheel, the corporation man who can charm his colleagues, while tramping them underfoot with his slip-on Guccis. His mecca is the conference.

"I've come a long way," said one spiralist. "My parents were working in the Northeast, my expectations were at best tradesman. When I'm at conferences I feel how far I've come." On the other hand, because his social mecca is suburbia he often ends up sounding exactly like Howard Weybridge.

I went to a conference on direct mail recently, where the spiralists were rampant. The "venue," as they would call it, was the Café Royal in London and it was all firm handshakes and announcing their names: "Vic Taylor. Pleased to meet you, Ji-ell" (always two syllables), accompanied by a card pressed into one's hand.

Another favourite gesture on seeing an acquaintance was the thumbs-up sign, or jerking their heads on one side and winking simultaneously. (The middle classes, particularly schoolmasters, tend to raise one arm at about twenty degrees to the ground.) The smell of Brut fought frantically with that of deodorant. Most of the spiralists had goal-post moustaches, and brushed-forward thatch-cottage hair, with that flattened lack of sheen from being washed every day under the shower, rather than in the bath. They all wore natty lightweight suits in very light colours as being more American in style.

On the spiralists' lapels are unfaded circles which have always been protected by conference badges. One can hear the rattle of Valium as they take off their lightweight long-vented jackets to reveal belted trousers. Their accent is mid-Atlantic: justified by the fact that they've spent a lot of time in "the States" (spiral-speak for America), which usually means a brief business trip or a cheap weekend on a Laker flight.

Their vocabulary (i.e. spiral-speak) is peppered with expressions like "product attributes," "growth potential," "viability" and "good thinking." Perhaps it is some unconscious search for roots, but whenever they meet, they start tracing advertising genealogies (That's Les Brace, he used to be Saatchi and Saatchi, Garland Compton, before they became . . .) with the same intensity with which Caroline Stow-Crat and her group of jolly nice girl-friends are always saying "Sukie Stafford-Cross, she was . . ."

Conscious of their seemingly effortless mobility, spiralists always have razors, toothbrushes, pyjamas and a drip-dry shirt in their briefcases.

Our third strand is the lower middles who don't rise, whom Orwell called "that shivering army of clerks and shopwalkers. You scare them by talking about Class war, so they forget their incomes, remember their accents, and fly to the defence of the class that's exploiting them." They are also the sergeant-majors, the police sergeants, the toastmasters, Prufrockian, neatly dressed, cautious, thrifty. "In the old days," as Len Murray, the trade-union leader, pointed out, "they had an affinity with the boss, who saw them as people who could be confided in and trusted. They haven't the bargaining power, now there's more education about. The nineteenth-century entrepreneur has gone, and in his place have come huge management empires, where the smooth pegs thrive in round holes."

If the ex-working-class spiralist's mecca is the conference, the lower middle's mecca is the "function," where in hired tails or dinner jackets they play at gracious living and the "Ollde Days." Howard Weybridge goes to lots of such events and rather takes them for granted. But Bryan Teale's ambition is to be president of the Stationery Trade Representatives' Association for one year and stand with a chain round his neck, beside Jen Teale, who has a little chain and a maidenhair corsage, graciously welcoming new arrivals, and being stood up for and politely applauded when they come into the dining room. Throughout the five-course dinner which starts at 6:30 they will "take wane" with each other and various dignitaries and past presidents and their ladies down the table. As this is a Ladies Night, each Lady will get a gift of a manicure set or an evening pochette in uncut moquette by her plate. Later there will be Ollde Time dancing interspersed with popular favourites. Bryan will "partner" Jen in the valeta. They both enjoy "ballroom dancing." The conference gang, on the other hand, would bop until their thatched hair nearly falls off. The difference between the lower-middle "function" set and the spiralists is that the former crave the "dignity" of a bygone age, while the latter are geared towards America and the future.

But the real battleground in the late 1970s is between Bryan Teale's "function" brigade of clerks and insurance salesmen, and the skilled manual workers one rung below them. For a long time the skilled worker has been earning far more money than most clerical workers, and because the former tend to live in rented council flats, rather than paying commercial rents or buying houses on mortgages, and have all the kiddies at state schools, they have far more money to play around with.

One notices too that, in the light of extra cash, people tend to think themselves far higher-class than the sociologist considers them to be. The financially disadvantaged lower middle class may feel not only envy but under social threat from the skilled working class, men who tend to consider that class depends not so much on education and income as on production and consumption. Large number of miners interviewed for a recent survey called themselves "upper-middle-class" whereas the Census would have placed them at upper-working-class.

Barriers

Although the barriers are slowly breaking down, there are still jobs from which you will be excluded if you come from a particular class. Many firms in the City—stockbrokers, insurance and shipping brokers, commodity dealers—still appreciate what they call "polish and mixability" (which is a euphemism for "upper- and upper-middle-class background") beyond academic qualification.

The discrimination, however, is now going both ways. A company director recently said if he interviewed two equally well-qualified graduates, one working-class and one from a public school, he took the working-class boy, because he'd had to fight harder to get there. Nicholas Monson, an Old Etonian, was sacked from his provincial newspaper because of what was loosely called his "background." A fortnight later he was told by a London advertising agency that his credentials were fine, but he couldn't have the job because the staff objected to Old Etonians.

You can't get a job as a disc jockey if you're upper-class, nor as a television reporter. This is particularly so if you're an upper-class woman. You may look glamorous but you mustn't sound it.

Many people, particularly rock stars, find they can only get into high society if they go abroad. Vidal Sassoon went to America, which he described as "a society where there are no class barriers, where the cop's son can become president of a great corporation and where profit isn't a dirty word." Mr. Sassoon was wrong, there are plenty of class barriers in America, but he, as a foreigner, wouldn't be aware of them or feel self-conscious if he transgressed them.

But despite the film *Shampoo* (which portrayed the hairdresser as a super-stud) and Mr. Sassoon making the gossip columns as "millionaire crimper and health food freak inviting 400 close friends to the Hilton"—hairdressers will never be accepted completely by the upper and upper middle classes because of their pansified and plebeian image. Her hairdresser may be the recipient of Caroline Stow-Crat's indiscreet confidences, but he'll never be asked to dinner. Although as a token working-class, he might get asked to her wedding.

Manual work

> While I was at university, I took a vacation job. To a nicely brought up girl from an academic family the horror of sitting at a conveyor belt eight hours a day packing chocolates was indescribable. I also remember the feeling of being a non-person to the manager and the secretaries of a small firm. I hope the custom of students doing manual work continues. For many of us it is the first time we have been in close contact as equals with the working classes.
>
> Letter in the *Sunday Times*

The inclusion of the words "working classes" is interesting. The girl who wrote this letter must have met people from working-class background at university, but then, perhaps by definition, they had already become middle-class. Recently, when a Sunday paper published a middle-class man's account of how he swept the streets for six months as an experiment, what came across was the monotony, the hard grind and the way people in the street behaved as though he didn't exist—was a "non-person" in fact. Evidently the only compensation for working in a factory is that it teaches you to lip-read.

If the career is the supreme reality to the middle classes, the worst thing about the working classes, according to Ernest Bevin, was their poverty of ambition. They are far more interested in good pay than "job satisfaction." In a recent survey, 96 per cent of clerks interviewed thought pay was less important than prospects, but only 20 per cent of the manual workers wanted to be promoted to foreman. Promotion would involve too much commitment to the management and much less overtime pay. If Mr. Definitely-Disgusting is made a foreman, he finds himself in an ambiguous position. The management thinks of him as a junior executive, but he wants his fellow-workers to think of him as one of the boys. He also finds he has to cajole and threaten to make the slacker on the assembly line pull his finger out. The only thing Mr. D.-D. is really good at is assembling cars—and he doesn't do that any more. If he works too hard, even on the factory floor, he'll show up his colleagues and they'll resent it. To rise is to feel less secure; paranoia is the disease of the upwardly mobile.

If Mr. D.-D. wants to get on, therefore, it's far easier to become a shop steward and rise through the unions—then he can have a chauffeur-driven car, expense account, lunches, first-class tickets, trips to Brighton, Blackpool and abroad, and the ear of the Prime Minister without losing the respect of the shop floor.

For the middle classes it is much easier to move upwards. By hard work and a bit of luck, a man in Unilever can become managing director of sausages at twenty-eight, then move on through soap and toothpaste up to the central board.

Monitor commissioned a recent advertising survey which goes as far as to say that the belief in greater social mobility for the working classes is principally held by the middle classes. The tradition of the working classes is a fatalistic acceptance of existing hierarchy and status. Mr. D.-D.'s hopes for the future are based on the price he and his mates can get for the work they do. This is emphasised by the belief that they will do better by collective bargaining under appointed union leaders, who often manipulate their demands, rigging ballots and forcing them to come out on strike. Striking is also a good way for union leaders, shop stewards, pickets and even Mr. Definitely-Disgusting to get on telly, and have Auntie Edna ringing up from Darlington after *News at Ten* screaming excitedly: "We've just seen you." Even Mrs. Definitely-Disgusting was asked for her autograph the time she attacked a picket with her shopping bag during the lorry drivers' strike.

As work on the whole is hell, the working-class man likes to keep home and work quite separate. Mr. Definitely-Disgusting comes home, having been bossed about all day, and wants his tea on the table. Nor does he see work as a place where he makes new friends or joins social clubs. He couldn't go to one of these clubs in his overalls, all sweaty from work, and once he's out of the place, he doesn't want to have to go home, clean up, change and come back. Firms' social clubs and societies are for this reason almost exclusively middle-class.

When work is so exacting, monotonous and unrewarding, it is hardly surprising that workers seeing people having candle-lit dinners, frisking on sun-drenched beaches and driving blondes in fast cars every night on television often fail to clock in in the morning. At British Leyland, if Mr. Definitely-Disgusting works for three months without taking a weekday off, his and Mrs. D.-D.'s names are included in a draw for a fortnight in Majorca. For those who can go for two months without playing hooky, there's a chance of five days in Belgian beer halls. If you don't go to work because you're ill, the working class refer to it as being "on the sick," which sounds awfully slippery.

Within the working class itself there are also numerous hierarchies. We know of the Respectable and the Rough, and those in work despising those who are unemployed. There are also great divides between skilled, semi-skilled and unskilled. There is a lot of kudos in being skilled, as my hairdresser pointed out: "My dad works at Vauxhall on the cars—skilled, of course. Then there's my father-in-law on nights at Fords, earns £200 a week, but he only does two hours a night, spends the rest of the time learning Spanish. He's skilled too."

There is also status in having the power to paralyse. The biggest rewards go to the workers who, if they stop work, do the most harm to the country collectively. Thus, miners, power men, dockers, engineers and lorry drivers are the new elite who can bring the country to its knees. While the wretched postmen, firemen and ambulance men have no clout.

Choosing a career

Dive Definitely-Disgusting wants to be a helicopter pilot; he doesn't know how to fly, but they'll learn him. A few years ago he might have gone into "The Print" as he calls newspapers, but they're not taking on any more apprentices; or he might have trained as a motor mechanic, because it would have been his only chance of handling a car, but now his father's got a second-hand Vauxhall, the job has rather lost its appeal.

Mrs. Definitely-Disgusting, who accompanied Dive to the interview with the careers officer, thinks he ought to learn a trade, then he'd be skilled, definitely. Dive rather likes the idea of being a tool-setter, which he thinks is somefink to do with chisels and hammers, like, and he enjoyed woodwork at school. He might go in for television repair, then he can mend the knocked-off telly when it goes wrong, and he's quite drawn to electronics, because he thinks it will involve somefink like that spaceship in *Star Wars*, and it'll help him mend the knocked-off Hi Fi when that goes wrong, like.

Yet looking for a job at sixteen, Dive Definitely-Disgusting may be luckier than little Wayne Teale, who's been persuaded by Jen and Bryan to stay on at school until he's eighteen, presuming there must be some lollipop at the end. A headmistress at a comprehensive school admitted that she uses class as a carrot, telling her girls: "If you stay on longer and take final examinations you'll get a job in a better firm, and make nicer girl-friends and meet a better class of man." In reality, as the careers officer pointed out, it's easier to get a job at sixteen because the employer feels he doesn't have to pay you nearly as much as an eighteen-year-old.

Alas too, today's more straight and sober teenagers are reaping the wild oats sown by the last hippy generation, who were so restless that they dropped out of any job after three months. In the end employers got fed up and now tend to employ Old Age Pensioners, rather than office juniors—they're more reliable, they're grateful for the work, and they don't feel jobs like making the tea and doing the post are demeaning.

Even so Sharon Definitely-Disgusting will probably end up in an office or a shop, which she always refers to as a "booteek," unless it's Woolworth, where she will call herself a trainee buyer. Mrs. D.-D. would rather she worked in an office. If "they learn her to type" she'll become a "sekkertry," go straight into Class III Nonmanual, and cross the great manual divide. She'd quite like Sharon to become a hairdresser—"skilled" again—and then she could do Gran's hair on the weekend. But Sharon doesn't like the idea: On your feet all day, and you have to work Sa-ur-days. She'd enjoy doing something with kiddies. (For 80 places last year Wandsworth Borough Council had 900 applicants.) She'd do anything not to have to work in a factory, or for some reason in a laundry, nor would she touch nursing—far too many soap-dodgers. But nursing is still very popular with West Indian young who regard it as a step up from Mum who used to clean wards when she first arrived from Jamaica.

Ten years ago, Sharon Definitely-Disgusting's ambition would have been to become an air hostess, but as it would take her away from her steady boy-friend for such long stretches, she'd prefer to be a ground hostess. Mrs. Definitely-Disgusting likes her at home, anyway. She'd like Dive to get on; she doesn't have any real ambitions for Sharon. One working-class school leaver in a very depressed area of the North managed very creditably against a lot of competition to get herself a job as a hotel receptionist. Her parents refused to let her take the job, they thought it would make her "too posh."

Women

The greatest feature of occupational change in the last twenty-five years has been women of all classes going out to work, the telling statistic being that three-fifths of all working women now take non-manual jobs, while three-fifths of all working men do manual work. This is reflected in the vast shift to and swelling of the Census Class III (non-manual). With increased technology, most of the Class I and II jobs have gone to men, with women filling the increasing array of lower white-collar jobs. Consequently schools, for the first time, are taking seriously the fact that women will work before and after they're married.

One of the great job phenomena of the seventies is the way the upper classes have taken up cooking for money. All the debs take *cordon bleu* courses automatically now, instead of learning to type and undo the flowers. All their mothers cook like mad because they've got upper-class husbands with picky appetites to please, and have to organise grand house parties and dinner parties without servants. Therefore it is like falling off a log for them to cook for other people. The result is Caroline Stow-Crat organising directors' lunches and working wives' buffet parties, starting take-away food shops and running Mrs. Nouveau-Richards's dinner parties.

Fiona Stow-Crat goes and cooks in chalets in Switzerland for free skiing, or in villas in Spain or Majorca in the summer, and is known as a jolly good sort. She was fumbled on the last night by one of the husbands in the kitchen, but turned her head away because her mouth was full of left-over Coq au Vin.

Like the upper-class man who can't cope with the six-year training for a lawyer, the upper-class girl is incapable of long-term sustained effort. If she works in an office, as has been already pointed out, she's always on the telephone, or vanishing on Friday and not coming back till Tuesday, or, far far worse, not recognising any difference socially between Sharon Definitely-Disgusting in the typing pool, whom she describes as "absolute heaven," and Thalia Upward, who's doing significant research in the art department. As the principal of a smart London secretarial college can be heard saying on the telephone: "Saturday morning, oh, that wouldn't suit my girls, they go to their country estates on Friday."

My husband had one secretary who always used to ring up her mother when she was going home for the weekend and arrange to have the train stopped, because the railway ran across their land.

The upper classes sometimes impose their tastes as interior

decorators. "I let Caro Stow-Crat have Carte Blank," says Mrs. Nouveau-Richards. The Marchioness of Tavistock advises Aston Martin on their colour schemes. Sometimes they run dress shops from which the hoi polloi think they can buy upper-class taste, but in which they get ripped off just as much as Oxford Street. Nude modelling used to be O.K. for the wilder element at the beginning of the seventies. By the middle seventies women's lib had arrived and any kind of modelling was dismissed as pandering to sexism. But now Antonia Fraser's daughter and the Earl of Dudley's niece are modelling, people have got bored with women's lib and it's quite smart to be a sex object again.

"Mayfair Mercs," who are the glamorous social climbers invented by *Harper's* and are the female equivalent of spiralists, go into advertising, pop music, commercial radio, television, or else shop for Arabs. They also become stylists in advertising, which means they impose their frightful lower-middle-class taste on all the sets in television commercials and press ads.

It seems insane, by the way, that all the lower-middle and lower-class girls who come from Epping and Romford and the East End work in the City with upper- and upper-middle-class men, who wouldn't dream of marrying them; while all the upper- and upper-middle-class girls who live in Knightsbridge, Fulham and Chelsea can't face going any farther east than Mayfair on the tube, and therefore work with all the middle- and lower-middle-class spiralists in advertising, whom *they* wouldn't dream of marrying either.

Upper- and working-class husbands don't like their wives going out to work. They want them waiting when they get home, always with a clean house, regular meals and the children under control. Only in the middle classes is an outside occupation for a woman a sign of status. Samantha Upward hates saying she's "just a housewife," although, for her, taking an interesting job is less of an economic necessity than it is for Mrs. Definitely-Disgusting.

Mrs. Nouveau-Richards has absolutely no desire to work. She saw her own mother working her fingers to the bone, and considers she's very lucky to be a "lady" (she emphasises the word) of leisure.

Some upper-class wives tend only to play at jobs. They counter depression when the children leave home by doing charity work, sitting on committees, marriage guidance counselling, visiting the old or spending one day a week in a smart boutique or a bookshop. "I wouldn't possibly have time to do a job," said one upper-class woman, "If you have a private income you have far too many letters to write."

In the office

The middle classes tend to take work home from the office and not take nearly so many days off. The working classes, feeling out of their depth socially in offices, do best in back-room jobs—one remembers the spiralist who felt he had to switch over to admin. in order to get on. The lower middles do best in sales and P.R. because they're so pushy. Gideon Upward is too laid-back to sell, but he has polish and self-confidence which make him good as an account executive, "liaising" with the client.

According to a fascinating book called *Managers and Their Wives* by J. M. and R. E. Pahl, the working-class woman like Mrs. Definitely-Disgusting would loathe the firm's dance. But Jen Teale would adore it, the atmosphere is lower-middle anyway, and she likes to practise socialising in a formal atmosphere. Often she's been a typist before she was married and feels very much at home.

Samantha Upward would hate any of Gideon's office parties if she were asked. She would feel underrated and neglected. She doesn't like being defined by *who* she is rather than *what* she is. She can't bear being treated just as Gideon's wife.

Mrs. Nouveau-Richards has a ball, and kisses all the directors on the mouth.

Jen Teale, because she is house-and-kitchen-proud, enjoys entertaining Bryan's colleagues at home. She has read magazines and seen commercials emphasising the wifely role when the boss comes to dinner, and knows about cooking food that is delicious but not so obviously expensive that Bryan would be thought not to need a raise.

Samantha Upward doesn't mind entertaining, but she finds it more of a bore than an ordeal. She regards Gideon's boss as such a tedious little man.

Jen Teale, who would love Bryan to get on, gives him more practical help than Samantha gives Gideon. Because they don't often entertain, she discusses work with Bryan in the evening, and being an ex-typist, helps him out typing reports when his secretary is off with the curse.

The most terrible story is told of the very shy wife of a spiralist who was bogged down by several little children at home, but who was invited to her husband's annual dinner dance. As he was doing well, she made a tremendous effort, buying a new dress, going to the hairdresser's and arranging for her mother to baby-sit, and scouring the headlines for conversational fodder. The great day dawned and on arriving at the dance she discovered she was sitting next to her husband's boss. Despite her trepidation, they got on terribly well, and it was only during the main course, when suddenly everything went quiet, that she realised she had cut up all his meat for him.

When Jen Teale worked in an office, she was a flurry of daintiness, fingerettes so she didn't have to lick her finger to turn a page over, plastic soap dishes, a shoe bag for her outdoor shoes, a mauve office cardigan to stop her good clothes getting dirty, a floral plastic sponge bag and a blue plastic container for her Tampax, in case anyone should see anything. When she went to the ladies' she rustled lavatory paper very noisily from the moment she shut the door and sometimes coughed, too, so no one would hear anything. Afterwards she washed both hands with soap and water, unlike Samantha Upward, who only bothers if there's someone there.

Chapter 7

SEX AND MARRIAGE

As was pointed out at the beginning of the previous chapter, the chief factors affecting social mobility are career and marriage. If Sharon Definitely-Disgusting blossoms into a beauty and lands Georgie Stow-Crat, her future will be completely different from that of her brother Dive, who marries a factory girl. If you marry beneath you, and have plenty of money, it is possible to yank your partner up to your own level. By the time King Cophetua had given the beggar maid a few elocution lessons and smothered her in diamonds and sables, she was probably indistinguishable, save for a few "ta"'s and "pardon"'s, from the other ladies of the court. But take a plunge both in class *and* financial status, and it's a different matter. If Queen Cophetua had fallen for a beggar, however handsome, and then been cut off with 10p. and forced to live on his lack of income, they would have both vanished into obscurity.

Although kings have married beggar maids, and peers' daughters eloped with garage mechanics, the fact that gossip columnists get so excited when this happens stresses both the news value and consequently the rarity of such an event. Most of us commit endogamy—which is not a sophisticated form of bestiality, but merely marrying someone of the same class. In fact, a genealogist called A. R. Wagner has gone so far as to say a social class for him means "an endogamous class, one, that is, whose members normally marry within it." The main reason why the classes have tended to pick partners in the same stratum is to exclude the classes below. The upper classes, for example, married each other to keep their land to themselves. The bourgeoisie did the same because they didn't want to share their capital with the working classes.

There has been much written about the social mobility triggered off by the sexual revolution of the sixties, with working-class lovers surging up from the East End; public school boys melting down their accents; and upper-class girls, in a glow of egalitarianism, taking on a string of down-market lovers: lorry drivers one year, Negroes the next, and beards the year after that. But as *Harper's* has pointed out: "Her final choice remains strangely unaffected. Somewhere there is a chartered accountant with her name on it." Or in Fiona Stow-Crat's case, it's back to Squire One.

Courting

The working classes get off the mark very early. Dive Definitely-Disgusting, having gone to school locally, meets the same members of the opposite sex all the year round. He goes about in mixed gangs at first, then one day on the way home from school, after knocking off Zacharias Upward's cap, offers to pay the bus fare of one of the girls and has the mickey taken out of him by all his friends. From then on he and the girl go round entwined like a three-legged race. As neither has a telephone at home, they spend hours on the doorstep necking, or gazing into each other's eyes like cats. If they ever do talk on the telephone, the conversation is punctuated by long, long pauses. Embarrassed by tenderness or compliments, they indulge in permanent badinage and backchat. This behaviour in extreme form was ritualised by the punk rockers: "When you fancy a girl, you spit in each other's glasses, then the boy punk says, 'Do you?,' the girl answers, 'Yes,' and you go up to the toilets." Jen Teale is very strict with Christine and hangs around at teenage parties, finally falling asleep at two o'clock in the morning. Naturally Christine reacts against Jen, and she and her friends escape to London, live in hostels, go in pairs to wine bars and pick up men. They are very keen on what they call "Chinese Nosh" or a "meal e-out," and use expressions like "a curry" or "a wine." Having been told since childhood to behave like little ladies, they are the most overtly flirtatious of all the classes, fluttering their eyelashes, pulling faces and rolling their eyes like Topsy, which they call being "animated." When she goes into a party or restaurant Christine always looks round to see what effect she is having on men. The upper classes never bother—and they never fidget either. Zacharias Upward starts courting much the latest. The middle classes haven't the self-assurance of the upper classes, and, locked into a single-sex school, Zacharias makes do with Thalia's friends who've been asked to stay in the holidays. Howard Weybridge and his friends are much better off. Too inhibited to pick each other up, and considering it common anyway, they have evolved an elaborate system of legitimate pick-up places: tennis clubs, rugger, golf and hockey clubs, where sporting events take place to heat the blood, followed by drinking to release the inhibitions before anyone can get going. Jim Callaghan, who was working-class, had to join the tennis club in order to court Audrey, who by his definition was middle-class because her parents had a car and a char and went on holiday.

Later the upper middle classes also escape to London, where they share flats with other girls and boys of "roughly the same sort of background" (their euphemism for "the same class"). They tend to meet the opposite sex through work, nurses going out with doctors, secretaries with bosses.

The upper classes have far more confidence. They all know each other anyway, and their parents, whom they call "wrinklies" or "jarryatrics," have full enough social lives not to bother themselves too much about their children's morals. They worry far more about drugs and car smashes after drinking than loss of virginity.

Georgie Stow-Crat meets girls at dances in the holidays, at the Fourth of June or Scotland in August, and at the Feather's Ball, once described by the *Observer,* in very unsmart terms, as the "do of the year for those of first-class stock."

Unlike Thalia Upward, Fiona Stow-Crat, if she sees a boy she likes, will "dance over and hope he notices me. If that doesn't work I find out someone who knows him, and get that person to introduce me. If he still isn't interested I give up."

When they're older, the upper classes meet skiing, shooting

and at various up-market occasions like Ascot and Henley. At
parties they go in for lots of horseplay and shrieking. Linda in *Love
in a Cold Climate* was more attractive to the opposite sex than the
much more beautiful Polly, because she was a "romper"—almost
a sort of chap. The upper classes are inclined to lean out of windows
and pour champagne and cigarettes on tramps and parked cars, or
to charge around at dead of night changing road signs. The sexes
also meet each other at drinks parties in the girls' flats in Knightsbridge and Belgravia. Even if the party isn't being given in her flat,
the hostess sends out "At Home" cards, and the recipient automatically runs her thumb over the words "At Home" to see if they're
engraved.

The season

Up to the late fifties most upper-class girls "came out." One's
mother, who'd been presented herself, presented one to the
Queen, and the Nouveau-Richardses bribed some impoverished
upper-class woman to do the same for Tracey-Diane. In 1958,
however, the Queen abolished the whole presentation ceremony,
which meant that anyone could become a deb, the season was
swamped by social climbers and lost any kind of cachet.

Despite this setback, a few hundred girls still come out every
year. The procedure is to write to Peter Townend, the social editor
of *The Tatler*, for a list of "gairls" doing the season. Then follows
a string of luncheons where the mothers get together to see that
party dates don't clash, and make sure that their daughters get
asked to as many things as possible. Clued-up mothers have stickers
printed with their own and their daughters' addresses on. The
minute the first luncheon reaches the coffee stage, out come the
diaries and everyone charges round seeing how many stickers they
can get into other people's diaries.

Many of the upper classes sell farms or woods to pay for dances.
It is also necessary to suck up to Peter Townend in order to get your
daughter's picture in *The Tatler*. He can also produce young men

out of a hat for dances whose background, education, regiment or sheer cash flow make them eligible. Most of the young men live in the country or a precious stone's throw from Harrods.

One of the great dangers is that one's daughter may fall in love with one of them at the beginning of the season and wreck her chances with other men. "Don't you dare go steady," I heard one mum say recently, "just like the lower classes."

One has the feeling that the mothers enjoy the season almost more than the daughters. Many of them, still youngish and pretty, suddenly have the chance to meet up with old gairl-friends and flirt with old flames.

And at the end of the season, I asked a deb's mum whether she felt all the expense had been worth it.

"Oh yes," she replied, "the gairls have all had such fun, and, at the worst, they'll have built up a network of jolly nice gairl-friends."

"And even if they do go astray," boomed her friend, "one knows they'll go astray with the right sort of chap." (Which is back to endogamy again.) When I went shooting in Northumberland I encountered a good example of this concern.

"Who's that ravishing girl who's been staying with Elizabeth?" asked one of the guns.

"Oh, she's being stuffed by a man who says 'cheers' and 'pardon,' " said another, "so her parents sent her up here to see if Elizabeth could find something more presentable."

Rough diamonds are a girl's best friend

"When the mind is full of tit and bum," a friend of mine once said, "it tends to be a-critical." Meaning that in the first flush of love, you don't mind what class a person is. The fact that he's not "the right sort of chap" makes him even more attractive. When they are young, the insecure of both sexes tend to drop class. Older upper-class men love going to bed with working-class girls. It reminds them of Nanny. For the same reason, they adore big strap-

ping Australian girls. One Australian journalist went to interview
an earl about wealth tax, and only moved out six months later.

Equally, going out with a yobbo gives the middle- and upper-
class girl a feeling of superiority. She finds the working-class man
more respectful but at the same time more dominating than his
public school counterpart. (Geoffrey Gorer claims that the skilled
worker has the highest sexual energy—so she's on to a good thing.)

It should be pointed out here that the working and upper
classes tend to be far more chauvinistic than the upper middle and
middle classes. This is perhaps because they are more reactionary,
but also because they tend to have everything done for them by
their mothers or nannies; whereas the middle-class mother, struggling for the first generation without servants, is much more likely
to have made her son run around fetching and carrying for her. The
middle-class man will therefore be far more prepared to reverse
roles. This is important because it is crucial to an understanding
of the different class attitudes to sex, dating and women in general.

The first great love of my life was a miner's son who'd become
a millionaire. I was working on a newspaper in Brentford. He
passed by me in the street in a vast open dark green car, and
screeched to a halt. I bolted into my office but when I sidled out
two hours later, he was still waiting. He was the most handsome
man I'd ever seen, and it was all very disgraceful and wildly exciting. He took me straight back to his house, whereupon he told me
to go and make him a cup of tea. I was far more shocked than if
he'd tried to seduce me. None of my stuffy middle-class boy-friends
had ever bossed me round like that.

We went out for nearly three years. Whenever he went abroad
on business, and, I suspect, pleasure, he never wrote. This broke
my heart. I only discovered years later that he was ashamed of being
ill-educated. He was shocked if I said "blast," and would never
come to any of my parties, although I was dying to show him off,
because he was frightened of not knowing how to behave. He went
to see his mother every day.

He was bossy, yet socially tentative, prudish yet unfaithful, and
mother-fixated—all working-class qualities—yet we had three mar-

vellous years. He was incredibly generous, showering me with presents, which cost a fortune and which were returned (my middle-class background again) whenever we had our periodic bust-ups. And he was far more masculine, more reassuring and more fun than any of the uptight barristers, stockbrokers and account executives I'd run about with before. If he had asked me to marry him, I should certainly have said yes, but he had the good sense to realise we were far too different for it ever to work.

For when the class war and the sex war are joined, hostilities always break out in the end.

Alan Coren reports that when he was at Oxford upper-class undergraduates screwed nurses and married upper-class girls, while working-class undergraduates married nurses and screwed upper-class girls, yelling "One for Jarrow" at the moment of orgasm.

Richard Hoggart, that champion of the lower orders, alleges that one of the most valuable characteristics of working classes is the ability to take the mickey and say "Come off it," which the middle classes usually translate as having a bloody great chip on one's shoulder. This trait frequently comes out in working-class intellectuals when they shack up with middle-class girls. One remembers John Osborne's Jimmy Porter constantly mocking his gentle, long-suffering wife.

Another example of working-class chippiness coupled with macho occurred recently with a beautiful girl-friend of mine who was running two men at once, one of them an underwriter and the first man ever to wear full eye make-up to Lloyds, and the other a working-class pop music promoter. One day the Lloyds underwriter took her for a row in Hyde Park. They were just pulling into the shore when the music promoter leapt out of the bushes where he'd been lurking and pushed the underwriter into the lake, where he stood spluttering and threatening to call the police.

"If he'd been working-class," said the music promoter later, "he'd have slugged me back. I didn't throw him in the water because I was jealous about you—but because he was upper-class."

If Zacharias Upward goes out with Christine Teale, Gideon and Samantha will talk scathingly about "not quite P.L.U. [People like Us], darling" or "rather Pardonia," and pray that Zacharias will grow out of it. Middle-class parents also become particularly lenient in the face of eligibility. If you go out with someone much grander than yourself, you tend to take on some of their mannerisms. Friends noticed that when Roddy Lewellyn was taking out Princess Margaret, he assumed the patrician poker face, used the pronoun "one" instead of "I" and started walking around with his hands behind his back like Prince Philip.

The date

When Dive Definitely-Disgusting takes a girl out on a date he's likely to be much cleaner than Zacharias Upward, who often goes out straight from the office. Dive has a bath and a good scrub before getting dressed for the evening. He'll reek of Brut and over-scented deodorant and wear an open-necked shirt to reveal a hairy muscular chest clanking with medallions. He'll be extraordinarily generous with drinks, but he won't give the girl dinner (having already had high tea so as not to drink on an empty stomach), because he's frightened of "resteronts," as he calls them. (Harry and Gideon call them "restrons.") Dive can't understand the menu if it's in French; he doesn't know how to order wine, or how to eat asparagus, and is terrified of making a fool of himself asking for steak tartare to be well done or complaining that the Vichyssoise is stone cold. This is why many restaurants qualify food on the menu, like "chilled" watercress soup, and probably explains the popularity of melon because it's the same in French and English.

Being taken out to dinner is such a treat to Sharon Definitely-Disgusting that she always works her way straight through the menu, and always has pudding. She won't comment on the food, or say "Thank you" afterwards. One working-class girl I know went out with a lower-middle sales rep who had an expense-account acquaintanceship with "resteronts." "He was so charming and well-spoken," she said afterwards, "and such a gentleman. He kept

telling me what knife and fork to use, and correcting my conni-
nenal accent." Georgie Stow-Crat, in fact, would never correct
pronunciation or comment on table manners. If his companion
wants an "advocado pear," let her have one.

The manager of our local restaurant is a great observer of dating
couples. "You can always tell a girl who's escalated," he says. "She
talks direct to the waiter, instead of letting the man order for her.
Artichokes are a great leveller, I saw one girl trying to eat the whole
thing."

"People who belong," he went on, "always hold their coats in
mid-air when they take them off. The nouveau riche never say
'Good evening,' are curt with waiters, snap their fingers and then
over-tip. They also put vinegar on their chips."

Both Christine Teale and Sharon Definitely-Disgusting tend to
prefer sweet drinks to dry: sweet Cinzano, martini, Baby Cham and
orange (a sort of Doe's fizz), Tia María, crème de menthe. If they
drink gin, it's with orange.

Sharon also likes a man to be neatly dressed on a date. "If he
had a holey sweater, or holey jeans I wouldn't entertain him," she
says. "And he must be clean. I couldn't stand all those rockers a
few years back with dirty hair. I like a boy with a bit of life in him,
but not rough." She would also say: "I've got a snapshot of him
indoors" (which is working-class for "at home").

Christine Teale refers to a boy-friend over twenty-one as a
"boy" (e.g. "I'm going out with a wonderful boy"). Most people
say "boy-friend" or "man." The upper classes when they're trying
to be democratic and trendy say "guy" in quotes. One should
never talk about an "escort." According to *U and Non-U Revisited,* one should say "male companion," which seems a bit
pedantic. Most people merely say the person's Christian name, and
leave you to guess whom they're talking about. It is also vulgar to
say "May I bring my girl?" as opposed to "a girl" when you mean
a girl-friend.

Unlike the working classes, who don't bother about the mor-
row, Wayne Teale tends to be tight with money. To splash it
around is both prodigal and cheap. He won't buy a girl dinner, so

he'll put on a paisley scarf, which he calls a "cravat," tucked into a sweater, and take her to a bar where he knows the landlord by his Christian name. This he calls "social drinking." If he's over thirty, he might wear a white orlon jersey which he'll call a "roll-neck" ("roll" to rhyme with "doll") sweater, because a touch of white is so flattering close to the neck after a certain age, and the collar hides the wrinkles in his throat. He refers to a girl as an "attractive young lady." He would prefer her to wear a skirt rather than jeans, even though his trouser creases are sharp enough to ladder her tights. He's also read somewhere that it's common to say "perfume," but "scent" sounds too foxy, so he settles for "fragrance." Gideon would probably say: "That's a nice pong."

Caution is the watchword of the lower middles. Wayne daren't be romantic, in case some unsuitable "young lady" traps him into matrimony. He would call it getting "invole-ved," with a long "o." His girl-friends have corrugated left breasts from being pressed against the pens in his top pocket. He doesn't resort to insults and backchat like the working classes, but his conversation is arch, and rather hearty with an air of continual interrogation. He will use expressions like "Chop-chop, young lady," or, even worse, address his girl-friend as "woman." She will say in reply: "Stir your stumps, Wayne Teal." It is frightfully lower-middle to address people by both their Christian name and surname. Any money Wayne makes will be spent on what he calls "home-improvements" or on his car, which has a Christian name and is always referred to as "she."

Zacharias Upward likes entertaining girl-friends in his flat, where he can show off his gourmet cooking. This is cheaper than going to restaurants, saves on petrol and is much nearer the bedroom. All his friends say Zach is very "hos*pit*able" (the upper classes emphasise the first syllable). Howard Weybridge's idea of a really exciting date is to ask his girl-friend to freeze on the touchline while he grapples muddily with a lot of other fifteen-stoners on the rugger field. Later she will be expected to talk to rugger wives about deep-freezes, while he frolics naked in a plunge bath with the rest of the team, and then make one warm gin and tonic last all evening while he downs pints and pints of beer. In summer she might get taken to cricket, which is sometimes warmer but goes on longer.

Georgie Stow-Crat will be very generous to his girl-friends, like Oscar Wilde, who, when asked why he gave champagne to a barrow boy, replied, "What gentleman would starve his guests?" Georgie can't cook, and would starve in a well-equipped kitchen. So, as he is too thick to make conversation for very long, he takes girls to dine in a nightclub or disco. As the upper classes tend to leave London at the weekend, Fridays and Saturdays are less good. To win Georgie, you'd probably have to engage Snipe's affections too.

Who marries whom

"Education!" I was always led to suppose that no educated person ever spoke of notepaper, and yet I hear poor Fanny asking Sadie for notepaper. What is this education? Fanny talks about mirrors and mantelpieces, handbags and perfume, she takes sugar in her coffee, has a tassel on her umbrella, and I have no doubt if she is ever fortunate enough to catch a husband, she will call his father and mother Father and Mother. Will this wonderful education she is getting make up to the unhappy brute for all these endless pinpricks? Fancy hearing one's wife talk about notepaper—the irritation!

Uncle Matthew in *The Pursuit of Love*
by Nancy Mitford

As the upper classes all know each other, they get in a panic if their children get engaged to someone they haven't heard of.

Georgie Stow-Crat plays around with girls of other classes before and after his marriage, but he'll try and settle for one of his own kind. For what are a few nights of passion for a lifetime at the end of the wrong table. Lord Lichfield took out a string of models and actresses, but he ended up with Lady Leonora. More recently the Marquess of Druro married the Princess of Prussia. The Duke of Roxburghe married Lady Jane Grosvenor, while Prince Michael of Kent chose an Austrian baroness. As the aristocracy are forced to straphang through life like the rest of us, they are closing their ranks, and marrying the sort of gairl who will bring some cash or land with her, or as one aristocrat put it, "can make a decent lunch for a shooting party," preferably from the same class. "The reason my marriage came unstuck," said one friend, "was because I was upper-class and he was only landed gentry."

The moment Georgie Stow-Crat gets engaged he takes the girl to meet Nanny, which is far more of an ordeal than meeting Caroline. What the upper classes really dread is their child falling for someone middle-class.

"A thoroughly conventional man in good society," said Edward Lyttleton, an ex-headmaster of Eton, "would rather that his son should resort with prostitutes than that he should marry a respectable girl of distinctly lower station than his own; indeed it is not going too far to say that he probably would rather his son should seduce such a girl, provided there were no scandal, than marry her."

In order not to be continually irritated by class differences, the aristocracy often marry rich Americans or foreigners, whom they can instruct in upper-class English behaviour without being too insulting: "In England, Ortrud, we have a funny national custom of not saying 'horse racing.' "

If Georgie Stow-Crat did marry down, he would probably choose a very beautiful girl, which is why the aristocracy is so good-looking. In general, good-looking people marry up—Tony Armstrong-Jones and Captain Mark Phillips being notable examples—and the insecure and ugly tend to marry down. Just as they dropped class while dating, they tend to pick a partner who'll look up to them and make them feel superior.

When people get married for the first time late in life—in their forties or fifties—parents are inclined to waive class prejudices out of sheer relief that their child is finally off their hands.

It is debatable whether the middle classes have any real desire to land an aristocrat any more. As has been pointed out already, the lord is no longer the favourite hero of romantic fiction (unless he's in costume, of course) and has been replaced by the middle-class doctor or surgeon.

Heather Jenner told me her marriage bureau clients "don't give a hoot" what class people are any more. "Why should they want to marry a lord and cope with a falling-down overgrown house? On the whole, blue-collar men are far better at giving a woman a good time. One upper-class woman was so fed up with the sexual and financial ineptitude of the aristocracy she put 'Working Class Only' on her form."

On the other hand, another girl who ran a marriage bureau, discovering she had a baronet among her clients, promptly whipped him off the books and married him herself. Then another friend of mine, born on a council estate, can pinpoint the moment she fell in love with her future husband, who is a peer. "He signed a cheque to pay for our dinner with his surname only." Finally, one has only to read the small ads in *The Tatler* — "Very attractive blue-blooded academic in his early thirties, equally at ease on the hunting field or engaged in economic and political discussion" (sounds hell)—to realise that class does have a pull, the Blue Bloody is still holding his own against the Blue Collar.

The upper-middle-class man, preferring to get his career to-gether before settling down, tends to marry late, between twenty-eight and thirty-two; his bride will be in her mid-twenties. Often they live together first, particularly if one set of parents disapproves. Then gradually, out of sheer force of habit, or desire for grandchildren, the parents come round.

Samantha Upward, who's always taught Zacharias to be un-snobbish, finds the thought of being a mother-in-law awfully trying. First there was Zulunka from the Fiji Islands, who was really wonderfully dark, but who spoilt it all by referring to all those nice Africans as "no-good blacks." And now there's Mikki (who's really called Enid), who appears to have no surname. Mikki does some-thing nebulous in the music business, is totally uncultured, but full of pretensions. In referring to herself and Samantha collectively as "middle-class folk like ourselves" she is obviously totally unaware that Samantha's family is much better than hers is. Even more maddening, Gideon obviously thinks that Mikki is quite quite perfect, particularly as she doesn't wear a stitch in bed.

The lower-middle parents, being materialistic, aren't sure whether to oppose early marriage as unsound financially or welcome it as better than premarital promiscuity. One lower-middle spiralist said the reason he finally decided to marry his wife was that she'd been brought up in a careful household and therefore would be a good manager of his money. Believing in deferred satisfaction, Wayne tends to be engaged for several years, rather than live with a girl, so he can put a deposit down on a house. He will "study for exams" in the evening, his fiancée will work in a bar and bank the lot, so they will have enough money to move into a "perfectly decorated home." His fiancée can't stand disorder—she must have everything nice. Whereas the upper-middle girl who wanted to get married in a hurry would be perfectly happy to move into a rented box in Fulham and run up an overdraft doing the place up, or expect Daddy to fork out for carpets and things later.

The Nouveau-Richardses will be absolutely furious if Tracey-Diane doesn't marry up. In the same way, the middle-class Princess Grace was livid, having hooked a prince herself, that her daughter settled for a middle-class industrialist.

Parents are very seldom cross about upward mobility. Even when engagements are broken off, parents make social capital, like the mother who went round telling her friends: "It's such a bore having to pick all the coronets off the linen."

Dive Definitely-Disgusting marries the earliest of all the classes. This is probably due to frustration. The working classes have got nowhere to make love—probably no car, no flat. If they go home Mrs. D.-D. and all the children are watching the telly and it's too cold outside except in summer. They also started dating earlier anyway, and if they do screw they often don't bother to "take precautions," get pregnant and can't afford abortions.

"I didn't *have* to get married, I married for love," a working-class minicab driver told me the other day, as if it were the exception to the rule.

Engaged at seventeen, Sharon Definitely-Disgusting gets "eternized" at eighteen, which means she receives an eternity ring from her betrothed. At Christmas and birthdays she will send him a four-foot-square card padded with red satin, saying "To my Darling Fiance" (without the accent).

The word "fiancé," perhaps because so many people live together now, has become distinctly vulgar, particularly when it is pronounced "fee-on-*cay,* " with the weight on the last syllable. Debs get round it sometimes by saying "my fiasco" or "my intended."

The wedding

The wedding is one occasion when the classes meet head-on. People who marry up choose tiny churches or have registry office weddings so they don't have to invite less grand relations. It doesn't matter having common friends, everyone thinks one's frightfully democratic, but common relations are quite a different matter. Wedding presents aren't displayed either, because they might cause derisive mirth at the reception.

Embarrassing relations are less obvious at a stand-up reception with food you can eat with your fingers, so people's table manners don't show up—and with any luck working-class relations will push off early because they hate not being able to sit down.

There will invariably be a panic about protocol. One girl said her mother pored over *The Tatler* for months, studying every detail of the weddings, muttering firmly: "We're going to get this right." "We even," she went on, "put a sleeping pill in Granddad's cocoa, the night before, because he refused to wear morning dress."

When John Betjeman married an upper-class girl he drove his mother-in-law insane at the pre-wedding party by wearing a made-up bow tie on elastic and flicking it all the way through dinner.

Conversely, an example of aristocratic indifference to other people's opinions also occurred at a recent stag party held in a private room at a club. The men had just finished dinner, and the bridegroom's father, an old peer, suddenly beckoned to a waiter and said: "Pot."

"We're not allowed to supply it, sir," said the waiter nervously.

"Don't be bloody silly," roared the Earl. "I mean pisspot." Whereupon a huge chamber pot was brought down from one of the bedrooms, and the Earl proceeded to use it, in full view of the other guests.

The upper classes get married in the country in their own churches. As they are accustomed to giving and going to balls and big parties, the wedding is not such an event as it would be in a middle-class family. Quite often the bride wears her mother's wedding dress, and a 200-year-old veil of Brussels lace held in place by the family tiara. (One upper-class bride was so relaxed she spent her wedding morning washing her horse's tail.) She doesn't usually have a long engagement or any of the hassle of finding a house, because her parents or her in-laws have already given them a "place" with lots of "pieces" in it.

The wedding invitations are engraved in black, the service cards have the Christian names of the bride and bridegroom (pronounced "bridegr'm," not "bridegrume") printed at the bottom. Flowers in the church are usually something unostentatious like lilies of the valley, with the bride's bouquet (pronounced "book-ay," not "buke-ay") of white roses or spring flowers.

The men wear their own morning coats. There are usually hordes of little bridesmaids called Lucinda and Henrietta, a page with patent-leather hair wearing a replica of a Blues and Royals uniform, and a Labrador looking sheepish in a regimental bow. No one minds about the music. "Here Comes the Bride" up, Mendelssohn down. The bride agrees to honour and obey. It used to be unsmart to get married at the weekend, particularly in London, as everyone had gone away. But now most of the upper classes and their show-business friends have jobs, it is considered perfectly all right. Saturday police have to be deployed from the local football match to deal with the traffic. Several of the guests arrive by helicopter.

After the service, the line-up to shake hands with the couple takes hours and hours. We queued interminably at a royal wedding a few years ago—it was rather like mountaineering. You crawled along for ten minutes, then turned into the next room to find another long queue, and then another up a staircase and then another. People kept giving up and doing U-turns to go out to dinner. One felt they ought to provide something to sustain one during the waiting: champagne at the foothills or brandy at the South Col.

At another very grand wedding, having been nervously practising my curtsy all the way, I found when we finally reached the bride and bridegroom that everyone was shaking hands with them.

"I thought we were supposed to bob," I muttered to a friend once I was safely inside.

"I was damned if I was going to bob to that jumped-up trollop," said my mate. "And after that everyone followed suit."

The reception at an upper-class wedding is a very cheerful occasion, once again because everyone knows each other, and it doesn't matter that there's no introducing. None of the women look the least self-conscious in hats, the cake is decorated with white flowers, and often cut with the bridegroom's sword, the nearest it ever gets to active service. Really grand weddings include busloads of tenants from both families. Usually they sit around with red faces, shiny blue suits and well-greased hair. But at Earl Grosvenor's wedding recently, morning coats were hired for all the tenants so they wouldn't feel out of place, and they were all flown down by aeroplane.

The latest trend is to have a wedding followed by a small luncheon for the stuffier relations, followed by an afternoon rest for the stuffed bride, followed by a huge booze-up in the evening.

Georgie Stow-Crat hates his honeymoon because he misses Snipe. Upper-class girls often take Teddy on honeymoon.

When Georgie marries Tracey-Diane Nouveau-Richards, no expense is spared. Tracey-Diane's tiara is so heavy her head droops like a snowdrop. The "floral decorations," composed of "Football Mum" chrysanthemums nurtured in Mr. Nouveau-Richards's conservatory, are described by the N.-R.'s friends as "tasteful."

Mrs. Nouveau-Richards has had orchids and maidenhair cor-
sages in little test tubes of preservative liquid made up for herself
and Caroline Stow-Crat, who surreptitiously tries to rip off the
maidenhair during the service, and only succeeds in burning a hole
in her new coat and skirt with the preservative. Signing the register
takes longer than usual, as Mrs. N.-R.'s hat gets stuck in the door.

Harry Stow-Crat has a wonderful time. There's plenty of champagne—Tracey-Diane's endowment of worldly goods means he
needn't worry about death duties any more. And Snipe gets into
all the photos with his back to the camera gazing at Harry.

The Upwards are simply furious they haven't been invited.

"I suppose they can't ask everyone," says Samantha bravely.

Although Mrs. Nouveau-Richards seems to have.

The upper-middle wedding is far more depressing. Samantha
and Thalia, wanting to be different and stress how "cultured" and
musical they are, choose hymns the congregation don't know.
Waiters keep the napkin over the champagne to hide the lack of
vintage. No one wears maidenhair behind their carnations apart
from a few déclassé cousins in lounge suits.

As the upper middle classes don't all know each other, but are
too grand for a sit-down meal, their weddings tend to be very heavy
going. The women's heels sink into the lawn, so they can't circu-
late. The merriment is not aided by a long speech from the bride's
parents' most upper-class friend. No one can clap properly at the
end because they're holding empty glasses. Thalia's husband hates
his honeymoon and thinks they're so called because they're so
sticky.

Howard and Eileen Weybridge's wedding is held in the function room of the Olde White Hart (circa 1937) with french windows opening onto the patio. The women look very self-conscious
in floppy hats, with too much hair showing in front. The bride
makes her own wedding dress or buys it off the peg. According to
one manufacturer, royalty influences far more wedding dresses than
show business, and the less virginal a girl is, the more covered up
she wants to look. Howard Weybridge and all his ushers are photo-

graphed outside the church in hired grey morning coats with maidenhair rampant behind every foiled carnation and their top hats on the sides of their heads. The reception starts off with sweet and dry sherry followed by Asti Spumante ("bubbly," as they call it, is too expensive); everyone sits down to lunch of a nice smoked trout, chicken and *bombe surprise,* after frightful rows over the seating arrangements. Likely to be local councillors or secretaries of the tennis club, who adore the sound of their own voices, the speakers go on for ever, and every dismally unfunny telegram is read out.

The bride's mother finds the "holl" occasion very "meuving." "It's such a nice opportunity to meet and converse with relatives," and Eileen's had "some wonderful wedding gifts." The father says "look after yerself," as Eileen goes away in the Austin Princess and a navy costume with beige accessories. The honeymoon is spent in the bridal suite of a hotel in Devonshire.

The lower middles are the tiredest when they get married, because they've decorated and renovated their new property (Georgie Stow-Crat would say "done up their new house") themselves, all ready to move in.

Bryan Teale has his stag party two nights before the wedding because Auntie Jean has to be met off the train from Scotland on Friday and the Volks has to be put through the car wash before they go away. No one wears a morning coat, the men are in three-piece waisted suits. The best man goes off to buy shoes with built-up heels on the morning of the wedding so his trousers hang better. The "bridal gown" is based on the latest royal soap opera with Mrs. Fitzherbert sleeves. The photographer snaps away throughout the service in all the most solemn moments, and the results are put in a white album with spider tissue paper. People are shown to their seats by "groomsmen" rather than "ushers." The service cards are printed in silver Gothic script and decorated with silver bells and the bride and groom's initials. The bridegroom has to remove his initialled signet ring to his right hand to make way for his wedding ring, and the happy couple, smothered in confetti and rice, leave the church in a white Rolls-Royce.

The reception is held at the Dainty Maiden Tea Rooms, and

thirsty cyclists who've ridden over from Godalming are told to go to the Hand in the Bush Tea Rooms down the road, as the place has been taken over for a "function." Sherry is followed by rosé or sparkling hock. Everyone eats ham, chicken and salad. The wedding cake is topped by a papier-mâché replica of the bride and groom, both wearing lipstick, and decorated with silver shoes, horseshoes and plastic flowers.

The bride, wearing a tangerine "skirt suit," and the bridegroom, in an even lighter-coloured and more waisted suit, go off to Majorca for a honeymoon, where the new Mrs. Teale loses her virginity on the third day.

The working-class wedding is the most jolly. Mrs. Definitely-Disgusting has even forgiven Stan for putting Sharon in the club —at least he's white. The hall is hired at the Goat and Boots, the bar is open all day, everyone sits down or dances—the working classes never stand because of their corns. Dad soon gets down to the piano and starts playing "golden oldies" like "You Made Me Love You." Auntie Eileen leads the singing. Even Mrs. Definitely-Disgusting is persuaded to do a knees-up. Sharon wears an Empire line dress to hide the bulge and feels sick all the time. The honeymoon is spent in Jersey. Having never been away from home before, Stan and Sharon are very homesick.

Sex

It is difficult to generalise about sex and class. Hunter Davies, a working-class writer so successful that he has certainly become middle-class in his life-style, in a *Sunday Times* piece expressed his bewilderment at his thirteen-year-old daughter going out with boys and demanding parties with drink. "Brought up on a council estate in the sixties," he wrote, "I married the school swot, it took me three weeks even to hold her hand. My dad knew what it was like to be me when I was courting, but things have changed so much in the last ten years that I haven't a clue what it's like to be Caitlin. She's a different age, a *different class*, a different society."

With the advent of the permissive society, one hopes that the young of all classes are getting better at sex, and more aware of "the great discovery of the age," as Hugh MacDiarmid called it. "That women like it too."

But there are still vast pockets of male chauvinism among the upper and lower classes, particularly in the North. It is possible that young Georgie Stow-Crat and Dive Definitely-Disgusting are fairly competent operators, having picked up a few tips from the cinema, but their fathers are probably still floundering around in the Dark Ages.

Harry Stow-Crat's attitude to sex, for example, is the same as that of our late lamented English setter, who was spoilt, goofy, terrifyingly tenacious and possessed of a totally unbridled sex drive. If he got on the trail of a bitch, he would charge across three main roads, race twenty miles until he caught up with her and then mount her from the wrong end. His libido was only equalled by his sexual ineptitude—rather like one peer who discovered after three years when no heir appeared that he'd been using the wrong entrance.

Another married aristocrat I know was so wild to pull a girl he'd had lunch with that he secreted them both into the Great Western Hotel by a side door without paying, locked himself into a bedroom, and was just settling down to work when the management rumbled him. Only a lot of fast talking and a fistful of fivers stopped him being arrested, and the most frightful scandal ensuing.

If Harry fancies a girl, particularly a lower-class one, he will pester her until he gets her, and then it's "wham, bam, thank you, ma'am." He's far too used to poor Caroline shutting her eyes and thinking of England to believe a woman should have any pleasure.

The telly-stocrat and the pop singer have the same exalted approach. "It's so easy," sighed one rock star. "You have all these groupies, there's no time to romance [lower middle for to "court"] on the road, so you just say 'get your gear off.'" A sort of "droit du singer."

My favourite minicab driver has a theory that tall people are good in bed because only they can reach the sex books that librarians insist on putting on the top shelves. But this doesn't explain why aristocrats, who are generally tall, tend to be so hopeless— maybe they never go into public libraries, or don't read anything except *The Sporting Life* and Dick Francis, like Harry Stow-Crat. Harry's sole aim is vaginal penetration—he can't even count up to foreplay. When a girl kisses him, she can feel his narrow stoat's head under his straight mousy hair totally devoid of any Beethoven bumps. As he thinks after-shave and deodorant are vulgar and doesn't have any of the middle-class hang-ups about being nice to be near, he might even be rather dirty.

Aristocrats often break their toes on stone hot-water bottles climbing into other people's beds at house parties. One wonders what the procedure is. Does the hostess sleep with the man in the right-hand bedroom for the first half of the night, and the man in the left-hand bedroom for the second half? Presumably anything goes, as long as you're back in your own room at dawn so as not to upset the servants. Most of the upper classes share their beds with their dogs for warmth. When a noble lover leaps into bed, and thinks he has encountered something interesting and furry, he may easily get bitten.

As they have all the freedom and restlessness of inherited wealth, there is a wild decadent fringe of the aristocracy, whose sexual appetites are so jaded that they're into every perversion under the eldest son. Having enjoyed beatings at Eton, both Harry and Georgie Stow-Crat adore being whipped. You can recognise an old school bottom—striped with red, white and blue weals—any-where.

Most newly created peers, who have been far too busy making it to the top to get any practice, are absolutely hopeless in bed.

The upper middles used to be even worse than the aristocracy. They were too inhibited even to have Harry's *joie de vivre:* their upper-middle lips were far too stiff for them to be any good at oral sex. Colonel and Mrs. Upward's generation must have had terrible sex lives because of overhead lights in the bedroom. Once they'd switched the lights off by the door, the room was plunged in darkness, so it was a miracle if they ever found their way into bed with one another. In fact, it's remarkable they succeeded in producing Samantha and Gideon at all.

Moving down the generations, Gideon is very enthusiastic, but a bit mainline—*Playboy* in the lavatory and a finger under his next-door neighbour's roll-on at New Year's Eve parties. He knows all about the middle-class sophistication and de-furred satisfaction and longs for Samantha to shave her bush off. She did once but it was awfully itchy, and as the whole family have baths together, it might have put Zacharias off his O levels. But she's frightfully understanding about Gideon's *Playboys* and allows him to do anything he likes to her in bed, shutting her eyes and thinking of Great Britain and the Common Market. She does her yoga every morning to keep herself young and attractive.

The best lover of all is the upper-middle-class intellectual. Having been made to run round by his mother when he was young, he's into role reversal and a woman having as much pleasure as a man. His already vivid imagination has been encouraged by voracious reading. He's just as randy as the aristocrat, but he tempers it with finesse and humility. Lucky the girl that lays the golden egghead.

A male stud who has done extensive field work agrees that middle-class intellectual women are also best in bed. The *Guardian* reader, he specifies, is the easiest lay of them all, because she feels she ought to be liberated and knows all about rejection and blows to the male ego. She always refers to coming as "a climax," says "penis" and "vagina" and talks about her friends having "lovely breasts."

The lower middles tend to be too cautious. It's all "nudge nudge" prurience and not much joy. Jen Teale is also terribly difficult to get at because she wears such an armour plating of full-length petticoats, corselettes, five pairs of "punties," tights with trousers (which she calls "punts") and "punty girdles." Bryan, on the other hand, sometimes forgets to take off his driving gloves. Dainty and fastidious, Jen would never make love during the curse (which she calls a "period") and she is "revolted" by anything slightly off-centre. Afterwards she says: "That was very pleasant, Bryan."

The working classes have a reputation for potency and being good in bed—a myth probably started by middle-class novelists and by graphologists who claim anyone with loopy writing must be highly sexed. Randy they certainly seem to be. According to an Odhams Survey, the working-class couple makes love more frequently than any other class, but the woman enjoys it less.

"We don't fight," said one builder's wife. "Only over money and sex, especially sex, he always wants it. He'd do it now if he came in and you weren't here."

Geoffrey Gorer maintains that the skilled worker (Class III) would appear to have more sexual energy than the other classes. But he says that there does not seem to be any factual basis for believing the working classes in general are more sexually potent. He quotes an upholsterer who only had sex three or four times a month, and a welder who only had it once a month (perhaps he got stuck).

Mrs. Definitely-Disgusting calls sex "having relations" or "inercourse." If there were any sexual problems, she would be far too embarrassed to discuss them. Mr. Definitely-Disgusting is not into foreplay, he uses that finger to read the racing results.

Marrying up

No one understands the nuances of class better than Chekhov. At the beginning of *The Three Sisters,* Andrey's fiancée, Natasha, is seen as a lower-middle-class social outcast. Everyone laughs at her, and the three sisters tell her her clothes are all wrong. Then she marries their brother, and gradually she gains ascendancy. She starts bossing the sisters, henpecking her husband and being beastly to the old servants ("I don't like having useless people about"). Soon she is cutting down trees on the estate and moving the sisters into smaller bedrooms. By the end they are meekly taking criticism from her about their clothes.

People who marry up are far more insistent than most on having their new status recognised. I'm sure the Beggar Maid, despite her lovesome mien, made a perfect nuisance of herself queening it all over everyone, and we have all seen how the middle-class Princess Grace became far more regal than royalty once she landed Prince Rainier.

One woman who married a duke suddenly insisted on having a room to herself at the hairdressers, "because I'm not just anyone any more." Often they can't quite master the new vocabulary.

"We're spending the weekend at Bath's seat," said a secretary who'd just landed a peer.

Women who marry up also become frightfully strict about their children's manners, because they're terrified that any lapse in behaviour will be attributed to a mother who doesn't know what's what. In the same way, stupid women who marry clever men are pushy about their children's education. Middle-class women who marry into the upper classes say "se-uper" a lot, and become very good cooks to cope with picky aristocratic appetites.

When men marry up, they usually move away from their home town, buy horses and farms and take up patrician pastimes like hunting and particularly shooting. They also become totally bilingual, putting on very grand voices when they're out hunting and lapsing into their mother tongue when they're talking to garage mechanics.

If you marry someone who constantly tells you you're pretty, you begin to think you are. In the same way, if you marry someone who thinks you're frightfully grand, you begin to believe him. As a result, lots of middle-class women married to working-class men get very smug and think they're far more upper-class than they really are. Men who marry up often put their wives on pedestals, and then run around with other women. Parvenus within marriage, in fact, are invariably unfaithful. It's a back-handed blow for the class war—John Osborne's Jimmy Porter is a classic example. So was President Kennedy. Upper-class women brought up to expect infidelity can handle this; that's why they build up that network of jolly nice gairl-friends to fall back on, and anyway they're so busy sitting on committees, organising charity balls and wondering what to wear at Ascot they don't miss sex much.

The middle classes like Eileen Weybridge and Samantha Upward can't cope at all.

"Oh, Charles," said one middle-class wife, "I can't bear to
think of your penis in Mrs. Peacock."

Which brings us to . . .

Adultery

Harry Stow-Crat has never been faithful to Caroline, like the earl
who made a good start to his marriage by asking all his old girl-
friends to sleep with him as a wedding present. Traditionally, as was
pointed out in the first chapter, marriages were arranged to improve one's cash situation and to increase one's land, and one got
one's fun elsewhere. Not all aristocrats are rich, of course, but it
is much easier to play around if you don't have a job, own several
places, have a helicopter to whisk your mistress round the country,
yachts to sail about the Mediterranean and plenty of cash to take
her to smart restaurants and hotels. Upper-class males also tend to
lead separate lives from their wives in any case.

"Where's Daphne?" I remember asking one peer. "Oh, she's
stalking in Scotland" came the reply (the prey wasn't specified).

Location can also curb the libido. One girl-friend of mine said
her lover, who was an Hon., wouldn't even hold her hand if they
were walking across the Knightsbridge side of the Park, but would
neck ferociously on benches on the non-smart Bayswater side (because he was unlikely to see any of his wife's friends up there). And
in the undergrowth of Wimbledon Common he would fornicate
freely ("because there's not the slightest possibility of ever bumping into anyone I know in the suburbs"). An aristocrat once came
up to London to take me out to lunch, and booked a table at a
restaurant in Holland Park, which he also regarded as suburbia and
quite safe. Alas, we couldn't get a taxi afterwards, and to his
extreme consternation, had to walk all the way to Knightsbridge
before he could find one.

Upper-class wives can occasionally be just as unbridled sexually.

One even has two telephone numbers, one for business and an unlisted hot line for lovers. She was livid with one editor (who'd been an ex) who rang her about a feature by mistake on the lovers' telephone. When one peer's daughter discovered her M.P. lover had ditched her and returned to his wife, she stuck a huge placard on his car, which was parked in the street outside his house, saying: "Do you really want to vote for an adulterer?"

The upper middle classes used to concentrate on their careers to keep sin at bay. But all changed with the advent of the country cottage. With Samantha in the country and Gideon at his little flat in the Barbican, the fun is unconfined, although Gideon's frolics are slightly inhibited when Thalia decides to leave boarding school early and take a secretarial course in London and live with Daddy.

The seven-year itch often finds some basis for truth among the middle classes. Samantha marries at twenty-four, has Zacharias at twenty-six and Thalia at twenty-eight. Three years later, when she's been married exactly seven years, Zacharias starts full-time school and Thalia goes to playgroup. Eureka, she has the house free for the first time in years, coupled with the feeling of nagging inadequacy that the children are no longer a full-time job justifying her being just a housewife. Hey presto, in moves the lover.

The upper middle classes, not having living-in servants, often have a sexual renaissance when the children go to boarding school and they have the house to themselves. On the debit side, one friend said it was very difficult to keep lovers at arm's length when one no longer had the excuse after a liquid lunch that one must rush away and pick up the children from school at four o'clock.

All adultery grinds to a halt during the school hols, which is the main reason—not tiredness—why mothers get so bad-tempered.

The lower middles tend to be too cautious to commit adultery, it might upset the extra-bright children. Occasionally they go to wife-swapping parties and pool all the children with what they call a "sitter." Bryan Teale, when not working out the commission he's made that morning, makes love in a car on the edge of the common in the lunch hour, which is why he furnishes his car with cushions and coat hangers so his cheap suit won't crease.

Working-class adultery, however, is much harder to achieve. No telephone to arrange appointments, possibly no car. Because of shift work and overtime, the lover never knows if the husband will be there or not . . . when the coast is clear the wife puts a packet of OMO soap powder in the front window (which stands for "Old Man Out"). Mrs. Definitely-Disgusting says she doesn't hold with it.

The upper and upper middle classes talk about "having an affair" with someone. The media and the trendy middle class call it "having a relationship."

In-laws and parents

Many working-class couples—unable to afford a place of their own —are still forced to live with one set of parents after they are married, often with the wife's mother bringing up the children. This is why the mother-in-law problem is more acute among the lower echelons, and is the basis for so many music-hall jokes. In the past when the mortality rate was very high, and husbands were likely to desert or be put off work, the wife's only protection was herself, so she clung to her own family, particularly her mother. As has been pointed out, many working-class men visit their mothers every day and, if their wives are working, go home for lunch. Although the old matriarchies are breaking down now that some couples can afford cars, and move to jobs away from home, work-ing-class mothers still tend to be far more possessive than middle-class ones. At Christmas and birthdays, they have truces with their sons' wives and they send each other large spangled "Dearest Mother-in-Law" or "Daughter-in-Law" cards.

Among the middle classes, the social gradations are so complex you often get both sets of parents thinking their offspring have married down.

"Oh, Zacharias has got a nice little wife," a mother will say. "We're getting used to her saying 'garridge' and 'port-rait.' " ("Lit-

tle," as in references to "little shopgirls," is always a euphemism
for "common.")

If, however, the "nice little wife" looks after her husband well,
and produces a son fairly quickly, she will soon be forgiven her low
caste. Heirs are a daughter-in-law's crowning glory. In many ways,
too, a slightly common daughter-in-law is preferable, as long as
she's respectful, because it makes the mother-in-law feel superior.
One girl-friend said she didn't speak to her husband for three days
after a weekend with her in-laws. In the middle of dinner, her
mother-in-law asked her to pass the cruet, and her son half-jokingly
said: "Oh, Angie thinks the word 'cruet' is common."

In the same way, if Thalia Upward were to marry Dive Definitely-Disgusting, she would start making Mrs. D.-D. feel that her
anti-black and generally xenophobic attitudes were uncouth. Mrs.
D.-D., in retaliation, would disapprove of the way Thalia made
Dive do the housework, get his own supper when she went to maths
workshops, and even went out to work when she needn't.

The middle classes, disliking friction, try to keep a superficial
peace with their in-laws, even if they disapprove. The upper classes
don't bother. A middle-class friend of mine was once very pointedly
told by her extremely grand old mother-in-law: "Divorce is considered perfectly respectable now."

On the middle-class front, one often gets antagonism between
two sets of in-laws, if the wife is working. Samantha's parents say:
"You must be getting *so* tired, and Gideon really ought to be able
to support you, darling." Colonel and Mrs. Upward, nettled by
such disapproval, retaliate with "poor Gideon being hampered in
his career by having to help with the housework, and cook dinner
when he gets home in the evening."

Parents whose children marry up and move away often complain that young people today are selfish and ungrateful. "He's
become like that Greta Thingamy," grumbles Mrs. Definitely-
Disgusting, "he wants to be alone."

One girl who married a man in the R.A.F. said it was a nightmare every time her working-class parents came to stay. "Dad

sneers every time Don brings out a bottle of wine at meals, and says: 'We *are* pushing the boat out, aren't we?' Then he expects Don to take him for a drink at the Officers' Mess. If only they'd behave like the jolly kind of people they normally are."

"My daughter goes to sherry parties now," said another working-class mother sadly, "and has a little car of her own. She asks me to go and stay but I don't go, I might show her up." Stay in your own world you're O.K., move up and you're out of step.

As Tracey Nouveau-Richards says: "If Dad wasn't my dad, I'd laugh at him myself."

One lower-middle girl I know describes a horribly embarrassing occasion when she got engaged to a peer and his father came for a drink to meet her parents. Her mother's first words were: "We're all of a flutter, we don't know whether to call you 'Your Grace' or 'Dad.' "

Divorce

As you go down the social scale, the more rigid and unforgiving you find the attitude towards infidelity . . . The upper-middle-class couple, according to Geoffrey Gorer, believe in talking over the situation if they discover one of them is having an affair. The lower middles would try and reconcile their differences and get over what they consider a passing fancy. The skilled worker might advocate separation but not divorce. But Social Classes IV and V would be all for punitive action: clobber the missus and clobber the bloke, and after that the only answer is divorce.

Of all the social classes, in fact, Class V clocks up the second most divorces. This is probably because they marry so young, often having to get married, and because they find it impossible to discuss their problems when things go wrong. The husband can't cope with the pressure of so many children, and as he often must take casual labouring jobs in other parts of the country, the temptation to desert and shack up with another woman is too strong. He can also get free legal aid and doesn't have to pay for a divorce, and finally, because the parental bond is so strong, it is quite easy for both husband and wife to go home and live with their own parents, whereas the middle-class wife, having achieved a measure of independence, would find this far more difficult.

What else wrecks a marriage? The middle classes mind most about selfishness, conflicting personalities and sexual incompatibility, while the working-class wife objects to drinking, gambling and untidiness, and the husband going out on his own with his mates.

Despite all the country cottages, Social Class I (engineers and oculists) has the fewest divorces, probably because they can't afford two mortgages and two sets of school fees, because no one's going to give them legal aid and because they think divorce would be bad for their careers.

According to Ivan Reid's *Social Class Differences in Britain,* lower middles get divorced more frequently than skilled workers. Maybe this is because the lower middles, working together in offices, have more opportunity to meet the opposite sex on a long-term basis, while the skilled worker is stuck on the factory floor assembling tools.

The aristocracy, statistically negligible though they may be, tot up even more divorces than Class V. Since the turn of the century, 33 per cent of all marquesses and earls have been married twice, 24 per cent of viscounts and 20 per cent of barons. That's why *Debrett's* is such a fat book, listing all the marriages.

"The reason for this," explained one life peer, "is that few blue-blooded aristocrats have inhibitions about what their neighbours think." Presumably if you live at the ends of long drives, the neighbours don't get a chance to see much.

Only 3 per cent of newly created peers get divorced—too busy getting to the top to have anything on the side, and too hopeless in bed for anyone to want them.

One of the saddest victims of the class war is the wife of the ambitious spiralist. While *he's* been living it up in foreign hotels, eating expense-account lunches and playing golf with the boss, she's been stuck at home with the children. He has a whole new life-style, and he wants a new wife to complement it, someone more glamorous and more socially adept. Husbands justify abandoning the first wife by saying: "Anita didn't travel with me," or "I married a local girl [euphemism for "common"] first time round."

People who've been married several times tend only to mention the grandest ex they've been married to. Woodrow Wyatt has had several wives, but in *Who's Who* only lists the one who was an earl's daughter.

Chapter 8

HOMOSEXUALITY

The middle age of buggers is not to be contemplated without horror.

Virginia Woolf

Heterosexuals, as we have seen, tend to marry and go out with people of their own class. But as Harry Stow-Crat might drop class if he had something on the side, because there would be less likelihood of his own set finding out, homosexual relationships (because until recently they were against the law in England) tend to be between people of different classes, simply for safety reasons. Harry Stow-Crat pursuing rough trade in Brixton would not be likely to bump into any of Caroline's friends, any more than Dive Definitely-Disgusting bouncing around in the four-poster of some stately home would be likely to meet any of his mates.

There are fewer homosexuals (about one in ten) around than heterosexuals. Therefore it's more difficult for them to find someone of their own class. Nor would you find a class of people more insecure socially than most homosexuals, and, as we've already pointed out, the insecure tend to drop class. The upper-class man having an affair with Dive Definitely-Disgusting is given a nice feeling of social superiority.

Perhaps most important of all, there is the psychological motive: if you're going to descend into the pit of Sodom you might as well degrade yourself further by dropping class. Hence the often tragic addiction of upper- and upper-middle-class queens to the criminal classes, laying themselves open to goodness knows what blackmail, beatings-up and being left trussed-up naked like a chicken for the char to discover in the morning.

Sometimes there are happier outcomes. A famous painter surprised a burglar rifling his house, and invited the burglar to stay: he did—for the next twenty years. Another friend has a running affair going with a wonderfully handsome married burglar. He was particularly enchanted the last time the burglar came out of prison "because he lied to his wife about the release date, and spent his first night out with me."

There's also no doubt there is something very attractive about a butch, muscular working-class boy. "I'm simply not turned on by people who don't have accents," said one aristocrat. While a middle-class man said his father "warned me never to look below for a friend—how wrong he was."

"If I want to attract a toff," said one East Ender, "I always thicken my accent, and talk about 'fevvers': they think it's marvellous."

On the other hand, the queen, whatever his class, tries to be more upper-class, ironing out his accent like mad and putting on what my East End friend calls a "posh telephone voice." Because the middle classes tend to articulate and emphasise their words more, the homosexual voice is often very difficult to distinguish from Jen Teale Refained.

The higher classes are attracted to the working classes not only because they like the butch image but also because, like women, they are drawn to people who give them a hard time. E. M. Forster, after years of falling in love with unreliables, said he was convinced that the working classes are incapable of passionate love: "All they have is lust and goodwill." Ironically, Forster later found happiness with a married policeman, who after Forster died said with typical lower-middle caution that he'd never realised Forster was homosexual.

But earlier Forster had advised the writer J. M. Ackerley, who suffered from a string of unreliable boxers, burglars, guardsmen and deserters, to bear in mind that the lower-class lover could be quite deeply attached to you, but suddenly find the journey up the social scale too much.

Certainly if Dive Definitely-Disgusting gets taken up by the upper-class fag Mafia he can lead an amazingly grand and glamorous life. I know a plumber who spends his weekends moving from one stately home to another, the sort of life Mrs. Nouveau-Richards would give her capped teeth for. Evidently a famous Oxford queen once took him to stay with Harold Nicolson, which he didn't like because Harold had made him go and put on a tie for breakfast.

According to Geoffrey Gorer, the higher the social class, or rather the more educated people are, the more likely they are to be tolerant of homosexuality. As he was basing his findings on the Census classifications, by the highest classes he would mean Gideon and Samantha Upward rather than Harry Stow-Crat. Certainly Jen Teale and the lower middles who don't enjoy sex and disapprove passionately of promiscuity would be the most intolerant, not being able to comprehend how anyone could do anything so "revolting" for pleasure. The upper working classes are also very intolerant. One thinks of the poor electrician who wrote to *Coal News* saying he was homosexual and pleading for acceptance, who was promptly pilloried and sent to Coventry by his work-mates. There is even less tolerance in the Midlands and Northeast. In Newcastle working-class homosexuals are so terrified of being rumbled they always take girl-friends with them to the gay pubs.

"I was chased by fifteen youths in Newcastle," said a cockney boy. "They wanted to beat me up because I was carrying a handbag."

Some policemen investigating a drug case went up to Wales incognito and tried to ingratiate themselves with the locals. But the locals automatically assumed they were homosexuals and resisted every approach, until the police imported some sexy police women.

London, of course, is much easier going. When I went to a C.H.E. (Campaign for Homosexual Equality) meeting in Streatham, I gathered that one lorry driver came up to meetings from Wales regularly, because "you can't come out in Cardiff." And the boy who worked in the London betting shop said that when he told his mates at work that he was queer, they were very understanding about it. "What they simply couldn't understand, and I think this is a working-class attitude, was how I could sleep with a man and not get paid for it." Whereas in the old days it was the great fear that one's daughter would become a prostitute, now it's the young lads, who are referred to as "rent boys," who run away from home, go up to what is known as the Meat Rack in Piccadilly and hawk their bodies to any likely buyer for £15 a throw.

One interesting point, however, is that the working classes seem to get less flak than other classes when they tell their parents they're homosexual. "My parents found out when I was about eighteen," said my East End friend. "This boy kept writing to me. We don't get many letters in our house, and I told Mum I was going to spend Easter with him. She said: 'Is there anything you want to tell me?' I said: 'No.' Well, I had a lousy Easter worrying about her, and the moment I got home I said: 'I *have* got something to tell you, I'm homosexual.' Her reaction was: 'Oh, thank God, I thought it was drugs.' I went to a shrink and he wasn't any help, so now everyone's accepted it. A lot of my gay mates are frightened of shrinks, the moment you tell them you're gay, they leap on you. There's a change in my dad too. Before, he was always very undemonstrative, but now we get on very well, and he often puts a hand on my arm and says: 'Are you all right, son?' My mum and dad don't mind what friends say, because they haven't got many friends, they're too much into the family."

One gets the impression that because the mother-son link is so strong in the working classes, a lot of them are subconsciously not displeased if their sons turn out queer; if this is the case, there won't be any daughter-in-law problems and there won't be the macho rivalry between father and son, when the son gets married to some lovely girl and starts jackbooting around the house. Since the working classes have large families, there'll also be other children to provide Mum with grandchildren, and there isn't this middle- and upper-class obsession with carrying on the line. Nor, like Jen Teale, do they care quite so much what the neighbours think; in fact, they enjoy their sons bringing home all these nice young men.

Further up the social scale, middle-class parents put appalling pressure on only sons who turn out to be "queer" and don't produce heirs or grandchildren to be boasted about at bridge parties.

"All hell broke loose," said one middle-class girl, "when my parents discovered I was a lesbian. They read some of my girl-friend's letters, and immediately started turning it all on themselves: 'What have we done to deserve this? Where did we go wrong?' They packed me straight off to a psychiatrist, but as they're both doctors, they made me use a false name. My girl-friend and I are still together after six years, but my parents won't accept her, or stop harping on it."

Rather like the lower-middle-class lesbian who fell in love with a married woman. When the married woman's daughter got married: "I was allowed to act as chauffeur, fetching the cake and the bouquet, ferrying the bride's mother to the Registry office, where I had to stay outside so no one would associate me with Pauline, then ferrying her to the reception. I wasn't allowed to that either. They were ashamed I looked too masculine and might shock the bridegroom's parents."

The upper-class attitude towards homosexuality is the same as it used to be towards heterosexuality. Marry well and produce an heir at all costs, and then do what you like.

Some of the happiest marriages, in fact, are when homosexuals marry upper-class ladies, a kind of "with my buddy, I thee worship." The sex side works, because the upper-class woman doesn't expect much, and the man just shuts his eyes and thinks of Benjamin Britten. The homosexual adores all the grand side of it, organising smart parties and inviting all his prettiest men friends. While the wife, used to the male chauvinism of the aristocracy, is entranced by a husband who can help her decorate her house, run her social life, advise her on clothes, cook delicious meals and provide hordes of endless personable young men to chat away amusingly for hours to all the girl-friends. The two classic examples of such liasons in modern literature are Lady Montdore and Cedric in *The Pursuit of Love* and Norman Chandler and Mrs. Foxe in *A Dance to the Music of Time.*

Samantha Upward, being very "aware," would be particularly nice to homosexual men, trapping them at parties, because she wants to show them that she feels no animosity towards men she knows can never find her sexually attractive.

Howard Weybridge "comes out" on the golf course at forty-five, and suddenly emerges at dinner parties in white suits with brushed-forward hair. His son, similarly inclined, would work in a prep school.

Bryan Teale would have an absolutely miserable time at the office party avoiding all the secretaries and longing to dance with one of the packers. If he's single, he also has problems when his boss gives him two tickets for a function. He can't take a man, and if he takes a girl, she's bound to get ideas and expect him to kiss her good night. If the office gets too much for him, he might easily become a male nurse or a purser, or work in the men's department in a department store.

Homosexuals, because they are insecure and sometimes effeminate and feel they have therefore to try harder, are often *raging* snobs. They worry terribly about accents, vocabulary and laying the table properly. They always write letters after dinner parties, and send you change-of-address cards saying "Crispin and Terence are moving to . . ." Because they have such good taste, their houses are often better-class than they are.

I think because it's euphemistic, Harry Stow-Crat would not use the word "gay," nor would he say "homo" or "lezzie." Harry Stow-Crat's mother would say "roaring pansy." Harry would probably say "homosexual" with a long "o"; Samantha, to show off her knowledge of Greek, would shorten the "o." Gideon would say "queer." Jen Teal would say "one of those Nancy boys." Mr. Definitely-Disgusting, luxuriating in alliteration, would talk about "effing fairies," like. An old-fashioned expression used to be: "Is he T.B.H.?"—meaning "To Be Had." Also in the old days, one used to say: "Is he *so?*"

Chapter 9

HOUSES

Though the pipes that supply the bathroom burst
And the lavatory makes you fear the worst
It was used by Charles the First
Quite informally,
And later by George the Fourth
On a journey north.

Noël Coward

It is not possible to gauge what class a person is just from the house he lives in. Some of the upper classes have execrable taste and don't give a fig about their surroundings, while some working-class people —perhaps a homosexual—may have an instinctive sense of what is beautiful. How people do up their houses is also considerably affected by fashion. A few years ago, flying ducks were only acceptable if they were outside and moving, now they've become fashionable kitsch, and the young and trendy, raising two fingers to convention, are putting them on their walls again. Or take someone who's just moved into a new house. The haste with which they explain away the ox-blood fleur-de-lys wallpaper in the drawing-room as the taste of a previous owner might be more an indication of social insecurity than the wallpaper itself.

Electric logs have long been considered a Jen Teale indicator. My husband once worked for a man whose son, an Old Etonian (whom I will call Ambrose), asked us to dinner. The other guests were a very smart couple, whom Ambrose was determined to impress. We arrived first to find him switching off some electric logs in the drawing room. He was worried that the smart couple might think them common. "My mother, being Spanish, has terrible lapses of taste," he said apologetically.

So the three of us sat frozen to death until the smart couple arrived an hour later. Instantly some devil overtook my husband, he crossed the room and switched on the logs.

"Have you seen Ambrose's mother's splendid fire?" he asked the smart couple.

There was a ghastly pause. Ambrose's face whitened like that of someone close to death. The merry flickering of the electric logs was nothing to the blaze of rage in his eyes. The evening was a disaster. My husband was fired within three months. And yet I know two peers of the most ancient lineage have electric-log fires. One even has bright blue water in his lavatory.

Nevertheless, the house that you live in, like the education you receive and the accent you speak with, is one of the determining factors that indicate the class you belong to. One girl was terribly keen on a tall, thin, very aristocratic-looking friend of mine until she discovered he lived in a bungalow in Sheen with his mother.

In Putney, where I live, the people who live in the big Victorian houses on the Common slightly, albeit unconsciously, look down on the large but semi-detached houses in the next road leading down to the Common, whose owners in turn look down on those living in similar houses in a street with slightly heavier traffic; the occupants of these look down on the people in the Neo-Georgian houses on the edge of the Common, whose occupants in turn despise the people in the terrace houses behind them, who won't have anything to do with the council estate beside the river.

In *Voices from the Middle Class,* by Jane Daverson and Katherine Lindsay, a journalist is quoted as saying:

A house is a complex thing, it represents a social position. We found living where we were [a smartish London suburb] without meaning to we had acquired several friends who see themselves as the same sort of people as we were because they live in the same sort of house. Painting and decorating is a middle-class thing. You say you've been decorating and you get an immediate response.

Harry Stow-Crat wouldn't dream of painting his own "hice" (as he pronounces it) or putting up shelves, and would regard any such activity as distinctly "working-class." But, as it happens, Mr. Definitely-Disgusting wouldn't bother to do up his house either because he considers it the council's responsibility. The moment he buys his own house, however, he crosses one of the great class divides from Council Tenant to Owner Occupier and starts to become bourgeois. He'll immediately drop the word "mortgage" in the public bar, and begin building a new porch or slapping different-coloured paint on the front of his house, to distinguish it from the houses on either side, and to show he's not Council any more.

The expression "they live in a bought house" would be a term of approbation from the working classes, but a term of contempt from the upper classes, who have usually lived in their own "hice" for generations, inheriting it, as they inherit all their furniture and silver. (One of the upper-class definitions of the middle classes is the "sort of people who buy their own silver"—particularly when they call it "cutlery.")

Another crucial point to remember is that the Stow-Crats of today were the Nouveau-Richards of a few hundred years ago. "How often have I wondered," wrote Lord David Cecil, "at the difference between the stately beauty of a great house, so exalting and tranquillizing, and the fierce, restless, unscrupulous character of the men who were so often responsible for its original building. Perhaps a gentler, more contented spirit would not have felt the urge and vitality to create such buildings."

Blenheim Palace, for example, described at the time as "England's greatest house for England's greatest man," was built to celebrate the new Duke of Marlborough's victories. Then there was the very rich Yorkshire baronet Sir John Smithson, who at the beginning of the eighteenth century married Elizabeth, the sole heiress to the rich and ancient Percy family. So great was the extent of their joint estate that Sir John was able to persuade George III to grant him the dukedom of Northumberland. Anxious to establish his new status, the first duke set about transforming Alnwick, the neglected castle of the Percys. Capability Brown (who'd been such a success at Warwick Castle) was called in to rebuild the towers and add seven turrets, and a complete new garrison of stone warriors was stationed on the battlements. At the same time Robert Adam arrived to re-Gothicise the interior. Everything was done to make the castle as luxurious and self-consciously picturesque as possible. And no doubt the old aristocracy, who regarded any peer created after the Middle Ages as an upstart, thought the whole thing both phoney and vulgar.

So it was that generations of new noblemen harnessed the best talents of their time, just as today David Mlirnaric and David Hicks move around forming the tastes of the uncertain and the newly rich.

In the same way the pop star who makes it big immediately buys a large house in the Thames Valley with high walls and installs burglar alarms and vigilante systems as daunting as any medieval drawbridge to keep out the fans. He will decorate it to the nines to impress other rising pop stars, and in his spare time take up market gardening, breeding race horses and farming. The Rolls is replaced by a Range Rover. The Showaddy Waddy even hunt with the Quorn.

What is regarded as the height of nouveau riche vulgarity today —the huge oval bed humming with dials, perhaps, or the onyx-and-marble double bath with 22-carat gold-plated mixer taps—will probably be considered exquisitely beautiful when it is unearthed from the rubble in the year 2500. Certainly the furniture and building trades would grind to a halt if it weren't for people erecting monuments to new splendour or ripping out the taste of previous owners because they considered it too grandiose or too vulgar.

Harry Stow-Crat does not refer to his house as a "stately home" but as an "istoric hice."

Although they may have originally been built as what Ivy Compton-Burnett called "huge monuments to showing off," few buildings quicken the pulses more than the great English country house, with its "towers and battlements . . . bosom'd high in tufted trees," its sneering stone lions at the gate, and long avenue of chestnuts leading up to the russet walls rising gently from soft billowing green lawns which eventually melt into the park. Vita Sackville-West points out that the best historic houses grew in a leisurely way over generations, sprouting a wing here, a tower here, like the oaks and elms that surrounded them. "There is no question of the period room, so beloved by professional decorators. Everything is muddled up: Jacobean paintings, Chippendale tables, chinoiserie wallpaper, Carolean love seats, Genoese velvets, Georgian brocades, Burgundian tapestries, Queen Anne embroideries, William and Mary tallboys and Victorian sideboards, all in a mixture to make the purist shudder." But it is this feeling that each succeeding owner acquired beautiful furniture and pictures as the taste and fashion of his generation dictated—and imposed his own taste—that makes up the glorious hotchpotch of the great house.

Lord Weymouth, who has contributed his own splendidly colourful murals to the walls of Longleat, says that everyone in his family "has been raised from birth to be an acolyte in the temple." This sums up the attitude of the aristocrat: good husbandry, rather than good husbands, or "Old Masters and young mistresses," as Peter De Vries called it. "I don't mind black sheep in the family," said Lord Carrington recently. "What I can't stand is people who don't put something back into the house."

Most upper-class houses therefore have a certain shabbiness about them. The festoons and rosettes on the ceiling show the traces of the years, the pink-and-white-striped silk cushions are falling to pieces, the faded red damask sofa is covered in yesterday's dog hairs. On the walls are squares of much lighter red flocked paper (like the circle on the spiralist's lapel) where a Rubens or a Romney has been flogged off to pay taxes. When you go to bed you draw the pale blue watered-silk curtains with care. The aristocracy believe in buying the best—silks especially woven in the colour they want—and then making them last. They'll probably only re-decorate their rooms every fifty years. Upper-class colours therefore tend to be faded into softness by antiquity—like a Beatrix

Potter picture. The faded rose-reds and golds of the Tailor of
Gloucester's coat are particularly popular, and ice blue is very in,
too, at the moment. Green is rarely popular because there's so
much of it outside in the park. In the upper-class London houses
(perhaps because their owners miss the green of the country) you'll
get a chilly Eaton Square eau de nihilism.

The floors are polished, and three-quarters covered with very
good, very old, patterned carpet. Caroline Stow-Crat wouldn't
dream of buying a modern patterned carpet, but Casa Pupo rugs
are somehow considered all right. Until recently she's resisted plain
fitted carpets, as being an example of the middle classes boasting
that they've got enough carpet to cover the entire floor. But convenience is a great leveller, and if you haven't got a servant to polish
the floor, you may sink to a fitted carpet. In the same way duvets
are being surreptitiously smuggled into four-posters, particularly for
the children, and the silver centrepiece in the dining room, which
used to be made up of forty individual bits and take two men three
days to clean, has now been lacquered over.

Caroline also resists any man-made fibres, and certainly anything plastic, which Harry's mother still calls "plarstic." The upper
classes wear leather on their feet and the elbows of their coats, but
not on their sofas or their backs. Their rooms tend to be very leggy,
like the bottom half of the paddock, because all the furniture has
long spindly legs. Huge libraries of memoirs and sermons, probably
acquired by the yard back in the eighteenth century, are kept
behind grilles like Snipe. The bedrooms have slots on the door for
the guest's name, and interlocking doors, so people can bed-hop
easily without the servants finding out. The ceilings are particularly
beautiful, so Caroline Stow-Crat can admire them when she's in
the inevitable missionary position. On the whole, the upper classes
prefer things to be either beautiful or functional. They wouldn't
hide the television in a repro cabinet, or the paper handkerchiefs
in the spare room in a dainty flowered box with a slit in it.

The rooms are lit by crystal chandeliers or candelabra or by
lamps with no tassels. Tassels on anything, umbrellas, lights or
chairs, are considered slightly flash. The bath and basin are always

white, the lavatory is white with a chain that pulls and a wooden seat which is often agonisingly cracked. All upper-class loos smell of asparagus pee in June. The kitchens are traditionally hellish because that was where the servants lived.

As the outdoor life has always been more important to English gentlemen than indoors, the field more alluring than the hearth, their houses tend to be terribly cold and smell of blasts of icy air. (One member of the landed gentry always asked you to bring old telephone directories when you went to stay, to feed an insatiable boiler.) On the walls they have huge paintings of battles, hunting scenes and their ancestors, gazing down and reminding them of their heritage. They also have portraits painted of their dogs, their horses and their children. As the latter go off to boarding school so early, it's important to be reminded what they look like.

The upper-class man always has a dressing room. Even though Harry sleeps in the same room as Caroline, he would refer to it as "Caroline's bedroom" if he were talking to an equal, "my wife's bedroom" if he were talking to a higher-echelon servant like the woman who organises people seeing over his house, and "Lady Caroline's bedroom" to a maid.

One very grand old lady said: "When Willy and I went to stay with some people in Norfolk, they didn't give Willy a dressing room but they provided a screen in the bedroom, so we managed very well." This was after they'd been married forty years—shades of the Definitely-Disgustings.

One of the ways the upper classes exclude the classes below is by pronouncing the names of their houses differently from the way they are spelt—Woburn, Holker, Althorp (pronounced "Woob'n," "Hooker," "Alltr'p") being typical examples. And because they have had their houses for hundreds of years, they also tend to take the beautiful things in them for granted, and tend not to comment on such things in other people's houses.

"Fellow praised my chairs, damn cheek," said a duke after a visit from a new neighbour.

Equally, it is not done to show someone over your new house, unless they ask specifically or they pay at the gate. There was an awkward moment when an actress we know, who was justifiably proud of her very expensively decorated house, asked an upper-class friend if he'd like to see over it.

"Whatever for?" came the curt reply.

In very grand houses, they have an estate carpenter permanently on the premises doing repairs. One friend got locked in the lavatory when she was staying in Yorkshire, and the host fed her bloody marys through the keyhole with a straw while they waited for the carpenters to come and free her.

Paying guests

The poor man in his castle
Sells tickets at the gate
While all the rich plebeians
Have fun on his estate.

Leonard Cooper

"Between the duties expected of one during one's lifetime, and the duties expected from one after one's death, land has ceased to be either a profit or a pleasure. It gives one position, but prevents one from keeping it up, that's all that can be said about land," said Lady Bracknell, admirably summing up the plight of the aristocrat.

In the old days, Harry Stow-Crat's ancestor would have looked out of his top window and owned all he surveyed; now he probably only manages it. Most of the upper classes are feeling the pinch, and the days when they could field a chauffeurs' cricket team against a footmen's are over. Only the hugely rich, like the Westminsters, are still not allowing the public to see over their houses. Some peers like Lord Montague and the Duke of Bedford, who obviously have a strong streak of showmanship in their make-up, seem to rather enjoy it. Others hate it, like an earlier Lord Bath, who was found cowering in a cupboard by one of the visitors, or Vita Sackville-West, who hid in the roses. Some peers try to keep up standards and shock visitors to the house by putting up signs

saying *lavatories* rather than *toilets,* but most of them descend to
the level of public taste by flogging the most appalling souvenirs:
key rings, caps, tee-shirts, replicas of the house in a snowstorm,
bottled Welsh or Scottish garden fragrance, in order to keep going.

Buying-up and doing-up

The upper middle classes, not subscribing to the law of primogeni-
ture, and tending to move where their jobs take them, seldom live
in the same house for several generations. They tend to start off
in a flat in Fulham, or some big town when they get married, then
move to a terraced three-bedroom house with the first child, then
to a five-bedroom house when the second child arrives, because
they need room for an *au pair,* or possibly for a lodger to help with
the mortgage. Samantha Upward prefers a student, so she can
combine altruism, free baby-sitting and help with Zacharias's
maths prep, which will soon—despite workshops—be quite beyond
her. To live in a house with more rooms than you have family is
regarded by the working classes as a middle-class characteristic.

The major change in the upper-middle-class house in the last
twenty-five years has been the kitchen, which used to be an air
force blue barracks where a sucked-up-to maid sourly banged sauce-
pans. In the seventies, this change was speeded up when financial
necessity, coupled with the absurd stigma attached to unpaid
domestic servitude, forced all but those wives with very young
children out to work. The status-conscious upper middle classes
therefore promptly re-vamped their houses. If Samantha Upward
has to sink to housework or cooking she must do it in congenial
surroundings. Kitchens therefore became more and more like draw-
ing-rooms, with sofas, low lighting, Welsh dressers covered in ornaments and books, pictures on the walls and a low pine table for the
children to play improving games.

As it was essential for the children to play on the ground floor
near their parents, the dining-room was also turned into a "playroom," and in order that Samantha needn't miss a word of the

intelligent dinner-party conversation as she was flambéing chicken breasts, or whipping the zabaglione, the kitchen was turned into a dining-room as well. The drawing-room by this time was feeling a bit neglected, and was consequently filled up with plants and natural earthy colours until it resembled Kew Gardens. The garden in its turn filled up with furniture, reclining chairs with gaudy seed-packet upholstery, stone lions, white wrought-iron chairs and tables, hammocks. What was once the "terrace" became the "patio," or as Mrs. Nouveau-Richards would say, the "pate-io."

A peer, recently flipping through a *Habitat* catalogue, remarked how extraordinary it was that the lower middle classes today furnished their houses with the sort of stuff you'd once only have seen in the servants' quarters. As stripped pine and William Morris are taken up by the lower middles, the upper middles have latched on to rattan, and Art Deco sofas and chairs, French and English antiques (when they can afford them), good Chinese furniture and Laura Ashley itsy-bitsy cottage prints (sort of William Morris Minor).

A word might be said here about the terms "drawing-room" and "sitting-room." Both seem to be perfectly upper-class except the "droin' room" would be slightly more formal and the "sitting-room" more easy and relaxed. You'd never have a "droin' room" in a cottage, for example. "Living-room," as a ghastly modern compromise, is extremely vulgar. So are "lounge" (except in a hotel), "front room" and "parlour."

In Samantha Upward's house, you would find a few antiques and some good china and silver. She thinks repro furniture is very common, and whereas she might hang reproductions in the lavatory or the children's room, they wouldn't be allowed in the drawing-room. Nor would a Victorian painting from her parents' house, of a four-year-old girl in a boat with a grizzled fisherman entitled "His Mate," get farther than the landing. All her curtains would be on brass rails. Her carpets would be plain but fitted, and relieved by a few rugs, and her counterpane would be distributed evenly over the whole bed, not mill-pond smooth and then edged in a fat sausage under and over the pillows. Since the middle classes discovered sex in the seventies, she'd probably have a bidet in the bathroom, next door to Gideon's and her bedroom. The bidet is a constant reproach as Gideon is usually far too tired and too drunk to want sex.

Samantha is gradually installing "continental quilts," as she insists on calling them, in every bedroom. She thinks the word "dewvay" is so vulgar. The most difficult Beethoven sonata lies open on the piano. Zacharias's cello is allowed to stay in the drawing-room among the *Spectators* and *New Statesmans*. Samantha would spend a lot of time removing book jackets to make the books look more read. Dried flowers, or honesty in a pewter mug, would gather dust on the window ledge.

In the lavatory downstairs, Gideon modestly records his achievements, with photographs of himself in hockey, rugger and cricket teams of his house at Rugby, of a freshmen's match. His dressing room would be the repository for all the atrocities little Zacharias and Thalia had given him and Samantha for Christmas over the years: china poodles, cats wearing bow ties playing the banjo, glazed china flowers, boxes encrusted with shells. He also has to put up with all rich Uncle Alan's paintings on the walls (these are whipped down to the drawing-room when Uncle Alan comes to stay), and a photograph of Samantha taken twenty years ago, and framed by herself at evening classes, when she had a beehive. Samantha waits till the daily woman goes home before loosening up the serried ranks of cushions on the sofa.

Upper-middle-class houses smell of beeswax, drink and sometimes cats.

On Saturday mornings all through outer central London— Fulham, Clapham, Islington and parts of Hackney—the streets are alive with the sounds of "gentrification," as coats of paint are slapped on the fronts of Victorian terraced houses, rooms are knocked through and the net curtains of previous occupants are shoved in the rag bag. The upper middle classes would far rather spend a bit of money knocking a Victorian or Edwardian workman's cottage back into shape than move into a modern house where everything worked, so they quite happily rip plywood and hardboard off doors to reveal the original mouldings, strip banisters and replace aluminium windows with wooden frames as close to the original as possible. Soon follow the French number plate, the brass letter box, and the trellis for the honeysuckle from the garden centre and a bay tree that quickly gets pinched. Blue tubs, bought cheap from the brewery round the corner, are soon filled up with bulbs or pink geraniums (Samantha thinks red ones are rather common). And on Saturday morning, Vivaldi pours out of the hi-fi into the street, and balding architects can be seen sitting in the window drawing lines at their desks and drinking coffee.

Having also cottoned on to the fact that they can get £25,000 tax relief for an extension, and with the price of houses being so prohibitive, my dear, and the traffic being so frightful we never get down to the cottage till midnight, the upper middle classes are beginning to sell up their "shacks" in the Isle of Wight or Gloucestershire, and build onto their houses instead. Gideon Upward and Zacharias are working so much at home now that they each need a study. And as Samantha so often wants to watch opera, and Gideon the late-night sport, it avoids so many rows if they have two televisions in different rooms. And now that Thalia's getting a bust it's not quite right for her to entertain boys in her bedroom, which calls for a second sitting-room where they can all play pop music as loudly as possible. As a result, £300 worth of clematis and hydrangeas are crushed underfoot, as an extension is slapped onto the patio.

One of the tricks of the middle classes is to buy their old houses, then form a pressure group to have their street declared a Conservation Area so as to stop the compulsory purchasers touching it or building flats nearby. But they then get absolutely livid when the council rather understandably drags its heels over planning permission for an extra music room or a new bathroom.

Don't say "Pardon," say "Surrey"

Merridale is one of those corners of Surrey where the inhabitants rage a relentless battle against the stigma of suburbia. Trees, cajoled and fertilised into being in every front garden, half obscure the poky "character dwellings" which crouch behind them. The rusticity of the environment is enhanced by the wooden owls that keep guard over the names of the houses, and by crumbling dwarfs indefatigably poised over gold fish ponds. The inhabitants of Merridale Lane do not paint their dwarfs, suspecting it to be a suburban vice, nor for the same reason, do they varnish the owls, but wait patiently for the years to endow these treasures with an appearance of weathered antiquity, until one day even the beams in the garage may boast of beetle and woodworm.

John le Carré, *Call for the Dead*

"Oh, look," said a friend as we drove through a rich part of Surrey. "All those houses have been Weybridged." This is a practice of the socially aspiring who've made a bit of money and want to shake off the stigma of suburbia by living in Sunningdale, Virginia Water or any rich dormitory town.

First you buy a modern house, which you refer to as a "lovely property," then you "age it up" to look like a Great West Road pub. Rustic brick with half timbering and leaded windows are very popular, with a lantern or carriage lamp outside the front door, and a name like "Kenilworth" or "De Cameron" carved on a rustic board. The burglar alarm would be discreetly covered by creepers. An alternative is white pebble-dash with a green pantile roof and matching green shutters with cut-out hearts, and the name in wrought-iron treble-clef writing on the front of the house. Wrought iron, in fact, is everywhere.

A few years ago, a Weybridged house would have had a chiming doorbell, but, suspecting this is a bit suburban, the owner has responded to an ad in *Homes and Gardens:* "No more electric bionic ping-pongs. . . . every lover of style can now capture the elegance and tranquillity of less hurried days with a real brass doorbell, complete with mechanism and most attractive pull arm to enhance your doorway."

The hall, as Anthony Powell once said, looks like the inside of a cigar box with a parquet floor, panelled walls and a very thin strip of carpet running up the polished stairs. At the top is a round window with a stained-glass inset. The Weybridged house smells of self-congratulation and Pears soap.

In the living-room (again, they've heard "lounge" is suburban but can't quite bring themselves to say "drawing-room"), you find wall-to-wall glossies and coffee-table books. On the walls are imitation candle lights, with fake drips and little red hats, bumpy white gold mirrors and pictures by real artists from Harrods and Selfridges. The carpet is tufted two-tone, the curtains pinch-pleated, the "settee" and "easy chairs" are covered in terra-cotta velvet Dralon. Repro furniture is inevitable to give a nice "Ollde Worlde" look: "period doors," a Queen Anne "bureau" and Regency Chippendale cabinets to hide the TV (the upper middles call it "the box," the upper class "the television") and the "stereo." Every piece of furniture has mahogany or teak veneer—the Weybridged house suffers from veneerial disease. A Magi-Log fire flames in the repro Adam fireplace—"the ultimate in realism," with incombustible oak logs knobbly with knotholes and twigs. The alternative might be a "feature fireplace" in stone. The *Radio Times* is wrapped in a sacking cover with a thatched cottage embroidered on the front. If you came for drinks, you would be offered goblets.

In the dining-room, lacquered silver candlesticks sit on the Elizabethan repro table even at lunchtime, and an Ekco hostess trolley keeps the rack of lamb, creamed potatoes and garden peas piping hot. There would be an overhead light, or more lights with fake hats and little wax drips, and six chairs with oxblood and silver Regency stripes.

Howard has a "den," where he's supposed to work at weekends, but in fact does nothing but read *Penthouse* behind Saturday's *Financial Times* and long to be asked to a wife-swapping party.

Poor Howard feels he is not "ollde" enough for the house, and if he plays with himself a lot, it might age him too.

The kitchen is usually very pretty, and quite indistinguishable from the upper-middle or even modernised upper-class kitchen. Next door a "utility" room is filled with expensive machinery.

In the "master bedroom," tufted carpeted steps lead up to a dais on which a huge brass four-poster swathed in white Norfolk lace sits like a wedding cake. The lampshade matches the duvet cover and the wallpaper.

Next month Mrs. Weybridge will receive her eighth German porcelain coffee cup and saucer from the "Collector of the Month Club" special offer, and be able to hold her first coffee morning.

Better nouveau than late Victorian

The Weybridged house is very "ollde" and tasteful, as opposed to the Nouveau-Richards mansion, which is very plush, ostentatious and modern—another great monument to showing off.

Reacting against the in-and-out-of-their-houses familiarity of the working class, Mr. Nouveau-Richards has high walls built round his house, and it is burglar-alarmed to the teeth. Ten-foot-high electric gates protect him from the street. As he arrives in the Rolls he presses a button and the gates open. The drive is lined with toadstools which light up at night. The garage for five cars opens by remote control, and so you don't get wet a lift takes you up to the hall.

Every room in Mrs. Nouveau-Richards's house has a rake for the shag pile. The daily woman's visit is a sort of rake's progress, nor does she much like having to climb into the onyx-and-sepia-marble double bath to clean it, and having to polish up the 22-carat gold mixer taps with headworks of solid onyx. She nearly got her hand chopped off when she was shaking her duster out of one of the electric windows the other day. When she answers the telephone she has to say: "Mrs. Nouveau-Richards's residence."

In Mrs. Nouveau-Richards's lounge, acrylic pile tiger skins with diamanté collars lie on the ebony shag pile. Mrs. Nouveau-Richards reclines on the leather chesterfield, in front of the heated coffee table, while Mr. Nouveau-Richards revolves in his captain's club chair in deep buttoned hide. On the walls is black and silver flocked wallpaper. When the maid in uniform hacks her way through the "house plants" to bring in "afternoon tea," she is sent back because the sugar bowl doesn't match the teacups. A ship's bell summons people to dinner, and the naval motif is continued by a bar in the corner with a straw ceiling covered in lobsters. After a few drinks they crawl by themselves. In the bar, every drink known to man hangs upside down with right-way-up labels. Mr. Nouveau-Richards doesn't drink very much, because he knows it makes his face red and his accent slip. Off the lounge are the swimming pool, constantly kept by the pool attendant at eighty degrees, the solarium and the gym. The stables are built under the lawn, so the horses can look out of their boxes into the pool like Neptune's mares. In Mr. Nouveau-Richards's library, where he has bought all the books by the yard, he has eighteenth-century repro library steps. When he presses a button the entire works of Walter Scott slide back to reveal yet another bar. Even the goldfish tank is double-glazed.

Mr. Nouveau-Richards is very proud of his dimmer switches; in a mellow mood he'll give guests a *son et lumière* display. In every room, Musak pours out of speakers, even in the loos, which have musical lavatory paper, fur carpets and chandeliers. The lavatory has a wooden seat. Mr. Nouveau-Richards responded to an ad in *House and Garden:* "After years of mass-produced plastic, feel the warmth of solid mahogany. Each seat is individually sanded and french-polished. Hinges and fittings are made of brass, and we offer as an option at no extra cost a brass plaque recessed into the lid for your personal inscription."

Mr. Nouveau-Richards has "Piss Off" wittily inscribed on his.

In the "guest bedroom," as Mrs. Nouveau-Richards calls it, everything is upholstered in peach satin, with a peach fur carpet. The master bedroom, however, has a vast suede oval bed, so humming with dials for quadrophonic stereo, radio, dimmer switches, telephones, razors and vibrator (which Mrs. Nouveau-Richards uses for massaging her neck) you don't know whether to lie on the thing or hijack it.

Nouveau riche houses are always blissfully comfortable to stay in. "Chandeliers in the loo, and a bidet on every bed," said my mother after one visit.

A word about nets

The world is divided into "Haves" and "Have-Nets."

The upper classes never had net curtains because, if you lived at the end of a long drive, there was no likelihood of being seen and, never being worried about other people's opinions, you didn't give a damn if anyone saw what was going on anyway.

The upper middles, aping the upper classes, don't have net curtains either. They traditionally had servants to keep their houses tidy, so it didn't matter anyone seeing in, and, as they only had sex at night (unlike the shift worker coming home for lunch), they drew their curtains if they wanted privacy. Samantha Upward wouldn't dream of having net curtains, she wants the whole street to look in at the gay primary colours of the posters and the extra-bright drawings in Zacharias's playroom.

The middle classes sometimes have net upstairs. If Eileen Wey-bridge is changing out of her tennis shorts in the middle of the day, she doesn't want the workman mending the road looking in. If they have nets downstairs, they might explain it by saying they've got an American mother.

The rough friendly element of the working class, who float in and out of each other's houses, never bothered with net at all, and have an expression for someone putting on airs: "Net curtains in the window, nothing on the table."

It is where the more thin-lipped respectable elements of the working classes blend into the lower middles that net reigns supreme. You can see out and chunter over everyone else's behaviour, and twitch the nets to indicate extreme disapproval, but they can't see you. Suburban privet hedges and Weybridged latticed windows provide the same function.

Jen Teale, however, wanting to priss everything up and shake off the stigma of upper working class—which is a bit too close for comfort—hangs pink jardinière festoon cross-over drapes, which leaves three-quarters of the window clear. This allows space for "floral decorations" on the window ledge, makes the windows look "so feminine" and enables the neighbours to see how "spotless" (a favourite lower-middle word) her house is. Other examples of the lower middles trying to go one better are ruched nets, putting a row of package-tour curios on the window ledge outside one's nets or hanging one's curtains so the pattern shows to the outside world. Mrs. Definitely-Disgusting tried yellow nets once, but they made the whole family look as though they'd got jaundice.

Behind the mauve front door

Jen Teale, liking to have everything dainty, wages a constant battle against dust and untidiness. Bryan Teale sits in the lounge with his feet permanently eighteen inches off the ground in case Jen wants "to vacuum" underneath. In the bedroom a Dralon button-back headboard joins two single divans with drawers underneath for extra storage, into which Jen might one day tidy Bryan away forever. Gradually all their furniture—wardrobes, sideboards, cupboards—is replaced by fitted "units" which slot snugly between ceiling and floor rather like Lego, and leaves no inch for dust to settle.

As soon as the Teales move into a house, the upper-middle process is reversed: all the doors are flattened so the mouldings don't pick up dust any more, the brass fittings replaced by aluminium, which doesn't need polishing, and all the windows and old "french doors" (as Jen Teale calls french windows) replaced by double-glazed aluminium picture windows. Being hot on insulation, because they loathe wasting money, the Teales even have sliding double-glazed doors round the porch. Bryan does all this with his Black-and-Decker.

The mauve front door has a rising sun in the bottom left-hand corner of the glass. The doorbell chimes. The house smells of Lavender Pledge and Freshaire. In the lounge the fire has a huge gnome's canopy to concentrate the heat and keep smuts at bay. Beside it stands the inevitable Statue of Liberty combination of poker, brush and shovel in a thistle motif. On the walls, Bryan has put up storage grids, like vast cat's climbing frames, with compartments for the hi-fi, records, Scrabble, the odd spotlit bit of Wedgwood or "vawse" of plastic flowers (real flowers drop petals, and paper ones gather dust). A few years ago the Teales wouldn't have had any books—too much dusting—but as culture seeps downwards, there might be a few book-club choices tastefully arranged at an angle to fill up a compartment.

The lounge suite has easy-fit nylon William Morris stretch covers which have interchangeable arms that can be switched from unit to unit, or rotated on the same chair to give that straight-from-the-showroom look, which is the antithesis of the shabby splendour of the upper classes. Jen also rather likes the continental habit of offering lounge furniture as a group comprising three-seater settee, two-seater settee and one armchair called "Caliph." (Down-market furniture invariably has up-market names like "Eton" and "Cavendish.") There is also a Parker Knoll recliner in case an "elderly relative comes to visit."

As well as her books Jen also has her Medici prints and her Tretchikoff (under a picture light, to show there's no dust on the frames), and in the dining-room there's a David Shepherd elephant gazing belligerently at Bryan's vintage-car etchings. There is no bar; because the Teales are tight with drink, Bryan keeps any bottles in another room with measures on. Just as a guest is putting his glass down, a mat with a hunting scene is thrust underneath to stop it making rings on one of a nest of tables called "Henley."

The kitchen is like a laboratory. No ornaments alleviate the bleakness. As the lower middles disapprove of money spent on luxuries (and can't afford them so readily), Jen probably wouldn't have a washing-up machine. She doubts it would get things really clean. She washes, Bryan "wipes" with a "tea towel" rather than a "drying-up cloth." (Caroline Stow-Crat would call it a "clawth.") Jen also does a lot of "hand-washing" and, as she's very conscious of understains, she "boils" a lot. Friends say her whites are spotless.

In the bedroom a doll in frills, to show Jen's just a little girl at heart, lies on the mill-pond-smooth candlewick bedspread which is edged in a fat sausage under and then over the pillows. (Caroline Stow-Crat has a worn teddy bear.) "Robe units" with motifs and very shiny lacquered brass handles slot into the walls. Jen tidies her make-up away in a vanity case. The only ornament on her white Formica-topped vanity unit is a circular plastic magnifying mirror. When she makes up and brushes her hair, she protects her clothes from "dandruff" with a plastic pink cape. The matching bathroom suite, in sky blue or avocado, with a basin shaped like a champagne glass, has a matching toilet cover, toilet surround and bath mat in washable sky blue nylon fur. A Spanish "dolly" with Carmen skirts discreetly conceals the toilet tissue (pronounced "tiss-u," not "tishu" as Samantha Upward would pronounce it). Jen, being obsessed with unpleasant odours, has Airwick, pot-pourri and a pomander on top of the cistern, and a deodorant block hanging like a sloth inside. In the toilet there is bright blue water. Bryan and Jen prefer showers to baths, they waste less water, are easier to clean up after.

Although she keeps her house like a new pin, Jen always does housework in tights and a skirt rather than trousers. Her whole attitude is summed up by her feather duster, which keeps dirt at a distance.

The chrome squad

There was an advertisement recently in a magazine called *Home Buying* offering: "Modern houses in Wood Green, the ideal site for those who want a convenient rung on the home ownership ladder." Among the other attractions was "garage with space for work bench."

This was aimed at the spiralist who is continually buying houses, doing them up, selling them at a profit and moving on to a better part, which means a safer suburb, with a nicer class of child, more amusing parents at the P.T.A. and no danger of coloureds (although a black diplomat's O.K.). Usually the process is to start with a flat, then move to a terraced house, then on to a large "period semi," where you let off the top flat to pay the mortgage. Then as soon as the house is done up, you buy a cheap flat for the sitting tenant, put it on the market and look for an even bigger house. The process is basically the same as that of the upper-middle-class couple, except that the spiralist moves as soon as he's got the house together, while the upper middles wait until they've run out of room.

Spiralists like anonymous furniture—chrome, glass and unit sofas and chairs—because they can be shifted around to fit into any size house. Just as they often adopt a phoney American accent to hide the cockney or the Yorkshire, so spiralists embrace American terminology: "trash cans," "garbage," "closets," "chaise lounges" and "car ports." Even in the short time they stay in a place the spiralists are deeply competitive.

They are likely to buy a three-piece suite in a sale, then put it in a Harrods depository, so it can be delivered three weeks later in a Harrods van.

They are the estate agent's nightmare, because they never stop hassling and expecting more for a house because of another brick on the night storage heater. Evidently the upper middles treat the agent like a pro, because they're used to one chap doing one job.

Home suite home

When Mr. Definitely-Disgusting thinks of buying a house other than his own council house, he fills in a coupon and goes off and sees a show house on an estate called some grandiose name like

Northumbria, and puts his name down for it if he likes it. Attractions include "teak-laminated kitchenette, stainless-steel sink, coloured bathroom suite with matching vein tiles, veneered doors in the living-room, kitchen dinette and shower-room."

Ads in the "home-buying" press show neighbours looking welcoming and helpful in wide-bottomed trousers, so as not to intimidate Mr. Definitely-Disgusting, who is used to his friendly familiar street. In a comic-strip guide to "home buying," the solicitor has spectacles and brushed-back hair, and wears a suit and a tie, while the buyer has wide trousers again, an open-neck shirt and hair brushed over his ears. His wife has shoulder-length hair, swept back from her forehead by a barrette, and a skirt on the knees. This is presumably the ideal working-class prototype.

The Definitely-Disgustings hurry now and buy everything on sale. Up to their necks in installment buying, they get carried away by the ads and buy three-piece suites in deep-pile uncut moquette and wildly expensive domestic appliances, which go back when they can't keep up the payments. The house-to-house upstaging is as subtle as the spiralists'.

"You can't hang your washing out any more, because everyone'll know you haven't got a tumble dryer," said one wife.

Mrs. Definitely-Disgusting, on the other hand, buys a fridge for the first time and stands at the front door saying: "I'm worried the kiddies will catch their fingers in the door," just to show she's got one.

(My favourite advertisement of all time appeared in an Indian magazine showing a woman and child gazing admiringly up at a huge fridge, with the caption: "Just right for our living room.")

Mrs. Definitely-Disgusting's front room, if she's feeling flush, will be dominated by a black cocktail cabinet with interior lighting, containing every drink known to man, like the Nouveau-Richardses', and a glazed-tile fireplace with a gas fire (although the council are beginning to put in what is known as a "fuel alternative"). Most of the ornaments look as though they have been won at a fair, or bought for his mother by Zacharias Upward: china Alsatians, glazed shire horses, china ladies in poke bonnets and crinolines. Here also are the curios from a hundred package tours, green donkeys with hats on and panniers, matadors under cellophane, a mass-produced plastic bull with a piece of the next bull's back attached to its cock, fifteen glass fishing floats and ashtrays barnacled with olives (brought for Mrs. Definitely-Disgusting by various Samantha Upwards on their return from holidays) and souvenirs from trips to historic houses. There might be a few very small reproductions: Constable's "Hay Wain," Van Gogh's "Sunflowers" or "The Queen" by Annigoni.

The colours are garish, with everything—wallpaper, sofas and chairs—in different patterns. The carpet, a symphony of yellow, brown and orange exploding in circles, wouldn't cover the linoleum. On the huge colour television there might be some candelabra, or a carriage clock with the works well exposed by a Pyrex dome. Mrs. Definitely-Disgusting's plastic flowers differ from Jen Teale's in that they make no attempt to copy the originals; mauve snapdragons and blue roses, pink primroses and Day-Glo tulips would mass gaudily together in a sharply cut glass vase (Mr. Definitely-Disgusting would probably rhyme it with "praise"). In Mrs. Definitely-Disgusting's mother's house the decor would be mostly brown, from design and chip fat fumes.

The less respectable element of the working classes would have no ornaments or pictures, having smashed the lot during drunken brawls. The room would be furnished with a huge colour television and biked beans tins.

Working-class houses and flats tend to smell of cabbages and leaky gas and—Jen Teale, wrinkling her retroussé nose, would claim—dirt. (A major casus belli, one of the great rows in the class war, is the fact that Samantha Upward, Eileen Weybridge, Jen Teale and Mrs. Definitely-Disgusting all accuse each other of being sluts.)

Chapter 10

GARDENS

The Englishman traditionally loves his garden almost more than his family. It needs cherishing and tending, but doesn't answer back. It is hardly surprising, therefore, that class distinction should be almost more rampant outside the house than in. Once again, garden centres, like furniture shops, do a roaring trade because of snobbery—people ripping out the plants and paving stones of previous owners—that were "too ghastly, my dear." I remember being mystified once when a friend came to stay. We were having tea outside, enjoying the sunshine and the quiet (for once the aeroplanes were silent), when suddenly she fixed me with a beady eye, and said: "You know, it's frightfully common to have Peace in one's garden."

It was a few minutes before I realised she was referring to the beautiful pink and yellow rose next to the magnolia which flowers so gallantly and continually all the summer, which she thought vulgar, perhaps because it is so universally popular.

In the same way, Caroline Stow-Crat wouldn't touch gladioli, begonias, chrysanthemums, most dahlias or fuchsias (except in the conservatory). Also on the index would be gaudy bedding plants like petunias, French marigolds, calceolarias, cinerarias, calendulas, salvia, California poppies, zinnias, asters and yellow daisies, although Michaelmas daisies and white daisies are O.K. Colour would also be important: the white and green tobacco plants are much more upper-class than the red or mauve ones; dark red wallflowers better than yellow or mauve. Trails of pale blue lobelia are all right, but Oxford blue is very common, particularly when combined in military rows with white alyssum and scarlet geraniums. Caroline wouldn't be very keen on any flower of a different colour from that which nature intended: blue roses, brown irises, pink forget-me-nots or daffodils. Daffodils, and most bulbs, she feels, should be planted in long grass, not in flower beds. She hates tulips. If she had rhododendrons she would not have individual ones, but a thousand in clumps lining the drive. A friend once asked a West Country peer how he achieved his magnificent multi-coloured display.

"Oh, I move them around," said the peer. "When I want to change the colour schemes I just get sixty men up from the factory."

Some trees are also more upper-class than others; one thinks of the great flat-bottomed oaks, beeches, limes and chestnuts that look, as Taine said, as though they'd been tended for hundreds of years like the children of rich parents.

If you discount the ancient cedars of Lebanon planted by Capability Brown, indigenous trees are considered much smarter than foreign ones, which is why the white cherry scores points over the pink ones, and why the Stow-Crats tend to despise the silver birches, pines and conifers of Surrey. Weeping willow trees are all right growing "naturally" by a lake or stream, but a willow would be considered the height of vulgarity in the middle of a lawn, particularly if it were planted in a circle of earth. While the suburbs in spring with their candy-floss mass of blossom, pink and white cherry, dark pink crab-apple, almond, laburnum and lilac are quite beyond the pale. Pink hawthorn, although considered much more common by the upper classes than white, is for some reason more acceptable in the suburbs.

The names of buildings in the garden are also pronounced differently. Harry Stow-Crat says "garidge," Samantha Upward, wanting to show off her French pronunciation, says *"gar-arzh"*; the Weybridge set say *"gar-arge"* in order to upstage the lower middles, who say "garidge" like Harry Stow-Crat. Mrs. Nouveau-Richards has a "carport." Harry has a "gaz-ee-bo" in his garden; Samantha calls it a "summerhouse," while Mrs. Nouveau-Richards reclines in her "gayze-bow." Harry pronounces "loggia" like "lodger," but the Weybridge set call it "lowdjea" in case there is any confusion about paying guests when someone says Howard is relaxing on the loggia. A friend claims his very grand great-grand-mother used to refer to ants as "aunts," saying "there's an aunt-heap in the garden"—which sounds like a great fleshy pyramid of maiden ladies.

The point about the upper-class garden is that it should look as "natural" as possible, great sweeps of mown grass leading down to the lake, huge trees with new little saplings always being planted and nurtured, trout streams, parks full of deer, and cows, swishing their tails knee deep in the buttercups. Away from the house, there might be a series of flower gardens, divided by walls or hedges of box or yew; a conservatory full of nectarines, peaches and the oldest vine in Europe, a herb garden and a huge vegetable garden. Around the house, plants will grow in genuine Versailles pots, which are made of wood and square but narrower at the bottom and topped with balls. (All balls are very upper-class, says Harry Stow-Crat.)

But everything would be mellowed and weather-beaten, the walls and roof of the house "stained by time and many-coloured lichens, and overgrown with creeper to a richly variegated greyish red." The drive would be made of stone chippings or gravel—not black tarmac or concrete like a throughway.

The Stow-Crats are very keen on vistas. Through a gap in a wood you might see a temple of Flora, or a folly or a bend in the river.

The great gardens, in fact, show the ideal blending of classic and romantic. At Sissinghurst, Nigel Nicolson attributes the firm perspective of the vistas, the careful siting of an urn or a statue, the division of the garden into a series of small separate gardens to his father's classical influence.

But, in the overflowing clematis (Howard Weybridge would call it clem-a-tis) figs, vines and wistaria, in the rejection of violent colours or anything too tame and orderly, one discovered his mother's romanticism: "Wild flowers were allowed to invade the garden. If plants strayed over the path they must not be cut back. Rhododendrons must be banished in favour of their tender cousin the azalea, roses must not electrify, they must seduce."

The secret of their gardens is sweet disorder. Weeds in moderation don't matter, because the plants are so closely massed they don't show the earth beneath. A dearth of earth is very upper-class.

Sissinghurst, too, is the elder sister of the cottage garden—a law unto itself with all the flowers the Stow-Crats love jockeying for position: rosemary, drifts of lavender, ramparts of honeysuckle, an ancient wistaria, sweet peas, hollyhocks, lupins, delphiniums, pinks and mignonettes, love-in-the-mist and cornflowers, clove carnations, pansies, sweet william, white stocks and phlox, Canterbury bells and lilies; moss and plants instead of cement fill the cracks in the flagstones.

Percy Lubbock, writing about the "easy abundance" of a particular upper-class garden, realises that it's not the plants themselves but the way they are planted that matters. "Lobelia stripes, for example, and those marigold patches, which might have looked harsh and hard (one knows how smartly odious marigolds can look in an over-tidy garden), all rejoiced together, rambling and crowding in liberal exuberance. The gardener might wreak his worst will, but the free soul of the garden escaped him and bloomed tumultuously."

A garden like that, however, requires not just money and genius ("Planted 400 bulbs in the orchard this afternoon," wrote Vita Sackville-West to Harold Nicolson) but also gardeners you can bully.

In the old days, gardeners used to wash all the vegetables and take the thorns off the roses before they were sent up to the house. A handbook published in the eighteenth century advised them to look clean and neat: "Your employer will not wish to look on a dirty ragged uncouth grinning or conceited bi-ped, in his garden." They were also instructed to "put the manure on the flower beds early in the morning, so the putrescent vapours may not prove offensive to the owner of the garden and his friends."

But as "corsts" get higher and gardeners get scarcer, it is more and more difficult to keep up a large and beautiful garden. In the country, gardens tend to get smaller and smaller, and orchards bigger and bigger. Donkeys are becoming increasingly popular for keeping the lawn down. And I heard that mixture of concern and self-interest which always colours the master-servant relationship neatly summed up by a woman I met at a party the other day who said: "Our darling old gardener died last week—isn't it *maddening!*"

In Harry Stow-Crat's London garden you find a few bulbs in window boxes, followed by pink geraniums and ivy followed by irises and Albertine, a pale pink rose which stops flowering in June. After that the upper classes are always out of London, so it doesn't matter what their gardens look like.

In the country, the upper middles tend to have beautiful gardens with shrubberies and herbaceous borders more related to the house and not set aside in separate gardens, as they are in Harry Stow-Crat's place, although the vegetable garden will be separate. Plants and flowers grow round the house and on the terrace you might see imitation plaster Versailles pots by Julian Jenkinson, an Old Etonian who copied them very successfully from the authentic wooden pots at Lord Harcourt's place. The lawn will be well tended, but there will be more brown patches on the lawn because upper-middle-class dogs are less likely to pee in the house than upper-class dogs. As manure is seldom available all the time, there will also be greater interest in compost. The roses and dahlias will be very fine and the colours slightly brighter than in the upper-class garden. As we go down the social scale, gardens tend to become neater and gaudier.

Samantha Upward is very proud of her green fingers, particularly if she lives in London. She reads Wordsworth to her potted plants, rushes out with a shovel every time the police horses go by, and, by feeding Zacharias's daffodil with Liquinure, she won him first prize in his form's flower-growing competition. But, alas, the herb garden she planted so she could have all the ingredients in

Elizabeth David's recipes has been turned into a cat's lavatory by visiting toms.

Samantha knows that plastic flower pots and plastic hanging baskets are frightfully common, but such is the greenness of her fingers that she couldn't possibly afford pottery flower pots for all her plants. She's also far too soft-hearted to rip out that variegated horror donated by a neighbour that time she had shingles, or that rose that looked the palest pink in the catalogue but turned out bright crimson and horribly clashing with the Day-Glo orange rose beside it. She knows, too, that dear, funny John Betjeman said that every time he looked at a rhododendron, he thought of a stockbroker, so she moved her two mauve ones under the catalpa, but, alas, they're doing terribly well. At least she hasn't descended to crocuses in a wheelbarrow, or a plastic Venus de Milo like the one on the patio next door which melted at their last barbecue party.

Her garden would be really quite lovely if only she could stop the gardener who comes two hours a week from edging the lawn so the flower beds are never full up, and planting tulip bulbs in serried ranks like the ones outside Buckingham Palace. But if she checks him, she's terrified he'll take offence and not turn up next week.

Gideon and Samantha sit in their garden on a Sunday morning, swilling back the chilled white, saying "This is the life!" and watching the half leg of lamb rotating jerkily on the barbecue, wafting intimations of garlic, rosemary and envy into the nearby council estates.

The suburbs

The English suburban residence and the garden which is an
integral part of it stand trim and lovingly cared for in the mild
sunshine. Everything is in its place. The leaves of the virginia
creeper which climbs the rough-cast wall just below the best
bedrooms hardly stir.

J. M. Richards, *The Castles on the Ground*

Nothing has really changed in the suburbs. When we lived in a
working-class part of Fulham, no one minded that we never bothered with our garden. A few neighbours grew vegetables and fought
a losing battle with visiting tom cats, but the rest of us let the weeds
flourish and chucked our beer cans and spare rib bones over each
other's fences when we ran out of dustbin space. Only when we
moved to Putney, a Madam Butterfly land of cherry trees and
flowering shrubs, and inherited a beautifully kept garden, which we
promptly let go to rack and ruin, did we discover that gardening
here was taken very seriously indeed. Soon the whole street were
clicking their tongues over our hayfield of a lawn, and making
cracks about calling in the forestry commission to deal with the
weeds. Finally, a kindly neighbour could bear it no longer, and
found a gardener to come in three hours a week to sort us out.

More recently, the local conservation association, which howls
with protest if even a harebell is touched or a sapling uprooted on
the Common, produced stern proposals, which were circularised
round the district for the tidying up of the garden of the only house
along the Common that happened to be owned by the council.
This, they felt, was letting down the tone of the road by its number
of weeds. At any minute one expected the dandelion-detector van
to start policing the streets bleeping noisily outside the offending
garden. My husband suggested it would be far cheaper to declare
the garden in question an Area of Outstanding Natural Beauty:
then the weeds and wildflowers could riot unimpeded.

Though Putney is more upper-middle than suburban, the notion of not letting down the street is shared by the suburbs farther out. Few people here are dedicated gardeners in the winter. Unlike the upper classes, they stay inside in bad weather. But come the first temperate weekend, suburban man peers out of his window at his colourless plot, and thunders off to the garden centre to load up the car with bags of fertilizer, bedding plants, do-it-yourself cucumber kits and a plaster fig-leafless cherub to upstage the plastic dolphin regurgitating blue water on the patio next door.

The suburban gardener is deeply competitive: he doesn't want anyone else to let down the street, so that his own glory may be greater when his garden is the best. Rivalry is particularly fierce over roses. Hybrid teas and floribundas and dahlias mass in clashing colours above totally weedless flower beds. You can't get a lie-in at weekends either; it's like the pits at a motorcar rallye with the roar of all the mowers revving up, interspersed with the occasional excruciating teeth-grating rattle as they drive over the crazy pavement. Some people acquire a second mower for difficult patches as a status symbol.

The patio is a focal point of the garden, a mosaic of Italian tiles covered with plastic urns containing striped petunias, deck chairs with footrests, and sun umbrellas mostly bought with Green Shield stamps.

The Weybridged house has a circular gravel drive bordered by "rhodos"; "in" and "out" entrances with no gates; an up-and-over garage door; a swimming pool which, despite its barrage-balloon cover, is filled in winter with dead leaves and sparrows; and a dog yard for the terriers to dry off in. Having gone one step up from the suburban garden with its high laurel hedges, Weybridged gardens are often open-plan with no dividing fences at all, although there might be a hedge of conifers to shelter the roses from the wind, or interlaced larch fencing round the vegetable garden. Here Howard and Eileen Weybridge sit in their summerhouses admiring the well-tended lawns with their crazy pavement steppingstones; the conifers and golden willow in their little circles of earth; the

beautifully kept shrubberies full of pampas grass and bamboo; and
the thrushes pecking at the "rack of lamb" bone which hangs from
the dovecote (pronounced "dovecoat"; Harry Stow-Crat says
"dovec't"). A heavily ferned stream flows under a wooden willow-
pattern bridge and into a waterfall through the heaths in the rock
garden. Heather, except on the moors, is considered very vulgar by
Harry Stow-Crat. Even its Latin name, "Erica," sounds frightful.

On Monday, aping the upper classes, Eileen Weybridge feels
it her duty to pick up the litter dropped by trippers in the nearby
beech woods before she goes out to bridge or a conservative coffee
morning.

Believing that upper-class women spend their leisure hours
doing the flowers, the Weybridged middle classes are heavily into
flower arrangements by numbers, ramming salmon pink "glads"
into green foam blocks so they stand up in the plastic "dole-phin"
vase and pick up the apricot decor in the lounge.

Yellow "chrysanths" and button dahlias have always been a
talking point, too, when arranged in the white basket held by a
naked cupid on the dining-room table when Howard's business
associates come to dinner. While the orchids Howard has raised in
the "*con*-serve-a-tory" (the Stow-Crats say "c'n*serv*'tri") look so
well in driftwood in the vestibule. The expression "fresh flowers,"
to distinguish them from dried or plastic flowers, is also very Weybridge.

Although Jen Teale lives in a house with a number, she has
re-named it "Jenbry," which combines both her and Bryan's
names, which she puts in inverted commas on her notepaper. This
drives the postman crackers. Her wrought-iron gate also incorpo-
rates the name. On either side Bryan has built a bright yellow wall
shaped like a doily. A plastic flower-pot container holding a plastic
flower pot filled with purple and shocking pink petunias hangs by
the mauve front door. Jen remembers to remove the dead heads
night and morning. There are no creepers up the house; Jen doesn't
want earwigs in the bath. Most of the back and front gardens have
been crazy-paved by Bryan because it looks so much neater, but
there are a few crescent-shaped flower beds. They might have been

dug out with a pastry cutter. Here in neat rows in the spring stand military lines of blue grape hyacinths, yellow "daffs" and scarlet tulips. In the summer these are replaced by white alyssum, French marigolds, Oxford blue lobelia and scarlet geraniums or, by way of change, calceolarias and salvias. Jen loves bedding plants because once they've finished flowering they can be thrown away. There is not a weed in sight. The garden is oblong, regular and compact like a park garden.

When Bryan is not in his tool shed, he tends his "chrysanths" and his "toms" in the greenhouse. It's better than being dusted under. Occasionally, on summer afternoons, Jen and the family sit out on tubular-steel picnic chairs that can fold away neatly afterwards. There was a nasty moment once when "an elderly relative come to visit" got stuck in the couch hammock with aluminium frames. Harry Stow-Crat ties hammocks to trees.

As a first-generation gardener, Mr. Nouveau-Richards pulls out all the stops. Apart from illuminating his tarmac drive and Technicolor lawn with toadstools, he has all his flower beds floodlit, and coolie-hat lamps are stationed like streetlights round the garden.

Weeding, watering and edging are all done by electricity, which also keeps the earth warm under the cloches. In the propagating frames, all-night fluorescent lighting forces tulips into bloom in November, and vast strawberries to ripen in time for Christmas. Plastic grass lines the outdoor swimming pool (which is constantly kept at eighty degrees like the indoor one).

Mr. Nouveau-Richards reclines on the under-floor heated "pate-io" and plays with a computerised mowing machine, a new toy newly imported from Texas. He has just mixed a mint julep from his portable drinks trolley, which glides over tiles and shag pile and was described in the catalogue as "the ultimate way to enjoy a cocktail on the patio, an aperitif by the pool or those after-dinner drinks in the lounge."

Mr. Definitely-Disgusting hasn't got a garden, but he grows tomatoes and geraniums on his balcony, and he also has an allotment which means a lot to him. It is illegal to sell "produce" or "provender"—both very Jen Teale words—from one's allotment, but at least he can grow vegetables and flowers for all the family. Here stand neat furrows of potatoes, curtains of runner beans, rows of lettuces and "caulies" and at the end a blaze of annuals and bedding plants in primary colours to rival Samantha Upward's playroom. When he pulls up a lettuce he calls it "picking a salad."

Chapter 11

FOOD

"When a woman buying bacon asks for back, I call her 'madam,' " said a grocer. "When she asks for streaky I call her 'dear.' You can always tell the gentry," he went on, "by their knowledge of cheese. They don't have trouble saying the foreign names."

The food you eat often indicates what class you are; the way you eat it, namely your table manners, does so almost as much.

The upper classes, for example, don't have any middle-class inhibitions about waiting until everyone else is served, they start eating the moment food is put in front of them. This stems from the days when they all dined at long baronial tables, and if you waited for fifty other people to be served, your wild boar would be stone cold. Nor would Harry Stow-Crat comment on the food at a dinner party, because there's no point in congratulating your hostess on something that's been cooked by someone else. Equally, if he knocked his wine over, he wouldn't apologise, because, traditionally, there would be a fleet of servants to clean it up.

The ritual of table napkins is interesting too. The working-class man tucked a handkerchief under his chin to protect his shirt and waistcoat (he would never eat in a coat). The lower middles, daintily thinking "napkin" sounded too much like babies' nappies, and wanting to show off their knowledge of French, called it "serviette." The middle classes, wanting to go one up, talked about "napkins," but, being frugal, also wanted them to last a few days, so they introduced napkin rings, whereas the upper classes, who had plenty of people to do the laundry (Harry Stow-Crat's mother calls it "larndry"), had clean napkins at every meal, and regarded napkin rings as the height of vulgarity (one peer, when presented with a pair in a velvet box after making a speech, had to ask the mayor hastily what they were for). Even today Caroline Stow-Crat would rather use paper napkins than napkin rings. Mrs. Nouveau-Richards, having read in some etiquette book that the word "serviette" is common, calls them "s-napkins." In the same way, she only just remembers in time that dinner in the middle of the day is called "lunch" and talks about "d-lunch," which sounds faintly West Indian. Harry Stow-Crat's mother still calls it "luncheon."

Both Harry and Gideon Upward would lunch from one o'clock onwards, have tea around four, and dinner at eight to eight-thirty in the evening. The Teales would breakfast very early because they don't like to be rushed. So would the Definitely-Disgustings because Mr. Definitely-Disgusting has to get to work early. Both Bryan and Mr. Definitely-Disgusting probably have a cheese roll or a bar of chocolate at nine-thirty, followed by "dinner" at twelve and "tea" the moment they get home from work about six to six-thirty.

The worst thing about the working classes, complains Caroline Stow-Crat, is they never know when to leave. If she asks them round for a quick pre-dinner drink, they've always had their tea first and are all set to carry on drinking until midnight. Samantha Upward gets round the problem by asking Mrs. Nouveau-Richards at seven, then lies that she's frightfully sorry, she and Gideon have got to go out to dinner at eight-thirty. Unfortunately, Mrs. Nouveau-Richards spoils everything by asking if she can see round the kitchen, and discovers three large baked potatoes and a casserole cooking in the oven. Samantha stands on one leg, and says: "The *au pair* has the most enormous appetite."

Then there's a whole different ball game about what to call the courses. Caroline Stow-Crat would never use expressions like "starter" except in quotes, or "the soup" or "an appetiser." She would talk about the "meat" or "main course" or "cold cuts" but never the "entrée" or "the roast." (The middle classes say "joint.") Nor would she refer to chicken or grouse as "the bird" or "poultry," although Harry might use the word "poultry" as a farming term. Howard Weybridge says "polltry" or "casseroll" with a short "o." Everything from lemon water ice to jam roly-poly, Caroline would call "pudding." She would never say "sweet" or "dessert." Cheese would be served after pudding, never before. Then, to muddle everyone, this might be followed by "dessert," which is fruit, even bananas, being eaten with fruit knives and forks.

A few months ago, I went to the annual general meeting of the "Istoric" Houses Association, a gathering bristling with members of the aristocracy and the henchmen who organise the people who see over their houses. Having been gossiping in the bar, I arrived late for lunch, and found a fat lady henchman sitting by herself, the rest of the table having gone off to help themselves to pudding.

"Who else is sitting here?" I asked. "Anyone exciting?"

"Well, ay don't think they were ducal folk," she said, "because they were holdin' their knives like pencils."

Indeed she was right.

One of the great class divides, along with living in a "bought house" and saying "pardon," is the way you hold your knife. The lower echelons hold them like pencils, the upper and middles to a man putting their first finger (the one Mr. Definitely-Disgusting uses to read with) on the knife where the handle joins the blade. Harry would also turn his fork over to eat his peas, if he felt like it, and pick a bone, behaviour that would horrify Jen Teale.

Michael Nelson, in *Nobs and Snobs*, tells a story to illustrate what a gentleman his grandfather was. When sitting next to his hostess, he saw a slug on his lettuce. Rather than embarrass her, he shut his eyes, and ate it. "And my grandfather," the story ends, "managed not to be sick until after dinner."

Whilst it is a touching story, I think this was the act of a gentleman, but not necessarily an aristocrat—the two are not synonymous. In my experience Harry Stow-Crat wouldn't swallow a slug or eat anything he didn't like. Nor would he ever resort to the lengths of a Jen Teale who once dropped in on my brother and his wife and was asked to stay for lunch. To eke out the sausages and mash, my sister-in-law fried three kidneys, which this Jen Teale was too polite to say she couldn't eat. In silent glee, my brother watched her whip a kidney off her plate, when she thought no one was looking, and hold it in her hand all through lunch. Afterwards, she sidled inch by inch towards the fire, and choosing a moment when my sister-in-law was pouring out coffee, flicked the kidney discreetly with a brisk backhand into the flames, whereupon it let out a prolonged and noisy hiss.

If someone else was paying for lunch in a restaurant, and the food wasn't up to scratch, Mr. Nouveau-Richards would complain noisily to the waiter. Harry Stow-Crat would keep his trap shut. If, on the other hand, he was paying, he would never be too embarrassed to complain, like Gerald Lascelles, lunching at the Ritz, who sent a trout back because it was too small. Or the crusty old baronet who peered into the communion cup at early service and because it was only a quarter full, bellowed: "That's not enough."

If you stayed with the Stow-Crats you would go in to dinner at eight on the dot, because it's inconsiderate to keep the servants waiting, and you wouldn't sit around the table swilling brandy until midnight, because the servants want to clear away. But the men would stay behind with the port for a while, and grumble about estate duty, while the women would go into the drawing-room and probably grumble about constipation.

Things are changing, however. These days you find far more upper-class people telling the hostess her food was lovely, because she's probably cooked it herself—and if you've spent two days slaving over a dinner party you want a bit of praise. In London fewer and fewer men wear black ties, although the upper classes and upper middles still tend to in the country, with many of the women still sticking to their horse-blanket-long skirts and frilly shirts.

With the inroads of women's lib, upper-middle women are less and less often shunted off to drink coffee by themselves after dinner, the merry-tocracy in particular believing in a port in every girl, and as the husband often cooks the dinner to cries of approval which his wife would never get, he's the one who needs to go upstairs and tone down his flushed face.

The other great change in the upper-middle-class life-style is the swing back to traditional English food. In the fifties and sixties, on those three-week holidays to various costas, the wives picked up tips for five-course dinners. If you put garlic and green peppers in everything, it showed you'd travelled. Samantha Upward even used the same plate for all courses, so you could still taste the squid vinaigrette and the beef provençale when you were eating your *Poire Belle Hélène.*

As a reaction to all this, the trend now is for simple English cooking designed to bring out the flavour of good food instead of concealing it in a cordon blur of cream-and-wine sauce with grated cheese and bread crumbs on top. At dinner parties, Samantha now serves fish pie, pink beef and, particularly, English lamb (she and Gideon have had best end of neck four times during the last five times they've been out). And for puddings, it's treacle tart, jam roly-poly and bread-and-butter pudding, which at a time of national unrest reminds Samantha of Nanny, childhood and security.

Meanwhile other trends move downwards. The patrician habit of not commenting on the food, for example, is reaching the suburban spiralist belt. "Dinner gets more elaborate," said a wife on a Neo-Georgian estate, "but people pretend not to notice; it's all passed over to prove we're used to brandy in everything, and avocado pears."

And although the Surrey commuters are still wafting out garlic like dragon's breath, a sort of last gaspacho—the return to traditional food is just reaching the Weybridge set. Determined not to let the Chancellor ruin their "wholl" new fun life-style, they are into communal dinner parties with one wife cooking each course, and all keeping a stern watch on anyone getting too elaborate and putting in too much cream.

The foreign-food bug, in fact, has just filtered down to Jen Teale. She has started tarting up the stew with package Hungarian Goulash, and finds that Chicken Marengo mix gingered up with garlic salt makes a nice change from an "assorted platter of cold meats," and all these mixes do save bothering with messy ingredients. Packet *Boeuf Bourgignon* was a smash hit, too, the time

Bryan's boss came to dinner. Bryan's boss's wife also admired Jen's table. Pink paper napkins in the glasses, a matching pink doily in the basket under the slices of "crusty bread," pink flowers in the centre of the table, and pink needle-dick candles casting a lovely light. Jen, who believes things that look good, taste good, had decorated everything with radish flowerets and cucumber hearts. And her new Tupperware Jel'n Serve bowl set the orange mousse in a rose shape and Jen garnished it so prettily with piped cream and mandarin segments. The one bottle of table wine looked so attractive in its basket and Jen made sure no one got tiddly by serving little glass bowls of crisps and nuts with the Bristol Cream before dinner.

Jen's knives have stainless-steel handles and resemble fish knives; the forks look like tridents and have long thin handles to keep you farther away from the messy food—on the same principle as her feather duster. Jen never "cooks," she always calls it "preparing a meal." After she'd been to a "resteront," she'd expect the waiter to say "Enjoyed your meal?" The word "meal" is a convenient cop-out when you don't know whether to call it "lunch," "dinner" or "tea." Bryan's Rotarian father says "repast."

The Nouveau-Richardses still overdo their dinner parties— smoked salmon and caviar soufflé to start with; sole flamed in brandy with a Pernod cream sauce; *boeuf en croûte;* and a moated sugar castle for pudding. Afterwards all the guests are sick.

The Definitely-Disgustings don't give dinner parties. Everything is geared towards Sunday dinner. In the old days you were paid on Saturday night, rushed off to the pawnshop, got out your Sunday suit and then hurried down to the late-night market to buy food for "dinner" the following day. The warmth and friendliness of the pub often proved too seductive for the wage earner, and his wife would try to drag him out before he blued all his earnings. Charlie Chaplin remembers that when there wasn't enough money to pay for dinner, he and his brother were told to sit down to empty tables and clash their knives and forks together so the neighbours wouldn't realise they were going short.

Today the tradition is continued. Mr. Definitely-Disgusting

starts Sunday with a good breakfast—fried egg, bacon, beef sausages (because they're cheaper than pork) and fried bread. At twelve he goes to the pub, and is dragged home at two-thirty for the "roast and two veg," followed by apple pie and custard, or, as a treat in the summer, tinned peaches and cream. Having slept off the excesses while the family watched football on telly, he would then have whelks and two slices of wholemeal bread for tea, this being the only roughage he has had since last Sunday.

As one moves through the day, the class indicators come thick and fast. The higher classes have coffee for breakfast, the lower have tea, which they drink very strong and usually sweet. Jen Teale says she doesn't favour either a "cooked breakfast" or a "continental breakfast" and instead has "just a drink in the morning," meaning tea. (When Gideon Upward or Harry Stow-Crat use the word "drink," they mean alcohol.) Jen sometimes has "segments" instead of "cereal," which means tinned grapefruit pigs. Caroline Stow-Crat has Oxford marmalade on her toast. So does Samantha; she doesn't like it very much but she read somewhere that Golden Shred was common. Mr. Definitely-Disgusting has "two a drip, a chuck a bubble, and a cup of bug," which translated means two slices of bread and dripping, a plate of bubble and squeak, and a cup of tea (which rhymes with "flea," hence "bug"). Jen thinks the word "chuck" has a nasty derivation, so she says "portion." Samantha says "helping."

On to luncheon, where gentlemen, according to Harry Stow-Crat, never have soup—presumably because the upper classes were always out slaughtering wildlife, and soup would be difficult to eat if you were crawling through a bracken or sitting on a horse. He pronounces venison "ven'son," and truffles "true-ffls." Jen Teale, knowing the importance of eating a proper lunch, has frozen cod in cheese sauce boiled in a cellophane bag, which is indistinguishable from the dishcloths and tea towels she is always simmering on the hob. "On the weekend" she and Bryan sometimes have "an assorted platter of cold meats followed by the cheese board." As a first-generation "resteront"-goer, Bryan has picked up some of the ghastly terminology—"bill o' fare," "sweet 'n' sour" and "turkey and all the trimmings" (which means a teaspoon of cardboard packet stuffing and one burnt chipolata). He's very partial, too, to duck "allaronge" which is a piece of burnt duck covered with mandarin segments with a spoonful of sugar in the gravy. Jen, being a great reader of women's magazines, is fond of adjectives like tasty, beefy, crusty, crispy, garlicky and chewy. Along with the vast majority of her class, she is slowly poisoning her family with convenience foods, television dinners, packaged beef birianis, cake mixes and instant whips—a sort of national Chemi-kazi.

On to tea, which for the unwary is also full of pitfalls. It is very unsmart to call it "afternoon tea" to distinguish it from "high tea." Now that people of all classes in a hurry use tea bags, everyone puts the milk in second, so this is no longer an upper-class indicator. The upper classes drink China tea out of china teacups, "but it's awfully difficult drinking out of hand-painted cups," said one spiralist's wife, "so we have mugs when we're alone, and por-cell-aine when we have guests." (Caroline Stow-Crat calls it "porsl'n.")

Jen Teale's tea is a symphony of doilies under pastries and gâteaux, cake forks, scones (with a long "o"). She provides paper napkins and a knife even if you're only eating sandwiches—which she pronounces "sand-witch," like "spin-itch"; Caroline Stow-Crat says "sanwidge" and "spin-idge"; the Weybridge set say "sani." Mrs. Definitely-Disgusting says "butty" or "booty" if she lives in the North.

Jen would be shocked by Mrs. Definitely-Disgusting's milk bottle and bloater paste on the table, by the way she holds the bread in the palm of her left hand and spreads it with the right, and dips her biscuits in her tea, because of her sore teeth (spiralists call it "dunking"). Caroline Stow-Crat has Earl Grey or China tea the colour of washing-up water (just the colour Mr. Definitely-Disgusting likes his coffee). White sliced bread is particularly lower-middle because of its lack of roughage.

A fellow-journalist, however, tells a wicked story of the time he interviewed a famous romantic novelist who was also a passionate health-food freak. During the interview at her house, he was subjected to a long lecture on the merits of wholemeal homemade bread, but just as he was leaving, a little Sunblest van came jauntily up the drive.

"Surely," said the journalist in mock horror, "you're not buying sliced bread."

"Oh, that, darling," said the lady novelist airily, "is for the servants."

Chapter 12

APPEARANCES

Clothes

In the past fifteen years we've been through a complete sartorial revolution. There was the self-expressionism of the late sixties, when everyone did his own thing, followed by unisex and jeans for all classes and all sexes, followed by the punk revolt of the late seventies. And now, as Christopher Sykes has pointed out, after the age of turmoil, an age of conservative consolidation has set in. As a result, it is almost impossible to tell what class the young are from their appearance.

On the one hand, you have the tear-away from Eton wearing polyester trousers and shirts with key motifs to irritate the establishment; on the other, the working-class undergraduate, determined to identify himself with the establishment, who smothers himself in college regalia. The hacking jacket has just about filtered down the class system to Sharon Definitely-Disgusting, while Fiona Stow-Crat turns up at a party with bright purple hair wearing a leopard-skin rayon jump suit and gold stiletto-heeled boots. And although the upper classes usually settle down sartorially with marriage, I recently met an extremely grand, much-divorced old woman wearing orange satin drainpipes and a white tee-shirt with I AM A VIRGIN printed across the bust. Meanwhile the majority of parvenu Tory ladies living in Weybridge, terrified of betraying their origins by putting a foot wrong, dress exactly like the Queen.

Recently I went to a lunch party where some Americans had been invited to meet a duke's daughter. The daughter of the house, who was middle-class, called Rosemary, and equally apprehensive about meeting a member of the aristocracy, wore a tweed coat and skirt, flat shoes, a pale blue cashmere jersey and pearls. The duke's daughter roared up from a drinks party on a motorbike wearing a leather skirt, fishnet stockings, a tight black sweater and punk eye make-up. The Americans, who arrived just after her, made a justifiable mistake.

One comfort is that even the grandest people worry about what to wear. That scourge of the middle classes, Nancy Mitford, was thrown into total panic by a last-minute invitation to dine with the Duke of Windsor.

There is a rather touching story told me by one of the Queen's dressmakers. The Queen was visiting his shop and admired a very beautiful evening dress, glittering with crystal and rhinestone. When both the dressmaker and her lady-in-waiting urged her to buy it, she shook her head wistfully saying, wasn't it a pity, but really she hadn't got anywhere smart enough to wear it. What she probably meant was that it was too tarty and glamorously ostentatious.

Traditionally the aristocracy survived because they were the wiliest of the tribe and knew when to lie low. Let the nouveau riche swagger around in their finery, showing off their wealth, and getting their heads chopped off by royalty, or later by revolutionaries. Harry Stow-Crat's ancestors were prepared to dress up in their peer robes when the King commanded it; otherwise they camouflaged themselves and blended in with their surroundings. Thus today Harry is only copying his forbears when he wears a dark suit in the grey of London and green, dung-coloured or brown clothes in the country. There was an additional reason for this. Harry's ancestors lived on what they shot, hunted and fished. It was easier to land your prey—whether it was a girl in London or a salmon in the Tay —if you were indistinguishable from your background.

If there is one single class indicator, therefore, where clothes are concerned—it is colour. The upper classes tend not to wear crude, garish, clashing colours. Not for them the Day-Glo oranges or reds, the jarring lime greens and citrus yellows, the royal blues, mauves and cyclamen pinks. A friend of mine was once witheringly written "orf" as "the sort of girl who wears shocking pink in the country." Mrs. Nouveau-Richards can pore over *The Tatler*, and find out exactly when and in what styles different clothes should be worn, but while the photographs go on being printed in black and white, she'll never get the colours quite right.

Traditionally, too, because the upper classes believe in supporting their own industries, they regard anything that's lived—wool, leather, silk, cotton—as all right, but anything man-made—Crimplene, polyester or plastic—as decidedly vulgar.

At a meeting of the Historic Houses Association, Edward Montague, the departing president, and Clive Jenkins, the trade unionist, wore identical clothes—dark blue suits, slightly lighter blue plain shirts and dark blue ties with red spots. But because Clive Jenkins's materials were all man-made fibres, they looked somehow much shinier and less substantial.

The upper classes, as Michael Fish has said, also believe it is morally wrong to buy more clothes than you have to. So as clothes have to last, they have to be conservative and of decent stuff. It is a point of pride for Harry at forty to be able to get into the same trousers and coat he wore at Eton.

In fact, the higher up the social scale you go, the taller and more finely boned people tend to be, because of diet, work patterns and extra vitamins over the years. Harry has no bum, Caroline no bum or bust, both are tall and thin, so their clothes, which have the advantage of being very well cut, tend to look good on them and set them apart. Leanness, as Mrs. Gaskell pointed out, is a great aid to gentility. Even if Georgie horrifies his father by buying an orf-the-peg suit, he'll probably get away with it because of an etiolated figure and self-confidence. Aristocrats, even if they live in London and have little opportunity to take exercise, seldom allow themselves to put on weight.

Harry Stow-Crat is therefore very conservative in his dress. But from the way he describes what he's wearing, "black tie" for a dinner party, "white tie" for an official occasion, or a "morning coat" for a wedding, you'd think he was going about half naked.

One aristocrat I know got caught out very badly in this way. He was going to spend a weekend at a very grand house in the country and asked his batman to pack his dinner jacket. It was only when he was dressing for dinner he discovered his batman had taken him at his word and only put in the coat. In the end he was reduced to borrowing a pair of trousers from his host, which were midnight blue, half his size and about three times too large in the waist. No one made any comment at dinner or afterwards. Harry Stow-Crat's own dinner jacket is almost green with age and wear and tear. He would never call it a "dinner suit," or have one in midnight blue, particularly in terylene with braiding. Georgie, however, might easily wear a different-coloured velvet tie, but not a waterfall of duck-egg-blue frills like Jison Richards.

Harry, as has already been pointed out, would wear a dark suit in London, but he wouldn't call it a "lounge suit" or a "three-piece suit" or a "business suit." At the back he would have a slit (Bryan Teale calls them "vents"). The buttons on the sleeve would undo, and there would be a real buttonhole for a carnation in the collar, which he could do up in bad weather on a button hidden under the collar on the other side. He would still wear fly buttons rather than zips to protect his member for carrying on the line, but Georgie would probably have a zip, just as he might easily wear a leather belt to hold up his trousers. Harry would wear braces, which he would take off before removing his coat. His shirts would be striped, checked or plain-coloured, and never have pictures, patterns or initials on them—initials on anything are considered very vulgar. Harry would never wear a striped tie with a dark suit, but he might wear a Guards tie with a tweed coat in the country. Georgie probably wouldn't bother to wear a tie at all, but it is interesting that when the tieless fashion was at its height in the late seventies, girls started one-upping each other by wearing the smart old school, club and regimental ties their fathers and brothers had jettisoned.

Harry would wear one "han'k'rchif" (not "hand-ker-cheef") in his trouser pocket, and another in his breast pocket—not up his sleeve. But it would not match his tie, and it would be casually arranged just to show a tip of a corner and bit of fold. It would not be folded across in a white rectangle, as though, as someone bitchily said, "you'd forgotten to post your pools envelope" (although Prince Philip wears it this way), nor in a neat right angle, nor in a made-up mountain range on a piece of cardboard, like Bryan Teale. Mr. Definitely-Disgusting wears a handkerchief on his head at the seaside.

Pottering about at home, Harry would probably wear old corduroy (pronounced "cord'roy") or whipcord trousers, and a tweed jacket, which he would refer to as a "tweed coat" or, as he called it at Eton, a "change coat." He would never use the expression "sports jacket." He would never wear a blazer; in fact, he tells Georgie he would have been thrown out of the Guards for using such a word. He might occasionally wear a polo-neck sweater, but never in pastel colours or white and always in wool. He would call it a "polo-neck jersey" because the upper classes think the words "jumper," "sweater," "pullover," "slipover," "woollie," "cardigan" and particularly "cardi" extremely vulgar. He would never wear a mackintosh in London or call it a "raincoat" or, even worse, a "showerproof." He would never carry an umbrella in the country (only vicars are allowed this privilege) except at point-to-points or the races, or anywhere where a woman might be dressed up and need cover—on the moors they can drown. The umbrella would be black and without a tassel. He would wear gum boots in green or black, but never call them "Wellington boots" or, even worse, "Wellies." If he wore an overcoat he would refer to it as a "coat" or a "covert coat" (pronounced "cover"—to fox the unwary).

If Georgie wore just a shirt and trousers, he would take off his tie, undo the top button and roll his sleeves up to below the elbow. Mr. Definitely-Disgusting would do the same except that he'd roll the sleeve up above the elbow. Bryan Teale would leave his tie on and his shirt sleeves buttoned up. (What does it matter if his cuffs get dirty? Jen can drip-dry them in a trice tonight.)

If Harry wore a signet ring, which is unlikely, as he doesn't need this kind of status prop, it would have a crest, and be on the little finger on his left hand. Georgie might wear a wedding ring merely to irritate the upper middles, who all wear signet rings with crests on their little fingers and think it's awful to have rings, with initials particularly, on any other fingers.

Harry would probably still decant his cigarettes into a cigarette case, although Georgie wouldn't bother. Not long ago one officer in the Guards got frightfully bawled out for offering the Duke of Gloucester cigarettes in a packet. "You're not in the garage now," said his commanding officer in a furious aside. Mr. Definitely-Disgusting smokes his Woodbines between finger and thumb to eke them out, and curled in the palm of the hand to hide them from the foreman. Howard Weybridge and Colonel Upward smoke pipes, Mr. Nouveau-Richards smokes very expensive cigars and leaves the label on, like a signet ring. Georgie Stow-Crat would certainly smoke in the street if he felt like it. His mother would not. Harry Stow-Crat keeps his money in a "notecase," not a "wallet."

Gideon Upward, trying to be trendy but slightly out of date, would still be squeezing himself into jeans. He might wear a blazer but not with a badge, more likely a corduroy or a velvet coat, or last year's denim, which Samantha bought him: it has four buttons and a high neck and makes him feel slightly silly. Since Zacharias and Thalia went to boarding school, he can't afford to buy suits any more, so he wears his old ones. All his Christmas presents are chosen by Samantha, usually sweaters from Marks and Spencer, in colours which suit Samantha and which Samantha wears during the week, so they have two bumps in front when Gideon puts them on at the weekend. He has reluctantly started to wear part-nylon socks, because Samantha shrinks his wool ones to Action Man size in a few weeks. He knows that shirt collars ought always to be worn inside a coat and a sweater, and he never wears a hat, although when he goes shooting occasionally, his grander friends force him into a cap, saying: "You'll be frightfully cold, Gideon."

Howard Weybridge dresses straighter than straight, not unlike Colonel Upward. Howard wears regimental ties, golf-club ties and an old school tie if he's got one. Occasionally he wears a paisley scarf (which he refers to as a "cravat") with a brass scarf ring. At the pub he wears a very clean blazer and slightly too new cavalry twill trousers, although the nearest he's got to the cavalry is an hour-long horseback ride through the pine trees in Oxshott woods. He has never gone in for wide trousers, and his suede ankle boots are slightly too ginger. When he goes to Twickenham he wears a sheepskin coat, often with brown fur, and one of an assortment of hats—Russian fur, flat caps and deerstalkers. He wears huge riding macs, and his spectacles have no bottom rims to them. In bed he wears a red wool nightshirt grandiosely called a "sleep coat."

Mr. Nouveau-Richards wears too much jewellery, huge gold cuff links and a huge gold watch. He likes wearing bow ties so he can show glittering collar studs on his shirts, but if he wears a tie, he puts on a huge gold tie pin. In his early working-class days, like Mr. Definitely-Disgusting, he wore a tie clip and sleeve garters. He wears a camel-hair coat with a belt, and in the evening changes into a burgundy velvet smoking jacket, with his initials in frogging.

Jison Richards, as a member of the telly-stocracy, wears three-piece suits in white with a black shirt and no tie, or very light blue suits, with the jackets so waisted and with such long slits at the back they look like miniskirts. He used always to wear very fat, flamboyant ties borrowed from Wardrobe at the B.B.C. but the knot is getting slimmer. He often leaves his make-up on after a programme when he goes to the pub, to remind people he's a telly star.

The spiralist who is climbing very fast, but hasn't got the same kind of money as Jison Richards, studies the fashion magazines slavishly and coordinates carefully. He might select a neat check jacket to go with plain beige slacks, add a "wesket" to match the slacks, and the whole ensemble can double up as a business suit during the week. He's also very keen on herringbone suits, which, worn with a sporty cravat, will double up as a sports suit for leisure wear. He likes British accessories—a jaunty check cap matching the check insets of his high-button jacket or a Donegal tweed hat with the brim turned down, worn with a matching coat and "holld-all." He's also heavily into luggage. Last year's gold plastic bag on a coat hanger has been replaced this year by a "travel robe" in tartan which has a handle enabling him to carry all his coordinates vertical. Nattiness reigns.

Bryan Teale is dressed from top to toe in drip-dry clothes. One day Bryan thinks Jen may well put him through the washing machine under the setting for "whites lightly soiled." Bryan wears burgundy Crimplene slacks which never fit because Jen brought them by mail order in the *Daily Mail,* rust cable-stitch cardigans and cavalry twill-style trousers in brown/black/lovat/fawn in 100 per cent washable polyester. He wears his Rotary badge on his lapel. He wears tartan jockey shorts. He also wears striped ties which the shop categorizes as a "club tie," but which have an old-school-tie look "that's very nice." Bryan also has a whole robe unit in the bedroom for his car wear: woolly hats, zip-up car coats, fake sheepskin coats for cold days, overalls to save his good clothes when he's lying under the car and driving gloves with holes in the back.

Gideon Upward changes out of a suit into old clothes when he gets home or at the weekends. Mr. Definitely-Disgusting changes out of old clothes into one of Gideon's old suits, which is a bit shiny but still has plenty of wear in it, that Mrs. Definitely-Disgusting bought at a jumble sale. She likes a good fight at the jumble on the weekend. Indoors Mr. Definitely-Disgusting always removes his coat, and sits in a waistcoat and collarless shirt; any shoes he wears inside the house will be called "slippers" (his bedroom slippers he calls "carpet slippers"). If he wears a shirt with a collar with a coat, he arranges the collar neatly outside the jacket. He always keeps his hat on in the pub.

Apart from the fact that Caroline Stow-Crat never wears manmade fibres except for stockings, it is far more difficult to tell the difference between her clothes and Mrs. Weybridge's, and even more difficult to distinguish Fiona Stow-Crat from Sharon Definitely-Disgusting. Caroline has a good dark fur coat for cold days in London but would never wear a fur stole, and particularly never call it a "wrap." Since sheepskin coats have sunk down the scale, the upper classes of both sexes wear a hideous quilted rubber coat called a "husky," not unlike Mrs. Definitely-Disgusting's dressing gown, except it is nylon and khaki. In the future we have to expect "husky knickers" to keep out the cold, which sound as though they'd be golden and furry and matted with Arctic snow, but turn out to be over-trousers.

Caroline would always tend to underdress. Except for a watch, or a small brooch, "nothing but pearls before sundown" would be her maxim. Her pearls would have little knots between each pearl. (The world is divided into have-knots and have-nets.) At night she would wear a lot of very good, inherited jewellery, which would add a lot of light to her face. She would never wear modern jewellery, and particularly never refer to it as "costume jewellery." After she'd been through her wild deb stage—and certainly after she was married—she wouldn't show cleavages or wear miniskirts, whatever the fashion. Nor would she wear see-through shirts. (She thinks the word "blouse" is very common.)

Caroline would also prefer the expression "coat and skirt," and although Fiona might say "suit," neither of them would ever say "two-piece" or "costume" or "skirt suit." Caroline might wear trousers, but never very tight, and never a trouser suit. Her shoes would be plain, and never too high, or two-tone, or decorated with bows, or with peep toes. Wedge heels and platform heels and coloured boots, particularly drum majorette white boots, would also be out. She used to prefer the word "frock" to "dress," but since Samantha Upward's taken up "frock" as being more old-fashioned and Kate Greenaway, Caroline's swinging back to "dress" again. Other expressions she doesn't use are "ball gown," "hostess gown," "evening gown," "housecoat," or "bathrobe" instead of "dressing gown." As she has very good legs, she doesn't need the flattery of dark stockings, but if she did she'd wear navy blue with blue shoes, rather than black, which she thinks are a bit tarty.

Samantha Upward is much more untidy in appearance. She is just emerging from her Third World ethnic phase, and still has a sloppy bra-less, long-straight-haired, intellectual earth mother look. She's not as good at staying on diets, or as naturally thin as Caroline Stow-Crat. She found those kaftans and peasant dresses almost better than Gideon's sweaters for covering up a multitude of tums.

At dinner parties she's weighed down with ethnic jewellery

picked up from various Oxfam or African project shops (which is the nearest she gets to abroad, now they're so poor). The difference between the upper middle classes and the lower middle is admirably illustrated by Shirley Williams and Margaret Thatcher. As Rebecca West pointed out to me in an interview: "Mrs. Thatcher has one great disadvantage—she is a daughter of the people and looks trim as a daughter of the people desires to be. Shirley Williams has such an advantage over her because she's a member of the upper middle classes and can achieve that distraught kitchen sink revolutionary look that one cannot get unless one's been to a really good school." The upper middles tend to be untidy, not only because they're more secure than the lower middles but because they like to look vaguely intellectual and because, unlike Caroline Stow-Crat, they don't feel they ought to set an example to anyone.

The middle middles try to dress just like Mrs. Thatcher, the Queen and Grace Kelly, very upper-classical. Eileen Weybridge wears velvet jackets over a shirtwaister pleated dress, or a blouse with a pussycat tie bow and a pleated skirt. When it rains she puts on a scarf decorated with snaffles and horse's heads, which she thinks give it a "very nice country look." She wears a camel-hair coat with saddle stitching in slightly too dark a shade, and a brown Melusine bowler hat for shopping. Her shoes are in slightly too orange a tan, and she spends days and days finding a matching "handbag." She rather lets the side down by buying an emerald green trouser suit with a matching peaked cap. In the evening she wears a polyester floral shirtwaister bang on the knee. She would never show bare arms after thirty-five.

Mrs. Nouveau-Richards, coming from working-class origins, likes to dress up whenever she goes out, even to the shops. In the evening she wears white or silver fox furs and a great deal of very flash modern jewellery, particularly diamonds. On her dresses she has lots of spangles and sequins, and her figure is as heavily corsetted as her ve-owell sounds, but inclined to break out above her stays like an overflowing ice-cream cone. She wears long coloured gloves with bracelets outside, and invariably very high-heeled shoes with straps round the ankles, and a spangled butterfly or a flower in her hair, which is peroxide blonde (just like Diana Dors). For coffee mornings, she wears a shrimp cocktail frock.

Jen Teale, like Bryan, lives in drip-dry coordinates—little terylene tops which she's always pulling down over the "derrière" of her terylene slacks when she is doing anything strenuous. As she hates untidy hair, she puts on one of those scarves with a fitted pleated centre, for tying under the hair. She wears rain hats which match her raincoat, and always carries a plastic transparent concertina hood in her bag in case it rains. Everything is washed after one wearing, and she never wears anything she buys from jumble sales until she's "hand-washed" it first. She always wears a bra and a panty-girdle, not only to keep Bryan and others out, but to make her figure as anonymous as possible. She's very keen on capes, because they don't reveal a single outline and yet look neat.

If Jen Teale wears a transparent shirt, she always wears a full-length petticoat and a bra underneath, so all you see is rigging. Even when she relaxes in the evening, her primrose brushed nylon housecoat is worn over all her underclothes. Although she's not a Catholic, she wears a gold cross round her neck to remind people she's a "nice girl." For weddings her "outfit" is a navy Crimplene two-piece trimmed with lemon, bought from a catalogue. Her uniform with a summer dress is a long white Orlon cardigan.

Mrs. Definitely-Disgusting only started wearing trousers a few years ago, when she was cleaning Samantha Upward's house. Like Caroline Stow-Crat, she always wears a scarf when she goes out, but hers is in shiny rayon and made in Hong Kong. Like Jen Teale, she buys by mail order; it's the only post she gets, filling in coupons in the *TV Times* while she watches *Match of the Day*. When she tries it on in the privacy of her own home, she finds the princess-line dress in dusky pink/African violet two-tone floral, in uncrushable polyester 100 per cent washable with figure-flattering panels, doesn't look nearly as good as it did in the *Daily Mirror.* Like Harry Stow-Crat, Mrs. Definitely-Disgusting has a change coat, in new

French navy with a nylon fur collar. She needed it to cheer herself up: her old burgundy barathea used to clash with her 'ot flushes.

Hair

How people wear their hair is an invaluable social litmus with men —less so with women. Although there are exceptions (Lord Weymouth may wear his hair long and in a million pigtails; Lord Lichfield, at least in his photographs, looks like a hairdresser), most of the aristocracy if they're over thirty-five brush their hair backwards, with the parting directly north of the outer corner of the eye, two wings above the ears, and cut just above the collar. Harry Stow-Crat wears his hair very shiny, probably as a result of Nanny's hundred brushes a night. Because he doesn't have much stress worrying about himself like the middle classes, or tend to work so hard, he seldom goes bald. If he did, however, he would never brush his hair forward to cover a receding hairline, or in strands over a bald patch, or part the hair above the ears and brush the remaining hair over his bald cranium like anchovies over a hard-boiled egg.

Aristocrats seldom wear their hair over their ears—Mr. Heath dropped a class or two visually when instead of brushing his wings back, he trained them forward in two tendrils over his ears. Nor would Harry Stow-Crat cut his hair short in front so it fell in a cowlick or in a serpentine ripple or in a just breaking fall-over wave. His sideboards would stop level with the entrance to the eardrum. Neither he nor Georgie ever combs his hair in public.

Georgie Stow-Crat might well have a fringe—not to hide a receding hairline, but because it was trendy. He would, however, start off brushing his hair back, and letting it fall forward, and it would be so well cut, and his features so lean and finely drawn, that the effect would never be like the lacquered thatched roof on top of a cottage-loaf of the spiralist. At the moment there seems to be a trend towards the Edward Fox short-back-and-sides look (inspired by his television appearance as Edward VIII). So soon, no doubt, Georgie will be looking just like Harry again.

Harry has his hair cut at least once a month when he comes to London. He refers to the man who cuts his hair as his "hairdresser," and asks him to "wash," never to "shampoo," his hair. He buys one bottle of Bay Rum each visit; it has a nozzle on it like Angostura bitters in cocktail bars. His hairdresser clips the hair out of his nostrils, but not his ears.

Gideon Upward's hair is still longer and more straggly than Zacharias's (because that used to be trendy in the late sixties). But it's getting shorter. He goes to the barber when he finds that his shirt collars are getting dirty on both sides. The barber is invariably Cypriot and near the office. After the perfunctory snipping and primping Gideon is asked if he wants "anything else," which means French letters, always prominently displayed alongside metal combs, razor blades and various cheap male toiletries. Occasionally in the privacy of his own bathroom Gideon will brush his hair forward, screw up his eyes and wonder when he'll ever get an opportunity to use one of those French letters.

The only men clinging to long straggly hair are middle-class left-wing trendies. As a reaction, the right-wing Howard Weybridge has his hair cut short. So does Mr. Nouveau-Richards, but having spent so much of his youth working hard to get to the top, he tries to stay young with Grecian 2000. Jison Richards, now he's a member of the telly-stocracy, brushes his blond streaked locks firmly forward to hide any incipient wrinkles across his fawhead and round the eyes. He washes and blow-dries it himself before television appearances, and keeps it in place with all sorts of toiletries. If he is not pulling a bird, he might even sleep in a hair net. He ages ten years in a high wind.

Mr. Definitely-Disgusting's hair is seldom cut and seldom washed. It falls out early, and what remains is coiled in oily strands inside some sort of headdress. He wears it very short.

Dive Definitely-Disgusting has a perm like a footballer. When it's just been done, he looks like a Tory lady—he always combs his hair in public.

Mrs. Definitely-Disgusting is also coiffure-mad—not only does she help in Mario's salon next to the fish-and-chips shop on the weekend, but most Fridays goes spangled peroxide blonde and bouffant, so that she and Mr. Definitely-Disgusting can be seen in all their glory at the pub music night on Friday evening, or the Working Men's Club. This bouffant remains till the end of the week, when it looks like a haystack ravaged by gales. I once heard a hairdresser claim that she has on occasions demolished such edifices only to find them full of a kind of maggots which feed on the lacquer. If Mrs. Definitely-Disgusting is not bouffant she wears curlers around the house and in the street, because it's cheaper than drying it by the gas fire and because Mr. Definitely-Disgusting's on night shift and sleeps during the day. This, however, is disappearing with affluence.

Jen Teale cuts Bryan's hair to save money—likewise that of the kiddies, who are all drenched in Vosene to ward off the dreaded dandruff (Caroline Stow-Crat calls it "scurf"). Bryan has a shower every day which flattens and brushes his hair forward automatically. If he is a salesman and goes to conferences, he has a razor cut. Jen wears her hair short because it's more hygienic and so much cooler in summer. She has a curly fringe halfway down her fawhead, and the side bits swept behind her ears, a style Caroline Stow-Crat would think very common. Once a year when she's feeling skittish she scrapes her hair into two bunches above her ears.

Eileen Weybridge has hair exactly like the Queen; so does her mother, with an additional blue rinse on her grey hair. Samantha's mother has hair like the Queen but slightly looser, more like Mrs. Thatcher, and she thinks blue rinses are very vulgar.

Samantha has a fringe on the eyebrows and wears her hair long, straight and mousy to match her dirndl skirt. She doesn't wash it more than once a week because it would destroy the natural oils. Occasionally she puts on a henna rinse, which Gideon is supposed to admire when she stands under the light. Now she's got bored with the women's movement, she shaves her legs with Gideon's razor, which she leaves clogged in the bedroom. She shaves under her arms too, but smells like a polecat when excited, because she wants to be natural and not use those horrible deodorants.

Caroline Stow-Crat's hair is worn with flick-ups and sometimes an Alice band. Like Harry, she has the sort of bone structures that can take hair worn orf the face—she doesn't need a forelock to pull to anyone—but recently she has taken to wearing a quarter fringe on either side, and Harry hasn't grumbled about it. She has her hair done quite often, partly for something to do and partly to catch up on back numbers of *The Tatler* and *Harper's*. Her hair is never in very good condition, as it spends too much time under a headscarf or a hat. A few years ago she would never have dreamt of dying her hair, but streaking looks so natural, and it does mean at least seven hours at the hairdresser's looking at *The Tatler* and *Harper's*. Her hair often smells of cigarette smoke from going to too many cocktail parties given by the Deputy Lord Lieutenant, Harry. She will go grey suddenly.

Fiona Stow-Crat washes her collarbone-length hair every day, so it always looks slightly untidy, and brushes it back in two wings like Harry. She has been known to dye it extraordinary colours.

On the whole, the aristocracy's hair is a sort of light brown, upper-class mouse. If Harry said one of his friends had brought a "blonde" to a party, the expression would be slightly dismissive because if she were anyone Harry would know her anyway. He would talk about "a pretty girl with dark hair," rather than "an attractive brunette." And if a girl had red hair, he'd call it red, he wouldn't have any truck with expressions like "auburn" or "copper."

Faces

The upper classes, as has already been pointed out, are tall and thin, and have narrow stoats' heads with very few bumps to them.

Their faces, therefore, tend to be narrow, with the skin more finely drawn over the nose and jawbone. Their eyes turn down rather than up at the corners, and although not very large, tend to be bigger than their mouths, which look not unlike the private parts of a female ferret. Often these hang open because they're not ashamed of their teeth. Big rubber-tyre mouths and large rolling eyes give a face a very plebeian look. Used to very cold houses, and an outdoor life, Harry Stow-Crat has the kind of delicate pink and white skin which flushes up at parties and in hot restaurants. From lack of stress, he tends to age more slowly than the other classes. Because he has a poker face you are less aware of his wrinkles. At fifty, he may look thirty-five, but when he laughs or gets angry his face suddenly breaks into hundreds of lines like a dried-up riverbed. Harry and Caroline both have very long thin feet.

As you go down the classes, people tend to be bulkier in the face, particularly round the jaw and chin. Mrs. Definitely-Disgusting's mouth disappears altogether once she's lost her teeth.

Chapter 13

VOICES

The men of Gilead said unto him, Art thou an Ephraimite? If
he said Nay, then said they unto him, Say now Shibboleth," and
he said Sibboleth: for he could not frame to pronounce it right.
Then they took him and slew him.

Judges 12: 5, 6.

When people talk about class barriers, they often mean sound
barriers. The story of the poor Ephraimite is one of the saddest in
the Bible, but such a universal one that the word "shibboleth" has
passed into the English language and has come to mean among
other things the criterion or catchword of a social group. Thus Jen
Teale would have a little eye-meet with Bryan if they heard Mr.
Definitely-Disgusting talking about an 'orse, and Samantha and
Gideon Upward would immediately identify a lower caste if they
heard Eileen Weybridge talking about zebras with a short "e" or
asking for "a portion of gâteau."

Your pronunciation and the words you use are so crucial for
determining your class that the subject has been already touched
on in numerous occasions throughout this book. For despite the
egalitarian revolution and the embracing of crypto-working-class
accents by some of the upper and middle classes, a person is still
often mocked because of the way he speaks. This very afternoon,
shouting across the road to an old colonel, I reduced two youths
in anoraks to fits of laughter. I could hear them mimicking me all
the way up the street. As Bernard Shaw said in *Pygmalion,* "Every

time an Englishman opens his mouth another Englishman despises him."

Things have certainly improved, however. Thirty years ago the announcers on the wireless still solemnly put on dinner jackets every night to read the nine o'clock news and spoke with an accent called "B.B.C. English," which was actually upper-middle-class (they enunciated far too well to be truly upper-class). Every young actor who wanted to get on ironed out his accent and tried to talk just the same. Pitman's agreed with them, so every secretary learning shorthand discovered that "bath" and "class" were pronounced with a long "a," because the squiggles depicting them went on the line rather than above it as they would have done if the "a" had been flat.

Then came the cultural revolution of the sixties and today; as a result, the English spoken by the B.B.C. (especially on television) has dropped to somewhere between middle and lower middle with dozens of announcers being matey and calling everyone "luv" and female interviewers with flat accents talking about "Ufrica" and "bunk balances."

What has also happened in the last twenty-five years is that people no longer despise you if you have a strong regional or lower-class accent, so long as you're successful and amusing. Everyone adores Twiggy and Zandra Rhodes. This social and cultural change has been described by Geoffrey Gorer as follows: "The young now like to call themselves upper-working-class. Twenty years ago, the bright young of working-class origin with intellectual gifts or talents would have been likely to acquire a B.B.C. accent and pass as upper-middle-class. Today they feel no need to hide their accent. They are the new trend setters."

Maybe. But if these new trend setters were not successful, I doubt if Caroline Stow-Crat or Samantha Upward (and certainly Eileen Weybridge) would ask them to dinner. And I suspect that as the country swings back and becomes more reactionary, not only Zandra Rhodes but all those upper and middle classes with their flat "a"s may begin to sound a bit dated.

In the present climate what people do object to now is the old practice of people changing their accents, as poor Mr. Heath learnt to his cost. Everyone thinks politicians are dishonest but when they have "dishonest" voices they are doubly suspect. Whenever he appeared on television, all classes sat listening to the ironed-out vowel sounds and the slow, low delivery (designed so that every word can be enunciated carefully) and gleefully waited for the first slip. But if people shrink from affected gentility, they also shrink from deliberate anti-gentility. Bringing your voice down is considered just as silly—like the girl in the sixties who had elocution lessons to try and get her accent made less patrician so she would be accepted at demos or Lord Stansgate calling himself Tony Benn and "yer know-ing" folksily all over the electorate.

But for all of us the whole subject is relative. All English people dismiss upper-class shibboleths they don't use themselves as "outdated" or "snobbish," while still regarding any word they themselves consider vulgar as "barbarous." Thus *I* think the word "luncheon" is pedantic, but the word "phone" is vulgar. Whereas my children will probably think "telephone" is pedantic.

Questions of accent are even more elusive. In a recent survey, 50 per cent of the people interviewed said they *didn't have any accent,* a statement with which the class above (and very likely the classes below them, too) would have certainly disagreed. In fact, everyone has an accent, from the Queen downward. It may not be regional, but there is certainly an upper-class, an upper-middle and a middle-class accent, which are all quite different.

The trouble with the upper class is they're inclined to change their vocabulary just to outsmart the lower classes. Now the word "loo" has sifted down and been taken up by *Daily Mirror* readers, the uppers have reverted to "lavatory" again. And you could feel the horrified frisson among the upper middles when Princess Anne was suddenly heard to say "ee-ther" in a television interview. They'd studied *Noblesse Oblige,* they knew the upper classes said "eye-ther": it was really too bad.

English snobbery about regional accents seems to be based on the proposition that they are O.K. if they're far enough away from

London. No one minds Irish, Welsh and Scottish accents half so much as Birmingham or South London ones. West Country and East Anglian are preferred to "home counties" suburban. If the B.B.C. wants a voice to represent the people, however, they go North and use one of their regional announcers, Colin Welland.

"I seem," he said recently, "to have cornered the market in the Common Touch."

But if accent does make the heart grow fonder, there are still a lot of people trying to get rid of theirs. One thinks of all the spiralists talking mid-Atlantic, and the union leaders learning all those long words (surely "indoostrial action" is the greatest euphemism of them all). Men promoted from the shop floor, egged on by their wives, are often sent by the management to elocution lessons. There was a piece in *The Sunday Times* recently about a cockney girl called Shelley who was trying to eradicate her cockney accent. It hadn't mattered when she'd had a backroom job in the bank, but now she was a receptionist at a ballet school and meeting people all the time, she decided she needed a new voice. "It's nice to improve," she said. "You're stepping upwards not backwards. It'll be useful for the rest of my life."

Rather like the schoolmistress who felt all her lower-middle vowels spilling out when she got angry in class, and the bank manager who felt his voice thicken when he had to talk to people about their overdrafts. We all know how our mouths seem to fill with marbles when we try to sound grander than we really are. Most people are bilingual, of course: telephonists, curates talking about carnal know-ledge with a long "o," airline pilots ("This is your Captain speaking"), demonstrators and women who tell you your train times over the tannoy all have special put-on voices.

Ironing out an accent can cut you off from your background. It didn't matter to Shelley because her parents were both dead, but the schoolmistress admitted that she was ashamed of her parents: "They have every awful pseudo-refinement of the lower-middle classes."

Harry Stow-Crat has a very distinctive accent. Because of his poker face, he only uses vowels that will hardly move his face at all. One opens one's mouth far less if one says "hice" rather then "house" and "aw" rather than the short "o." Thus Harry automatically says "orf," "corsts," "gorn," "clorth" and "lorst." This is, of course, old pronunciation: "Ride a cock horse, to Banbury Crorse." Harry also moves his face less by clipping his words: hence "Lond'ndri," "mag'str't" and "Charl't" instead of "Londonderry," "mag-is-trate" and "Char-lotte." He often uses a short "e" for "ay" like the old man who went into the village shop and asked for some "pepper."

"Red pepper or black pepper, sir?" asked the shopkeeper.

"Don't be ridiculous," snapped the old man, "I mean lavatory pepper."

The upper classes have frightful accents when they talk in a foreign language. As Harry Stow-Crat's mother once admonished him: "Speak French fluently, darling, but not like them." Upper-class accents may alter, but they are united in their absence of euphemism or circumlocution. They don't say "pleased to meet you," because they don't know if they are and wouldn't feel the need to resort to such flattery. They are not arch. They would never talk about "botties" or the "little girls' room," or ask, as Howard Weybridge might, if they can go and "point Percy at the porcelain."

Samantha Upward enunciates more clearly than the Stow-Crats. Her features are more mobile, she smiles more, her voice is less clipped. She is also less direct, talking about "having help" in the house rather than "servants," and saying "How's your glass?" rather than "Would you like another drink?" Because she is slightly unsure of herself, she would probably cling to words like "wireless" and "children" long after the upper classes were saying "radio" and "kids." On the other hand, she would clip her words far more than Eileen Weybridge—saying "'dmire," "s'cessful" and "c'mpete" rather than "ad-mire," "suck-sessful" and "com-pete." She wouldn't say "lorst" or "corst," but she would say "sawlt" and "awlter." Dive Definitely-Disgusting couldn't distinguish Samantha's voice from Caroline Stow-Crat's, but he would think Caroline sounded more commanding, and Samantha more hearty and jolly hockey sticks.

If you met Howard Weybridge you probably wouldn't be able immediately to tell what part of the world he came from: his voice would be very careful so as not to slip—a sort of Colonel Bogus. Mrs. Weybridge would articulate far more than Samantha Upward —she would talk about "coff-ee" and "syst-im." Eileen Weybridge also says "act-riss" (the flat-"a" brigade say "uctress"; Harry Stow-Crat says "actr's"). There was one Howard Weybridge living in Yorkshire who had a marvellously "haw-haw" voice, but slipped once at a dance when a fat teenager doing the Dashing White Sergeant with much vigour stepped back onto his foot and induced him to let out a most uncharacteristic yell of "booger."

Enough has been said about Jen Teale's refinement. All the main lower-middle genteelisms—"commence," "pardon," "serviette," "perfume," "gâteau," "toilet"—probably became currency to show off the speaker's familiarity with the French language. When it comes to "o" sounds, though, it is as if the English language had been deliberately invented to fox the Teales and the Nouveau-Richardses. In fact, I defy anyone to say the following list of words very fast three times without slipping: "Dolphin, dolt, doldrums, revolving, revolting, involved, holiday, hold, holly, whole, golf, gold." Class is a sort of sadistic *Histoire d'O*.

Mr. Nouveau-Richards packs Mrs. Nouveau-Richards and all his children off to elocution lessons when he becomes mayor, and takes a course in "public speaking." Mrs. Nouveau-Richards, opening the bring-and-buy sale, exhorts everyone to "give generously like what I have done." Mr. Nouveau-Richards ticks Jason off for talking too posh in the factory; it alienates the lads. "Sorry, Daddy," says Jason. "You shouldn't have sent me to such a good school."

Mrs. Definitely-Disgusting has a directness of speech not unlike Harry Stow-Crat's. She says "definitely" instead of "yes." Harry says "absolutely." She speaks in very short unfinished sentences, with a total disregard for syntax, and great use of conjunctions like

"so" and "but" and "like I said." Sentences are often left unfinished, she uses very few subordinate clauses, and punctuates with
words like: "Shame," "Just fancy," "Only natural, isn't it?" and
"Do you mind?" Statement and answer are often the same.

"I told you to hold on tight," she says.

"Why?" asks Dive.

"I told you to hold on tight, dint I?"

Dive often changes the first consonant and the final one—"I've
fort a' somefink" (I've thought of something)—and drops the middle one, as in "me-al" for "metal".

Mrs. Definitely-Disgusting is full of malapropisms. She's always
wanting to get up a "partition" or is "fumigating" with anger. She
also uses adjectives instead of adverbs. He cooks lovely, she dresses
fantastic. Because of her limited vocabulary she is likely to latch on
to a new adjective and flog it to death. The ghastly "caring" is
becoming a great favourite, with Express Dairies running a competition now to find your "caring" milkman.

Because Mrs. Definitely-Disgusting has received so many lectures from lefties on the dignity of the individual, she's quite keen
on the word "dignified" as the opposite to "common." When a
working-class girl played truant last April and posed naked on a
horse in the middle of Coventry, her mother said afterwards:
"Louise made a very dignified Godiva, we are not ashamed of her
showing her breasts, we are liberated parents."

One would have thought it was more the breasts that were
liberated.

Chapter 14

THE ARTS

Of all elite, the two that mix most easily are the aristocracy and the arts—Hamlet and the players—traditionally perhaps because they have the same bohemian disregard for other people's opinion and the same streak of exhibitionism. In the past, as we shall see later in this chapter, artists have been tragically dependent on the caprice of their rich patrons, but things have changed in the last century. Now successful writers, actors and singers no longer struggle, but are often far richer than the aristocrats. Mick Jagger now dines with Princess Margaret and has Patrick Lichfield as his best man. Elton John keeps his flat cap on throughout Prince Michael's speech because of a hair transplant he doesn't want anyone to see. And you even have a group of Etonians coming out of a punk concert nearly in tears saying, "We put safety pins in our ears, but they *still* don't like us."

The royal family have over the centuries been consistently resistant to the arts. George II hated all "boets" and "bainters." "Was there ever such stuff as Shakespeare?" asked George III. Although he did have a massive crush on Handel, and even re-wrote one of Dr. Burney's reviews of a Handel concert because it wasn't favourable enough.

Even today one has only to watch the jaws of the royal family absolutely dislocated with trying not to yawn at gala performances at Covent Garden. If you go to Buckingham Palace, you find red wallpaper flocked as in an Indian restaurant, pictures that all need cleaning and a band playing *South Pacific* and gems from *The White Horse Inn*. It is at this stage that someone always leaps to their defence and starts talking about Prince Charles's cello and Princess Margaret being a good mimic.

On the other hand, when one thinks of Lady Diana Cooper, Nigel Nicolson, Caroline Blackwood, Lord Ravensdale who, as Nicholas Mosley, writes novels, Lord Angelesey's military history, Lord Weymouth's murals and novels, the Sitwells, the Pakenhams, the Mitfords and many others one realizes that for a section of society that is statistically negligible the aristocracy have done pretty well for the arts recently.

The upper classes were traditionally patrons of the arts but because they have had their libraries and old masters and minstrels in the gallery for so long, like their gardens and houses, they tend to take the arts for granted. Unlike the middle classes—who today make up the audiences at the theatre, ballet and the opera, who tend to regard a knowledge of the arts and literature as a symbol of having got on.

In the same way, the lower middles who want to rise equate culture with the upper classes, and promptly start acquiring books, pictures and records. In the furnishing trade, bookshelves and record cabinets are actually categorised as "furniture for the better home." The more up-market the newspaper or magazine too, the more comprehensive the coverage of the arts.

Art

Crossing the threshold of Sotheby's one feels the sacred frisson, that special reverence evoked when great works of art and vast sums of money are changing hands. Of all the arts, painting is the smartest—because it involves the best-dressed people and the most money. Private views are far more frequently covered by the glossies than first-nights (which Jen Teale pronounces "preemiaires"), publishing parties or concerts. This may be because the best galleries are situated around Bond Street and Knightsbridge, only a stone's throw from the offices of *The Tatler*—and because all the elegant aesthetic young men with their greyhound figures and Harvey and Hudson shirts, who work in them, look aristocratic, even if they are not.

Caroline Stow-Crat often goes to private views when she's in London; it's nice to have a free drink and meet one's chums after an exhausting day in Harrods, and she likes bumping into all those old school friends of Harry's who in spite of being devastatingly handsome, somehow never got married. The upper classes, too, are very good at looking at paintings; they are able to keep their traps shut and whiz round galleries very fast. (Whereas Samantha Upward, brought up to fill gaps with conversation, can't repress a stream of "How lovely's.")

But what of the social standing of the painter himself? David Hockney is asked to the best parties, but "society is so constituted in England," wrote Samuel Rogers, "that it is useless for celebrated artists to think of bringing their families into the highest circle when they themselves are only admitted on account of their genius."

But even genius has to be tempered with charm. No one asked Hogarth to dine: he was the son of a tradesman. Sir Alfred Munnings, too, when he went to paint the Duchess of Westminster, had to eat in the kitchen.

Despite upper-class philistinism, it has always been a status symbol to have one's portrait painted to provide ancestors to be shown off by future generations. Elizabeth I epitomised royalty's attitude. There is no evidence that she had much taste for painting, said Horace Walpole drily, but she loved portraits of herself. Once a portrait painter became fashionable he went from one stately home to another, sucking up to duchesses—a sort of Toady at Toad Hall.

"I don't want to become a portrait manufacturer," sighed Hogarth. While Millais, succumbing to the inevitable tedium, admitted that the best bit was putting the shine on his subject's boots.

Harry Stow-Crat doesn't buy paintings—he inherits them.

Jeremy Maas, of the Maas Gallery, has a theory that art historians despise Victorian paintings and concentrate on Romneys and Gainsboroughs because this gives them access to grand houses, whereas the Victorian paintings are mostly owned by wool and steel manufacturers in the industrial North who are far less amusing to stay with.

Ballet

"I do not know anything about ballet, except that in the interval the ballerinas stink like horses," wrote Chekhov. Ever since then ballet has been prissying itself up, and has become a very lower-middle-class art, intensified by all those layers of tulle and the ballerinas walking around on tiptoe. Jen Teale loves "the ballet": all those good tunes, and something undemanding to look at.

"Have we come for the dancing or the singing?" Mr. Nouveau-Richards was overheard saying to his wife as they arrived at Covent Garden on the firm's tickets.

A recent survey of ballet audiences broke them down as 61 per cent upper-middle-class males, 19 per cent middle-class, 15 per cent lower-middles and only 5 per cent working-class, who presumably are the rough trade accompanying the upper-middle homosexuals.

Occasionally Covent Garden has gala nights, which Jen Teale pronounces "gay-la," presumably because of the number of homosexuals present. The effeminate appearance of the men puts off Harry Stow-Crat and the Definitely-Disgustings alike. "Pouffe's Football," Old Steptoe called ballet dismissively.

Actors

Until recently thespians were not considered respectable. A gentleman might go to bed with an actress and shower her with presents, but he did not make an honest women of her, and although a few aristocrats married Gaiety Girls, the parental opposition was stiff enough to discourage most Mrs. Worthingtons from putting their daughters on the stage.

Since the advent of the talkies, and even more so of television, things have changed. Acting is one of the most popular professions for girls from public school, and actors and actresses get lionised out of proportion to any other artists. (When Kurt Jurgens gets half a million for a coffee commercial it's hard to ignore him.)

Caroline Stow-Crat, however, still regards the show-business world with a mixture of excitement and horror. I remember a debs' mums' lunch at which they were discussing whether they could entice Georgia Brown or Paul McCartney to sing at some charity ball: "Anyway, Elizabeth can look after whoever it is," said the chairman. "She's *so* good with those sort of people."

The upper middle classes who, apart from homosexuals and the coach trade, are the only consistent patrons, tend to go to the theatre for a good sleep, but sometimes they manage to wake up for the last scene. Evidently when Chichester staged *Vivat Regina* some years ago, at the end when Elizabeth and Mary stalk out of opposite corners of the stage, Mary to be beheaded, one Tory lady was heard turning to another and saying: "That's exactly what happened to Monica."

Actors and actresses, although the good ones can adjust their accents to cross most class barriers, seldom appear upper-class because they are too self-conscious, too theatrical, too expansive of gesture and mobile of feature. Their diction is also far too good— the upper classes would never say "yee-eers" or "how-ers" for "years" and "hours." Actresses do this to make their parts longer.

Mrs. Nouveau-Richards loves "to do a show in town," and rustles a box of milk chocolates through the entire performance.

Literature

Like the actor, the professional writer wasn't always socially acceptable. The Elizabethans considered poetry, dancing and playing an instrument the sort of accomplishment rather like sex, which you did in the privacy of your own home but never for money.

Lady Mary Wortley Montagu said that it was contemptible to

write for money, and even in the nineteenth century Flaubert attacked the practice—though admittedly from the security of a large private income.

It was only in the middle of the nineteenth century, as Frank Muir has pointed out, that the habit of reading spread down the classes and became wildly fashionable, in a very minor way like television today. Another interesting point is that reviewers, bitterly opposed to emergent lower-middle-class writers, savagely attacked Keats for not being a gentleman and belonging with Leigh Hunt to what was derisively called the "cockney" school. "Cockney" in those days didn't mean working class but "genteel suburban." It is hardly surprising that Byron and Shelley, as very nouveau aristocracy (Byron inherited the title from a great-uncle, Shelley's grandfather managed to marry two heiresses), should initially attack Keats's poetry, not only because he was beneath them socially but, more dangerous, because he looked suspiciously like a far greater poet. Once Keats was dead he was no more competition, and it was much easier for Byron to leap to his defence in "Who Killed John Keats?" and for Shelley to write his elegy, "Adonais."

Recently a reviewer expressed amazement that Thomas Hardy could be simultaneously such a towering genius and such a raging mean-minded snob. But this seems quite logical. Any English novelist, if he is to draw characters with any accuracy, must be aware of the minutest social nuance. Most English writers, in fact, have been frightfully snobbish. All Shakespeare's heroes and heroines are upper class. Any working-class characters were just introduced to provide comic relief. "It's very tiring playing Shakespeare," grumbled one actress. "You only get to sit down if you're a king."

Pope always pretended to be related to the Earl of Down. Jane Austen was probably so obsessed with class because on one side she was related to an earl, but on the other side to a haberdasher.

Even today, a critic grumbled, the thing wrong with English writers is that they'd rather dine with a duke than with other writers, a sentiment echoed by Nancy Mitford's comment on Evelyn Waugh: "I feel he is all right with duchesses. It is the middle-class intellectuals who come in for the full bloodyness of his invective."

"If you stay with the Queen at Sandringham," according to Robert Lacey, "you will find an electric fire with three bars in your room, a fitted carpet, naval paintings on the wall and huge bookcases filled with regimental histories and army lists. But there are also more contemporary books put out for guests—Hornblower yarns and Nancy Mitford—all with the same simple book plate inside, 'The Queen's Book' in flowing white script which stands out of a black background." If an author goes to Windsor, he is likely after dinner to see his latest book laid out on a table in the library on a blue satin cushion. The Queen Mother is a Dick Francis addict, and is always presented with a copy on publication day.

Harry Stow-Crat reads *The Times,* the *Sporting Life* and the *Daily Express:* he has a soft spot for that Rook Woman. Caroline reads *The Tatler,* whose book reviews epitomise upper-class taste: a recent issue included a Standard Guide to Pure Breed Dogs, a book on heraldry, a history of the Isle of Orkney and a biography of the Pekinese.

Samantha Upward is a great reader; she also feels it her duty to buy books. She is very guilty about reading popular novels and thinks biographies are somehow more worthwhile. Virginia Woolf's letters (in fact anything about the Bloomsbury group) are ideal because they combine sex and culture. Samantha knows that literature is all about disadvantaged people struggling to make ends meet, so she would never admit to anyone that she finds Bertold Brecht a king-sized yawn. She always asks "creative writers," as she calls them, what they are "working on," but she'd *never* make the mistake of telling them she'd love to write a book if only she had the time. The Weybridge set buy "real coffee"-table books.

Jen Teale prefers to read home-improvement books, which she always wraps in brown paper, so the cover won't get "soiled." Bryan's home-library of do-it-yourself manuals and Reader's Digest condensed books are practically pushing the carved wise-owl book-ends off the colour telly.

Mrs. Nouveau-Richards is struggling with the first volume of "Prowst." Copying upper-class French mothers, she has stopped going upstairs every evening to kiss Tracey-Diane goodnight.

Music

There was one peer who only employed butlers who could play the piano in the key of C. He didn't give a damn if they could buttle, he merely wanted someone to accompany him when he played on the mouth organ. He, however, was the exception. Although Harry Stow-Crat sets a good example by singing loudly in church on Sundays, he is actually tone-deaf. His children sometimes learn an instrument at school, which is called "extras" and grumbled about when it appears on the bill.

Occasionally *The Tatler* cover a concert, but it's invariably for charity, some flaring-nostrilled Peruvian playing Chopin in aid of Father Mantua's mission in the East End, and all the audience surreptitiously looking at their watches, and wishing the still fat wad of pages the pianist still has to strum through would suddenly get thinner. Audiences, however, are much better mannered than they used to be. In the past musicians or minstrels just provided wallpaper music, a kind of Musak against which the audience laughed and talked. A good minstrel, of course, was part of an aristocratic household. Frank Muir suggests that William the Conqueror was so fond of his bard Taillefeau that he allowed him to strike the first blow at the Battle of Hastings. According to legend Taillefeau advanced up the beach singing ballads about Charlemagne, and was promptly struck dead by an enemy arrow. One suspects that if William had been that keen on his carolling, he wouldn't have exposed him to such danger.

Later of course there were fashionable musicians like Paganini who were very well paid and fawned on by aristocratic groupies. Liszt, in fact, was the first Beatle: society women brought special tweezers so they could pluck out his hair, and after a concert would fight for a fragment of the cushion he'd sat on. Kreisler was once asked to play by a fashionable but nouveau-riche American hostess. She would pay him 750 dollars, she said, but after the concert she didn't want him to mingle with her guests, in case he lowered the tone.

"In that case," replied Kreisler gravely, "the bill will only be 500 dollars."

In England music was traditionally only respected if it was imported. Italian castrati charged a fortune in the eighteenth century to give concerts to the rich and noble. The middle classes, it seems, had to make do with a lady from the local opera house.

"I detest these scented rooms," wrote Coleridge, "where to a gaudy throng, the proud harlot heaves her distended breast in intricacies of laborious song."

Opera, it appears, was something to be endured. The audience played draughts during the recitatives, and merely looked in for one act to be seen, to show off their jewels, and gossip. When a very grand but garrulous hostess asked Charles Haas, Proust's model for Swann, to sit in her box, he replied: "I'd love to. I've never heard you in *Faust.*"

Today the upper middle classes, liking their opera sugar-coated, regard Glyndebourne as the smart thing to do. They particularly enjoy picnicking with other middle-class people and writing down the names of the more attractive herbaceous plants in the garden on their programme. Today the only people who can afford Covent Garden are foreign diplomats, homosexuals and Samantha Upward's maiden aunts with plaits round their heads, referring to the singers by their surnames like prep school boys: "Isn't Sutherland too marvellously in voice?" There is always a mile-long queue for the loo in the interval, while all those Samantha Upwards who pretend to know the opera backwards mug up on the synopsis for the next act.

Mozart, Haydn, Vivaldi and Purcell are upper-class composers. Brahms, Mahler, Schubert and Beethoven are upper middle. Tchaikovsky, Grieg and Mendelssohn are lower middle.

Samantha would simply love to sing in the Bach choir. Her mother adores Gilbert and Sullivan. Howard Weybridge has a few classical records, *Peer Gynt,* the Moonlight Sonata and "Cav-and-Pack-them-in." He is also "very active" in amateur operatics. Jen Teale enjoys *Your 100 Best Tunes.*

Mr. Nouveau-Richards likes the cuckoo in the Pastoral Symphony and claps between movements. Tracey-Diane sways from side to side when she plays "The Lost Chord" on the pianola. Mrs. Definitely-Disgusting likes Mantovani and thinks Verdi's Requiem is a "resteront."

Television

Why did you choose such a backward time and such a strange land?
If you'd come today, you'd have reached a whole nation.
Israel in 4 B.C. had no mass communication.

Jesus Christ Superstar

Light-years above everyone else are the telly-stocracy. "When I go to the country," said Reginald Bosanquet, one of Independent television's most famous and individualistic newsmen, "I am more revered than the Queen."

"Every time Angela Rippon appears on television," confided a salesgirl, "we get people pouring in here trying to buy what she was wearing."

It's not just the telly-stocracy. Everyone who appears on television is somehow sanctified, albeit temporarily, with a square halo. It doesn't matter how inept one is, credit improves dramatically in the High Street. If ever I appear, my enemies in the council houses, who usually shake their fists at me because of my warring dogs, start waving and saying, "Saw you last night!"

Our particular part of Putney is known locally as "Media Gulch" because so many television stars, actors and journalists live here. You can only keep your end up, in fact, if you have the television vans outside your house at least once every two months, plus a gutted bus where all the crew retire every couple of hours for something to eat and hordes of men with prematurely grey hair and he-tan saying "Right" are draping plastic Virginia creeper over the porch to give an illusion of spring.

But apart from creating a new telly-stocracy, the looming presence of television has done more to change our social habits than anyone realises. When commercial television appeared in the sixties, it was hailed by Lord Thomson as the great leveller. Everyone could afford it. As a new and exciting medium, it seemed to epitomise the change from a rigid class system. In fact, it has enforced the divisions. Every day twenty-three million pairs of eyes stay glued to the commercial television screen. Advertising in particular makes people dissatisfied with life; the initial effect is to encourage them to go out and buy consumer goods formerly enjoyed by their social superiors. As they achieve these, and feel themselves to be going up in the world, television becomes their social adviser. It tells them where to go on their holidays, what car they should own, which wines to order, the appropriate fuel to burn, what furniture to buy.

Even more pernicious, television gives lots of advice on attitude and behaviour. Mrs. Definitely-Disgusting doesn't hit the roof any more every time Dive and Sharon come charging in with mud all over their newly washed jeans. She gives a crooked smile and reaches for the Daz. She feels guilty if her kitchen isn't spotless, and discontented if it isn't a modern one. If a horde of children drop in she doesn't tell them to bugger off, she fills them up with beefburgers.

Television has also created a new type of plastic family: smiling squeezy mums; woolly-hatted dads playing football and crumbling Oxo cubes; plastic dogs leaping in the air; plastic children stuffing baked beans; lovable plastic grans who are befriended by pretty air hostesses but are never sick. Why aren't we as happy as they are? thinks Mrs. Definitely-Disgusting. It isn't fair.

Television increases aspiration, but underlines the differences and has reinforced a strong Them and Us polarisation. Mr. Definitely-Disgusting can pile up goods till he's black and blue in the face, but it's still difficult for him to improve his status, cross the great manual/non-manual divide and join the martini set.

Television has created a battered victim, rendered insensible by a ceaseless bombardment of mindless hypocrisy. It is hardly surprising that so many children can't read or write, that few people can be seen in the streets of towns or villages after dark. The nation is plugged in. They are watching Big Brother.

Television forms the basis of nearly all conversations in offices and pubs. (A friend spent a week at a large holiday camp on advertising research and said people talked permanently in television jingles, one person beginning one, the next ending it.) Worse still is the effect on debate and argument; because of the law that requires television to be politically fair, all arguments end in compromises not in conclusions.

It is not just the lower classes who are hooked. The Queen is alleged to watch television to find out about her subjects down the hierarchy. One suspects she's an addict like the rest of us. Princess Margaret is also reputed to be an avid television viewer. A friend went to dinner when she was married to Lord Snowdon and the television stayed on the whole time before dinner, was carried into the dining-room and placed on the table on which they were eating, then carried back into the drawing-room immediately they'd finished.

Evidently, the whole royal family was livid about the spate of royal sagas, particularly *Edward and Mrs. Simpson.* Not because the events portrayed were so sensational, but because the actors playing themselves or their relations were, they considered, so common.

But half the fun of television is looking for the slip-ups. Recently when Thames serialized one of my novels they got the classes quite cockeyed. It was supposed to be about the Scottish upper classes, but almost the first shot was of a wedding cake with a plastic bride and groom on top. The hero kept calling the heroine "woman"; the heroine returned from her honeymoon landing on a Western Isle wearing a hat and high heels, and everyone waved their arms frantically in the air during reels at a ball.

Rebecca, on B.B.C. 2 recently, almost got it right. The only time they appeared to slip was when Maxim talked about "Cook," and when some very unpatrician extras appeared in the ball.

"It's impossible to make extras behave with any authority," said one of the cast. "They always look as though they'd got their costumes from Moss Brothers."

Chapter 15

SPORTS
AND PASTIMES

In the last fifty years there has been a complete revolution in sport throughout the world. This is particularly noticeable in England and can be directly attributed to the influence of two world wars and more generally to the advent of wireless and television. More evenly distributed affluence has created more time for "leisure," and whilst we have become more a nation of spectators than participators, less fashionable games and pastimes have through their exposure on the media led to a much more varied participating pattern across the classes.

The aristocracy seldom indulged in such games as football, cricket or hockey. Sport to them has always been closely linked either to survival—i.e. hunting, shooting and fishing—or to gambling, hence their traditional addiction to racing.

It was left to the middle classes, working through the medium of the public schools, aided and abetted by the church, who thought that violent athletic activity took boys' minds off masturbation, to champion the noble art of self-defence and later rugby football and soccer and "organised games." It should not be forgotten that one of the first Association Football clubs founded in this country were the Corinthians: a team of gentlemen. Team games which emphasised the manly virtues and social solidarity led naturally to the creation of exclusive clubs—almost a defensive movement. This sort of coagulation has always been peculiar to the

English—look at the regimental system of the army. Although this goes back much further, the values are the same. Never let the man next to you see you are afraid, and never let the side down: "Play up and play the game."

The social history of cricket is very complicated. It began as a peasant pastime, was only later taken up by the gentry and, today, with all the posturing and cuddling at the fall of a wicket that occur during a Test match, is fast going back to the peasants again. Exactly the opposite happened with rugger, which began as an upper-middle-class pursuit, was then taken up by grammar and then comprehensive schools and ended with the ultimate peasant adaptation of Rugby League.

One only needs to go to the University Rugger Match or any home international at Twickenham, "the last fortress of the For-sytes," as Christopher Laidlaw called it, to see the English middle classes in all their glory, and to realise that when the crowd howl for England they are really howling for the middle classes and the survival of middle-class values.

Today probably the only really smart game left is real tennis (royal tennis), possibly because there are so few courts. Hunting is no longer smart but bristling with Mr. Nouveau-Richardses and television stars. The Welsh miner in a red coat is no more an isolated phenomenon.

Fishing is not a sport either, although numbers of the lower classes who indulge in coarse fishing would argue that it is. Harry Stow-Crat has a beat on the Tay, but the fishing on either side is owned by Arabs and stockbrokers. Samantha goes to the fishmonger's, the Cousteau-Richardses go deep-sea fishing off Looe. Mr. Definitely-Disgusting sits all day under a green umbrella on the edge of a gravel pit catching inch-long roaches and throwing them back.

Harry Stow-Crat doesn't take much exercise. He plays billiards (not a sport), chemmy, backgammon (bridge is too difficult), polo, and might have rowed at school. He seldom rows after leaving university; that is left to the working-class clubs. He sometimes

hunts and takes a packet of pheasant sandwiches. He plays fives at
school and perhaps racquets, and occasionally tennis at weekends
and croquet (which he pronounces *"cro'*ky," not *"cro-kay"* as
Howard Weybridge would). He would never be seen dead on a golf
(which he pronounces "goff") course, and would soon be dead in
a squash court. He would never never jog.

Gideon Upward plays squash, tennis, cricket, rugger until he is
thirty ("Had to give up because of my knee")—never hockey,
which he regards as common and only played by minor public
schools, Indians and fat-bottomed female clerks from Barclays
Bank and fat-breasted female clerks from Lloyds Bank.

Howard Weybridge has a "Support Surrey Rugby" sticker in
the back of his car and enjoys "a few jars" at Esher Rugby Club.
He also plays "gole-f" if he can find room at Sunningdale alongside
all the bank managers playing against other bank managers, and
spiralists playing with their bosses and letting them win after a
tough fight.

Although they now allow the pro to drink in the bar, it is
evidently quite difficult to get into the Royal Berkshire or Sunningdale golf clubs. You have to be proposed and seconded by members
who've known you for a considerable time, fill in a form stating
your profession and where you went to school, and then get letters
of approval from between six and eight members saying you're the
right sort of person. At Sunningdale you actually have to play in
front of the management committee to prove you're good enough.

"What happens if a nice bricklayer wants to join the club?" I
asked the secretary at the Royal Berkshire.

"Well, it would be most unlikely," he said. "How could he
possibly know six of our members?"

Bryan Teale is too busy with "home improvements" and tinker-
ing with the Volkswagen to play with anything but himself. His
father plays bowls.

Mr. Definitely-Disgusting never does anything much out of
doors except kick balls against the factory wall during tea breaks.
He watches television all the time when he's not going to the dogs

or matches on Saturday afternoons or filling in his football coupons and placing bets. Harry Stow-Crat always pays his bookie before his tailor because it's a debt of honour. At the pub, Mr. Definitely-Disgusting plays darts, snooker and dominoes.

Horses

The horse was one of the first status symbols; like the car, it gave its owner mobility. Originally the upper classes were the only people who could afford horses, and many aristocratic titles come from riding, the French "Chevalier," for example, the German "Ritter," meaning rider, and the English Cavaliers. Sitting on a horse also enables you to look down on your fellow men. Horsy people invariably have that deadpan look one associates with the aristocracy.

Horses have always been a good way up the social ladder, as Mark Phillips recently showed us. In the nineteenth century the Rothschilds were accepted into the grandest Victorian society because the Prince of Wales was at Cambridge with Nathaniel Rothschild and shared his interest in racing.

Today show-jumping stars get asked to Princess Anne's pre-wedding ball and the livery stables are full of expensive horses acquired as status symbols by pop stars and actors who are too frightened to ride them.

Mr. Nouveau-Richards buys polo ponies, takes up hunting, slaps point-to-point stickers on the back window of his car and, even if he doesn't ride himself, struts around at local gymkhanas in breeches, having frightful rows with the collecting ring stewards and the judges when they don't put Tracey-Diane first.

Samantha Upward's father, like many another retired army colonel or brigadier, often finds an interest running the local pony club and bossing nubile little girls about. Competition is as fierce between the little girls as it is between the guns out shooting. There was fearsome grumbling at the local Putney show a few years ago because they all thought the jump in the Working Pony Class had been specially lowered for Princess Alexandra's daughter.

Harry Stow-Crat has his breeches made for him, and pays about £200 for black leather boots which have a garter strap that attaches to buttons on his breeches and keeps the boots up and the breeches down. Georgie Stow-Crat, however, who's feeling the pinch, has brought a pair of rubber boots so well made as to be indistinguishable from leather ones. Even he wouldn't resort to the stretch nylon breeches which show your pants worn by Mr. Nouveau-Richards. Georgie wears brown boots for polo and laced boots if he's in the cavalry.

When Mr. Nouveau-Richards goes out hunting he wears an ordinary white tie, instead of a stock, with his unauthorised red coat —like the show jumpers do on television—and carries his hunting whip upside down without a thong. Tracey-Diane looks like an advertisement in the back pages of a riding magazine. She wears thick eye make-up, dangling earrings and loose blonde locks flowing out from her black cap. Mr. Nouveau-Richards tells everyone she is "a marvellous horsewoman." Harry would say "a very good rider." Howard Weybridge calls it "horse riding" or "horse-back riding."

Samantha Upward carefully talks about "hounds with their 'waving sterns,' and 'pink' coats." She is rather shocked when Harry refers to "red" coats. Far too many nouveaus have started talking about "pink," so the upper class have reverted to "red." Harry also says his horse is "lame," whereas Howard Weybridge says his "mount" is "limping." Howard says: "I was thrown from the horse, which was very frisky."

Harry says: "My horse was too fresh and bucked me off/gave me a fall/I fell off."

Howard says his horse "jibbed at a hedge." Harry would say it "put in a stop" or "refused at a fence."

Howard's horse "gets the bit between the teeth." Harry would say: "It took off with me" or "ran away" or "I was carted."

Howard's horse "keeps rearing"; Harry's horse "goes up with him."

Shooting

"Hunting," wrote Bishop Latimer in 1820, "is a good exercise for a man of rank, but shooting is amusement equally lawful and proper for inferior persons."

Yet three-quarters of a century later shooting was the way in which the great landowners entertained their guests throughout the winter months.

The railway helped, as Jonathan Ruffer points out in *The Big Shots*, "so did technical improvements of the gun. You now combined the opportunities of a Vimy Ridge machine gunner with an infinitely better lunch. And finally, because Edward VII was too fat to hunt, he channelled all his enthusiasms into shooting—and it was natural that society should exert itself in pursuits which its champion made fashionable."

Edward VII kept all the clocks half an hour early so he got extra time shooting in the winter. Today people are just as keen. A friend of mine once asked the Macnab of Macnab, who's a brilliant shot, whether he really needed a secretary three days a week. "Of course I do," replied the Macnab indignantly. "Every day I have to write letters saying: 'Dear Charles, thank you for asking me to shoot on the fourth, I'm afraid I can't make it,' or 'Dear Henry, thank you very much for asking me to shoot on the eighteenth, I should be happy to accept.'"

All through the winter in Scotland and the North of England, in anticipation of the coming season, white plumes rise like smoke signals from various hills where the heather is being burned. It's all anyone talks about at upper-class dinner parties. If you're not careful you can burn a whole moor. (Harry Stow-Crat pronounces it "maw"; the middle classes call in "maw-er.")

At Sandringham and Balmoral, Robert Lacey wrote in *Majesty*, day-long shooting sorties take on the character of a military manoeuvre, with shooting brakes, vans full of beaters drawn by a tractor, and Land-Rovers which you clamber into, possibly to find the Queen sitting next to you.

Prince Philip is one of the best shots in the country, which means the world. Prince Charles, it seems, is all set to overtake him.

As soon as people start doing well in business, they take up shooting, and photographs of themselves knee deep in the bracken beside a grinning Labrador with its mouth full of feathers are placed on top of the piano. But the pitfalls are great for the unwary. Mr. Nouveau-Richards has no idea what to tip the loader, and keeps shooting his host's grouse, rather like poor Charles Clore asking a neighbouring gun if his loader could join them for lunch.

"Whatever for?" said the gun sarcastically. "Is he teaching you to eat as well?"

It is very smart to drink sloe gin at lunchtime but social death to turn up in gold boots and a shocking pink fun fur and talk throughout every drive, like Mrs. Nouveau-Richards.

Despite the Freudian terminology of shooting handbooks—all that talk about "pricked birds," "cocks only" days and "premature gun mounting"—women are expected to keep very much in the background. Their duty is to provide a good lunch, keep an eye on the dogs and occasionally load. "After August twelfth," sighed one Edwardian beauty, "wives and mistresses don't exist."

The exception was one Spanish prince who turned up to shoot in Yorkshire with a ravishing mistress, and missed everything he shot at on the first two drives. Bumping along in the Land-Rover to the third drive, the keeper heard scufflings and, looking round, saw the prince and his mistress humping away on a mattress of slaughtered grouse. After that he shot brilliantly.

Chapter 16

DOGS

"I can get on perfectly well with the people my children marry," said one aristocratic old woman. "What I find difficult is dogs-in-law." She was talking about the troops of Tibetan spaniels, dachshunds and fat irascible terriers who join the family circle with a new daughter-in-law.

The upper classes, of course, adore their dogs. In the country they usually have at least five (the way Catholics do with issue). The dogs coat the furniture with hairs and wipe their faces on the chair covers, and most of them sleep in the bedroom. (Sir Sacheverell Sitwell's Cavalier King Charles spaniels have a turquoise drinking bowl to match the bedroom wallpaper.) Their portraits hang under picture lights. Most of them are incontinent, but no one seems to mind very much. Randolph Churchill was once heard bawling out his dog for peeing on the sofa: "Get off, Boycott, you know you're only allowed to do it on the carpet."

Another old duke was absolutely devoted to a foul terrier called Spot, who was rotund, blind, incontinent, bit everyone and was over twenty. Finally, under extreme family pressure, the duke agreed to take the dog out and shoot it. Tears pouring down his face, he and Spot set out into the twilight. The family waited in anticipation, and jumped out of their skins when ten minutes later there was a feeble clawing on the door. It was Spot wanting to be let in. At the prospect of having to kill him the duke had had a heart attack. Spot lived on for several more years.

Walk through any upper-class garden and in a quiet shady

corner you will find a lot of little crosses marking the dogs' grave-yard. One I know in Lancashire includes a favourite parrot buried in a cake tin. A small tombstone in Sandringham bears the inscrip-tion: "To the Queen's faithful friend Susan."

On the whole, the upper classes prefer what they call "working dogs"—Labradors "to shoot over" (they never shoot "with" them), and Jack Russells, Norfolk or Hunt terriers, ostensibly to dig "Charlie" (as they call the fox) out, although they never do. Black Labradors are much grander than yellow, and are quite often in-vited without their owners to shoot in Scotland, and travel up quite happily on the train. Another Labrador came all the way down to London from Northumberland to be mated. The owner of the bitch booked a room overnight at the Turf Club (presumably in the name of "Mr. and Mrs. Smith"). Eight puppies resulted. The owner of a stately home once told me he had terrible trouble when members of the visiting public stretched out asleep on the grass in summer, because his Labrador always goes and lifts his leg on any bald head.

King Charles spaniels are very upper-class dogs. So are whip-pets, springer spaniels, pekes, dachsies, particularly long-haired ones. Hounds are never kept as pets, but "walked" as puppies in the summer. Upper-class dogs often have two addresses on their collars: one for London and another for the country. On the label should be engraved the owner's surname, address and telephone number. It is very vulgar to put the dog's Christian name in inverted commas, and to have anything other than brown leather collars. Tartan collars for Scotties or West Highland terriers and diamanté for poodles are also out. So are red barrels on the collar or red bows on long-haired dogs or topiary on poodles.

Upper-class dogs have only one meal a day and are therefore quite thin, like their owners. Snipe Stow-Crat is so well trained he doesn't need a collar or lead at all. (Jen Teale would say "leash." Mr. Definitely-Disgusting uses string and calls his puppy a "pup." He also talks about "pooches.")

It is very lower-middle to be frightened of dogs, or to go into queeny hysterics whenever a dog lifts its leg on your garden fence. Upper-middle dog owners are almost keener on them than the aristocracy. They don't have so many, so the affection is not divided and they don't keep them for working but to talk to and through. Colonel and Mrs. Upward address each other through their Dalmatian. Their daughter-in-law, Samantha, has an evening bag lined with congealed fat from bringing home chops and bits of steak for Blucher, her English setter. Dogs belonging to the upper-middle merry-tocracy always reek of garlic from having doggy-bag pork chops or chicken à la Kiev posted through the door to stop them barking and waking the nanny when their owners return home too drunk from restaurants to find their keys.

Dalmatians, English setters, cairns, golden retrievers are upper-middle-class dogs. The upper middles have also recently taken to foreign breeds—Weimeraners and Rottweilers—because the classes below can't pronounce them. Old English sheep dogs used to be upper middle but have lost caste since they appeared so often on television advertising paint.

Howard Weybridge likes Airedales and rough-haired terriers, Great Danes and Irish wolfhounds. They look so heraldic loping through the pine woods of Surrey. He also likes Irish setters and cocker spaniels.

Mrs. Nouveau-Richards loves Yorkshire terriers and poodles and all the show-off dogs like collies and Afghans.

Bryan Teale likes Dobermans and boxers because they don't shed hairs. Jen Teale hates dogs because they're so smelly.

Mr. Definitely-Disgusting belongs to the *Daily Mirror* Pets Club and loves all "pooches." But he's particularly partial to "Westies," as he calls West Highlands, and Alsatians because they're such good guard dogs. And of course you can't beat a good mongrel (though he frequently does). Mongrels (Mr. Definitely-Disgusting pronounces the first syllable to rhyme with "long," and Harry Stow-Crat, to rhyme with "dung") are sometimes called "street dogs," or "butcher's dogs," because they used to follow the butcher's van.

Nigel Dempster, in a recent piece on "In and Out" trends, said that mongrels from Battersea were very "In." On the whole, the upper classes don't approve of mongrels. I always pretend mine are lurchers when I go anywhere smart. Caroline Stow-Crat would swallow, then cover up her disapproval by saying: "But they're supposed to be awfully intelligent and loyal."

More pointed contempt was shown by a lower-middle woman who ran some boarding kennels. I'd sent my mongrel bitch there when she came on heat (Jen Teale would say "in season") because I didn't want her father, whom we also own, to get her pregnant. Unfortunately, it seemed we were too late. Ten days later the kennel owner rang up: "It's disgraceful," she snapped, "bringing cross-breeds into the world when there aren't enough homes for breed dogs. Why don't you have the father carstrated?" Harry Stow-Crat would never castrate a dog; it would be against his male-chauvinist principles.

It is pretty unsmart to show your dogs—rather like going in for a beauty contest—and also to enter your guard dog for what are called "o-bedience" tests.

Jen Teale talks about "veterinary surgeons" instead of "vets," and "lady dogs" instead of "bitches." Mrs. Nouveau-Richards talks about "doggies" and "pups."

Recently the paper reported that a Mr. Nouveau-Richards paid £100 for what he thought was a pedigree Labrador puppy for Tracey-Diane and it turned out to be a hamster.

Upper-class dogs have simple names like Badger, Ranger and Bertie. The middle class, however, are madly into the Victorian names which the upper middles were calling their children ten years ago: Emma, Jessica, Fanny, Cassandra, Sophie, Jason, and funny-ha-ha names like Wellington, Melchester, or Ugly for a pug.

The working classes either name their dogs according to their appearance—Spot, Blackie, Patch, Snowy—or try and upgrade them with names like Lady and Duchess. On Eel Brook Common at night it sounds like a mediaeval roll-call, with cries of "Rex," "Prince," "Duke" echoing plaintively through the darkening mist.

The upper classes don't like cats as much as dogs and tend only to keep them in the stables to keep the rats down. The more well-bred a cat, usually the more common the owner.

Mrs. Definitely-Disgusting refers to her cat as "Pussy"—e.g. "A neighbour took Pussy when I went on holiday."

Chapter 17

RELIGION

Frequent church-going becomes markedly less likely as one goes down the social scale. The upper classes regard it as a patriotic duty to set an example and go every Sunday, quite often to their own church, where they can have their own pew. As Douglas Sutherland has pointed out, the English gentleman knows that God believes in him; it is his duty in return to believe in God. He often reads the lesson, sings loudly but out of tune and tells the vicar to speak up if he can't hear the sermon. In return, his church expects financial support. The Queen always gives £1 to the collection.

Harry would never drive his Rolls-Royce on Sunday, because that day he goes to church. He only takes the Rolls on long journeys.

The Church of England is predominantly the church of the upper and middle classes. You find that the middle classes hog all the places on the parish council, act as sidesmen and churchwardens, while their wives, with their large well-stocked gardens, are responsible for the flowers in church and run fetes and jumble sales. The working classes feel intimidated and left out.

It's very vulgar to call a vicar "Vicar" to his face, rather like "Doctor" and "Teacher." You should call him "Mr. Upward" or whatever his surname is. If he's a canon you could call him "Canon Stow-Crat." On letters he should be addressed as "The Rev. Francis Stow-Crat," never "Rev. Francis Stow-Crat" or "The Rev. Stow-Crat." Despite its apparent social disdain of the working classes, the Anglican Church, since the introduction of the New English Bible, is getting more folksy and vulgar every day. We now have "Mother's Day" instead of "Mothering Sunday," to get it as far away from a church ritual as possible, and instead of a "Harvest Festival" we have "Harvest Home" or "Harvest Supper." In the towns they have plastic fruit, and lots of children arriving with apples on plastic trays. My sister-in-law in the country was asked to "bake a harvest pie for the harvest home." This is apparently another name for a quiche. If she wasn't up to a harvest pie, said the parish worker, a basket of provender would be very acceptable. Evidently the main excitement was some boys who were coming over from Uppingham to sing in the choir.

Next morning my sister-in-law's cleaning woman came in panting and puffing; she wasn't going to make a harvest pie for them foreigners, she said, and what's more she didn't like the vicar.

Any significance Easter may have had for the masses has disappeared under a mass of over-priced chocolate and Easter Bunny. And nothing can equal the spate of vulgarity which pours forth at Christmas, burying the country under a commercial avalanche of heavenly babes, yule logs, Santa and his reindeer crew, festive robins, jolly cardinals and seasonal cheer.

The Stow-Crats have a real Christmas tree from their moor in Scotland; it touches the ceiling and is decorated with candles and ancient peeling baubles. Snipe has a large mutton bone as a present, and Harry's few remaining tenants and estate servants shuffle in to collect their hams and turkeys and have a drink. In Putney we're lucky, too, because the children of our local telly-stocrat produce a pantomime for us.

Samantha's parents and Gideon's parents take it in turns to go and stay with Samantha and Gideon at Christmas. "Don't they realise you're working?" Gideon says furiously to Samantha every year. What he really minds about is not being able to drink himself stupid in front of his in-laws, and because Christmas goes on for so long he won't have a chance to see the secretary he fancies for at least ten days. Christmas staying with in-laws is invariably a nightmare—not enough to drink and Thalia breaks the crib Virgin Mary on Boxing Day. No one fights openly, but a muscle is going in both Samantha's and Mrs. Upward's face on the last day.

Gideon doesn't kick up too much because he knows Samantha's father is going to give him £500 to pay the school fees. (The middle class often use Christmas to hand over money, so the recipient won't feel any loss of independence.) In revenge, Colonel and Mrs. Upward take Zacharias and Thalia to the pantomime, where all over the theatre you will hear grandparents making cracks against their daughters-in-law.

"You would have had much better seats and been able to see, Thalia darling, if Mummy hadn't been so awfully vague about dates."

Samantha would have a real Christmas tree, and she would prefer candles, but as a result of pressure from Zacharias, and worry about the fire risk, she has this year stuck to fairy lights. She insists on Thalia and Zacharias writing thank-you letters to show how good their hand-writing is. She and Gideon always get glasses as presents to make up for all the ones smashed during the year.

Mrs. Nouveau-Richards has a vast silver plastic Christmas tree, groaning with tinsel and flashing lights. Jen Teale insists on a plastic tree too this year; she had to get last year's tree out by Boxing Day because it was moulting pine needles so badly. She hangs the Christmas cards from string across the lounge to avoid dust. Samantha regards Christmas cards as a marvellous excuse not to dust.

Christmas cards are a great class indicator in themselves. The higher classes like simple words inside like: "With best wishes for Christmas and the New Year" or "A Merry Christmas and a Happy New Year." If they have special cards printed, they only put their address at the bottom, and write in their Christian names, or their Christian names and surnames to those they know less well. The Weybridges have "Howard and Eileen Weybridge" printed as well, and cross out the "Weybridge" for their "very good friends." The Nouveau-Richardses have a very large card with a picture of jolly cardinals quaffing indifferent claret in front of a roaring fire, and a lovely poem about festive cheer, and "Hearty Xmas Greetings," plus their name and address in red loopy spangled writing inside. Jison, as a member of the telly-stocracy, often puts "Yours Aye" or "Sincerely Your Jason Richards" on his cards, which are usually of Santa with a red nose. Harry Stow-Crat would write "Love," particularly if he were writing to a girl. (He would say "Father Christmas" rather than "Santa Claus" or "Santa.")

The spiralists have a photograph of themselves and their family on the front of their Christmas cards, with a bigger and bigger house in the background as the years go by.

It is extremely vulgar to send your friends a Xeroxed letter bringing them boastfully up to date with all the doings of your family: "Daughter Avis is now chairwoman of the Surbiton Ladies' Guild and still joint chairperson with her brother Roy of my late, beloved Hector's company, Upstarts Polishing and Machine Tool Grinding Review."

Samantha Upward insists on buying cards to support a charity, the cards usually painted with someone's feet. Mrs. Definitely-Disgusting only sends cards to relations. She chooses one with "To a Very Special Daughter" for Sharon and "To a Fine Son" for Dive, and inside underlines the bits in the poem which she thinks are applicable. Sharon and Dive club together to send a "Dearest Nana" card to Mrs. Definitely-Disgusting's mother.

Eileen Weybridge thoroughly enjoys the festive season. Her house is a picture of "Yuletide holly rings, whitewashed twigs and tinsel and ribbon decorations" taken from *Good Housekeeping.*

She has also followed to the letter an article in the *Barclaycard News Magazine* on organising your Christmas menu, which starts off: "With a little planning, Xmas can be a holiday for all the family," and continues with instructions about embarking on a mammoth shopping spree with your Barclaycard, getting the family "to clean the cutlery in November," trying a "portion of Minty Ice Cream for dinner on 3rd of December, just to test it's acceptable for Christmas night" and making kedgeree on the 5th of December to go in the freezer for breakfast on Christmas eve. Howard Weybridge is delegated to cope with the booze bill with *his* Barclaycard, and even the turkey is cooked in advance and sliced ready for re-heating.

Jen Teale comes into her own at Christmas. Everyone com-

ments on the daintiness of her gifts. She knows that how you wrap
a parcel is so much more important than what's in it. Even boxes
of chocolates are now smothered in brightly coloured gift wrap (as
she calls wrapping paper) and topped with tasteful concentric circles of coloured ribbon, just like Harrods. She also "bakes all the
Christmas Fayre" without the aid of a deep-freeze, and stays looking lovely because she follows the *Woman's Own* guide for keeping
bandbox fresh over the festive season.

The Definitely-Disgustings have a real blow-out. They've contributed 50p. a week for a year to the Christmas Club to a fund
managed by some busybody, and this year Mrs. Definitely-Disgusting is personally going to see that the busybody doesn't abscond
with the lot on December 22, like last year's manager, who made
nine miles on the front of the local paper. Sharon Definitely-
Disgusting trails round Woolworths with a list which reads:

Nan: Devon Violets
Mum: Giftpack
Dad: Condor Tobacco
Dive: Brut
Auntie Dot: Thomas and Sarah's Brandied Peaches
Mr. Whiskas: Catnip Mouse
Patch: Bumper Xmas Dog Choc Drops

The whole family is glued to I.T.V. over the holiday, except
when Mr. Definitely-Disgusting, after a surfeit of turkey and all the
trimmings, snores his way like a good patriot through the Queen's
speech. Patch, having demolished the bumper Xmas Choc Drops,
the catnip mouse and a stolen turkey bone, is sick.

Chapter 18

DEATH

At last we come to Death the Leveller, who lays his icy hand on Stow-Crats and Definitely-Disgustings alike. Poets over the ages have been haunted by this equalising theme. Shakespeare wrote of golden lads and girls mingling in the dust with chimney-sweeps. Hardy wrote of the yokels William Dewy and Tranter Reuben lying in Mellstock churchyard beside the Squire and Lady Susan. But even if we are all equal in the moment of death, the living see to it that our departure is celebrated in very different ways.

Once upon a time funerals were occasions for great pomp—with long processions of carriages drawn by horses wearing floor-length ebony velvet, everyone including the children in deepest black, men and boys doffing their hats along the route and close relations going into mourning for several months. An outward and lavish display was regarded as a measure of the family's affection for the dead. But, like most fashions, it filtered down the classes until today only among the working classes, who are usually much closer to their families, and like any excuse for a party, does the tradition of the splendid funeral linger on.

Attitudes have changed too. In Victorian times, everyone accepted and talked naturally about death—with the rate of infant mortality it would have been impossible even for a child to be shielded from the subject. Sex was the great taboo, with copulation never mentioned and babies being found under gooseberry bushes. Today everyone talks about sex and birth quite naturally. It is death (like class) that has become taboo. Perhaps it is because most people no longer believe in an after-life that they cannot face up to the terror of death, and so sweep everything under the carpet. In the old days, a man died surrounded by his family. The Victorian deathbed was one of the great set pieces. Today, according to Geoffrey Gorer's excellent book *Death, Grief and Mourning*, it is rare in the upper middle and professional classes for a bereaved person to be present at the death (less than one in eight, in fact).

The undertaker would pick up the body from the hospital, and none of the family would pay respects to it. In the same way, Samantha Upward or Jen Teale, even if her mother died at three o'clock in the morning, would be onto the undertaker in a flash to get the body out of the house. The Definitely-Disgustings, however, would be much more likely to be present at the death, and to visit the body if they were not. When I worked on a local paper, whenever a working-class person died I was always invited in for a cup of tea to admire the corpse lying in his coffin in the sitting-room. As cremation gets more and more popular, too, the ashes tend to be left with the undertaker, and even a grave to mourn at is disappearing. According to our local undertaker, the middle classes often prefer not to watch that poignant final moment when the coffin disappears through the doors. They specify beforehand that they don't want the coffin to move, and troop out while it's still on its platform.

Fear of expressing unhappiness is also a characteristic of the upper middles—the stiff upper-middle lip again. Geoffrey Gorer said his own sister-in-law didn't even go to her husband's funeral; she was so terrified of breaking down in front of all her friends and relations and, wishing to spare the children such a depressing experience, took them for a picnic. Yet as a bereaved person, she found herself shunned like a leper. Only if she acted as though nothing of consequence had happened was she again socially acceptable. Thus, not only death but overt suffering is taboo. Perhaps this explains the plethora of euphemisms surrounding the subject. Howard Weybridge never "dies"; he "passes away" or "passes on" or "passes over" or "goes to God" or "to his rest." Death is even described as "falling asleep." "Flowers" become "floral tributes";

even the undertaker prefers to call himself a "funeral director" and describes a burial as an "interment."

Harry Stow-Crat's father, Lord Egliston, would have had a nice end to his life. He has made everything over to Harry to avoid estate duty, and all the family have been frantically cosseting him to keep him alive the required five years. "My father's great dread was going senile," said one aristocrat, apologising for his father, who was happily exposing himself in the orangery. "But now he has, he's enjoying himself enormously."

Harry might not bother to pay for an insertion in the deaths column. If he did, it would be simple, saying where his father had died and where and at what time the funeral would be held. Gideon Upward would also put his mother's death in *The Times,* and he might add her age (Samantha certainly would, out of spite) and the fact that she was the widow of Colonel Upward. Howard Weybridge would use the *Telegraph.* Jen Teale would use the local paper, and add a sentence about "passing peacefully away" and being "the loving mother of Bryan and the devoted granny of Wayne and Christine." The Definitely-Disgustings would proba- bly throw in "a happy release" and "a special auntie to Charlene and little Terry" and a "thank you" to the doctors and district nurses concerned.

When a peer, or peeress in her own right, or a baronet dies, it is customary for letters written to members of his or her family to be addressed using the titles by which they were previously known until after the funeral. Consequently, if a friend wrote Harry a letter saying how sorry he was about Lord Egliston, he would address it to the "Hon. Harry Stow-Crat," and if *The Times* re- ported the funeral they would describe him in the same way. At the memorial service a fortnight later, he would be called "Lord Egliston."

Lord Egliston's funeral would be simple. Harry would wear a dark suit and a black tie; Caroline would dress soberly but not in black. Relations and friends might have to walk across the fields while the coffin was carried to the family church, which means Gucci shoes sinking into the cow-pats. Although it is more upper-class to be buried than cremated, it is frightfully smart to *have* to be cremated because your family tomb is so full of your ancestors going back to the year dot that there is no room for you. Lord Egliston might just squeeze into the family mausoleum. The headstone, when it was up, would bear a simple inscription: "Henry George De Vere Stow-Crat, 5th Baron Egliston, born April 12, 1905, died April 23, 1979." Harry, when his time comes, will probably have to be cremated and put in the family crypt. People would probably send flowers picked from their own gardens, with plain cards, saying "With love" or "In memory," in their own writing, not in the loopy writing of the florist. Being old-fashioned, like the working classes, they might also send wreaths. Afterwards, everyone would go back to lunch or tea, where, depending on the stuffiness of the family or on the intensity of the unhappiness, a certain amount of drink would be consumed.

When very important men die, what diplomats describe as a "working funeral" takes place, which means that heads of state from all over the world meet on neutral ground, and while pretending to admire the wreaths, the Chinese and American foreign secretaries can discuss matters of moment out of the corners of their mouths, without appearing to fraternise.

The upper middles would probably drink themselves silly at the funeral, although a few years ago this would have been frowned on. When my husband in the sixties announced that he intended to leave £200 in his will for a booze-up for his friends, his lawyer talked him out of it, saying it was in bad taste and would upset people. The same year his grandmother died, and after the funeral, recovering from the innate vulgarity of the cremation service, during which the gramophone record stuck on "Abi-abi-abi-abi-de with me," the whole family trooped home and discovered some crates of Australian Burgundy under the stairs. A rip-roaring party ensued and soon a lower-middle busybody who lived next door came bustling over to see if anything was wrong. Whereupon my father-in-law, holding a glass and seeing her coming up the path, uttered the immortal line: "Who is this intruding on our grief?"

Today, however, anything goes. Samantha Upward would probably get drunk out of guilt when her mother died. She had taken her mother in when she was widowed and bedridden, but it hadn't been a success. Having lived apart for so long, it was a terrible shock when they had to live together. The upper middles have little respect for the wisdom of age, and Samantha got very irritated when her mother gave her advice about the children or running the house, and Samantha's mother missed her friends in Bournemouth terribly. Our local undertaker also said that the better educated people are, the more matter-of-fact they are about death. They treat the undertaker like a professional and let him get on with it, not quibbling about the price. Usually only the family sends flowers; everyone else is asked to send the money to charity instead. A month later everyone gets smashed out of their minds once again at the memorial service.

When Mr. Nouveau-Richards dies of a heart attack, Mrs. Nouveau-Richards is worried about how she should arrange things. They don't report smart funerals in *The Tatler* for her to copy. She turns up at the church in deepest black with a huge picture hat and lots of make-up. All Jison's telly-stocratic friends turn up and keep a weather eye out for photographers and television cameras. The men wear light-coloured suits and cry a lot. The girls also wear deepest black and picture hats, but cry less, in case their mascara runs. Mr. Nouveau-Richards's business colleagues send wreaths, with black-edged funeral cards with "Deepest sympathy" printed on them. The flag at the Nouveau-Richards Inc. building flies at half-staff. Mrs. Nouveau-Richards insists on the undertakers wearing the full regalia of top hats, pinstripe trousers and umbrellas.

After he was buried in the cemetery (Caroline Stow-Crat calls it a "graveyard"), Mrs. Nouveau-Richards would have a splendid tomb built in strawberry roan marble and engraved with ornate sentiments about Mr. Nouveau-Richards "crossing the bar to his eternal rest" and being "the beloved father of Jason and Tracey-Diane."

The Teales would be very stingy and question the price of everything. Jen thinks death is "not very naice" and would expect the undertaker to do everything. She wouldn't want the hearse outside the house, she and Bryan would drive the Volkswagen to the funeral. After all, there's nothing to get upset about: Bryan's mother was "very elderly" and had been a "senior citizen" for a long time. There would be no sobbing at the funeral; that's what the Definitely-Disgustings do. And Bryan's mother would probably be cremated, as it's cheaper, although if she did have a grave, Jen wouldn't want the bother of tending it, so instead of earth or grass, the flat bit would be sprinkled with emerald green chips which serve the same function as plastic grass. Floral tributes would be particularly tasteful, and Bryan would probably wear a black armband on his sleeve, or a black diamond sewn on by Jen, for a few weeks afterwards.

The Definitely-Disgustings really push the boat out. "I'm going to Florrie's funeral tomorrow," I heard one working-class Yorkshire woman saying. "It should be a good do"—a sentiment that would never be admitted by the middle classes.

Mr. Definitely-Disgusting even insured for the purpose of being buried right, but, alas, with the cost of living, the policy seldom comes anywhere near covering the cost of the funeral, which means Mrs. Definitely-Disgusting is likely to be left penniless and in debt. The problem, said our local undertaker, is to stop people over-spending in a fit of over-emotionalism. Often they get quite annoyed: "Are you trying to tell me my missus doesn't deserve the best?" said one man.

One engine driver's widow, who could ill afford it, forked out for six cars and a very expensive panelled coffin. Afterwards she came and thanked the undertaker, adding that it was worth it—"Even if I have to go out scrubbing for the rest of my life to pay for it."

In the old days the streets used to be sanded to deaden the sound of the horse's hooves. And even today whole streets in the North and in Wales will show solidarity by drawing every curtain from the moment the hearse leaves the house until the funeral party returns.

The working classes still send funeral cards with poems inside and pictures of lilies and purple prayer books on the front, which are displayed on the windowsill outside drawn curtains. Often the men go out specially to buy a black suit, and often as many as six cars filled with tearful relations follow the hearse. Frightful rows ensue, too, because someone who thinks he's important enough to travel in the second car only gets a seat in the third car. Invariably, it's the forty-second cousin once removed who screams and cries the loudest because he's been on the booze since dawn.

There was a cockney gypsy funeral for a man who had married again after his first wife died. On one side of the grave lined up the first wife's family, on the other the second wife and her family, both glaring across at each other. As the coffin was lowered, the first wife's son shook his fist at the second wife, hissing: "He's gone to lie with a good woman now." Whereupon the son of the second wife nipped round the back and pushed the first wife's son into the grave and jumped on top of him. A glorious free-for-all resulted, which was only stopped by the arrival of the police.

With the floral tributes, the working classes really come into their own. Once again, because of their diffidence about expressing themselves verbally, they spell it out with flowers. On the hearse are likely to be cushions and pillows with "Mum" written across; empty chairs saying "We'll never forget you, Dad"; teddy bears or favourite dogs for the death of a child; bleeding hearts, harps with a broken string, all made entirely of flowers. Around the Elephant and Castle, people often pay tribute to a man's profession. One East Ender had a whole market stall of fruit and vegetables, with all the price tickets, made entirely of different-coloured carnations, which took six men to lift onto the hearse. A landlord is often given a glass of foaming beer made entirely of white and brown chrysanthemums, while a bookie might have a floral winning post. One East End boxer had his last fight almost to scale, with a ring, a referee and two boxers—all made of daisies. A florist told me the working classes would consider it insulting to give someone a small posy of spring flowers. If an old-age pensioner comes into the shop and you steer her towards something that looks within her price range, she still insists on buying long-stemmed "Football Mum" chrysanthemums at £1 a flower.

The party afterwards will be a terrific booze-up with crates and crates of beer and masses of stodgy food. One scrap-metal merchant even put up a marquee in his garden. Everyone gets plastered and then does song-and-dance acts.

David Storey told me of how he once went to a friend's funeral in Yorkshire. Not knowing the dead man's family, it was only after freezing beside the grave for twenty minutes that he discovered, on asking one of the mourners, that he was attending the wrong funeral. "Never mind, lad," comforted the mourner. "They'll all be meeting up at the Black Bull same as us afterwards."

After the funeral Sharon and Dive would club together to buy Mr. Definitely-Disgusting a headstone, perhaps inscribed with the words: "Have a good sleep, Dad." They would also put another entry in the local paper thanking everyone for their condolences and floral tributes. A year later, it would be considered very remiss if an "In Memoriam" notice didn't appear in the same paper.

> God took Dad home,
> It was his will,
> But why that way,

We wonder still. Always in our thoughts, fondest love, Doris, Dive, Sharon, Auntie Edna and little Terry.

Quite often there will be additional notices from several other members of the family. Because the working classes tend not to take part in local government and parish affairs, birth, marriage and death, or when one of them gets caught nicking a television, are the only times they get their names in the paper. Howard Weybridge might put an "In Memoriam" to Eileen, or to his brother who was killed in Korea, in the *Daily Telegraph*.

But finally our heroes get to the Other Side. How will they fare in the after-life?

Harry Stow-Crat is thoroughly enjoying himself. He is just expressing delight at the prospect of seeing Snipe and Nanny again when suddenly a beautiful angel flaps past, and Harry can't decide whether to take a pot at her or ask her out to luncheon. Jen Teale is speechless with admiration at the whiteness of the angel's robe and wonders if she used a bio wash. Mr. Nouveau-Richards, having examined the burglar alarm on the pearly gates, is boasting to God how much better his own gates on earth were wired up against intruders, and how none of the pearls are as big as the ones he gave Mrs. Nouveau-Richards for their silver wedding. Jison Richards is just about to ask Jesus for an in-depth interview. Howard Wey-bridge is enjoying a round of golf with the Holy Ghost, and Mr. Definitely-Disgusting is having a lovely time playing "Roll Out the Barrel" on the harp and filling in his football coupon for the match against Limbo this afternoon.

Only Samantha Upward looks perturbed. Who would have thought, she keeps murmuring to herself disconsolately, that God would say "Pleased to meet you" when we arrived?

References

Introduction

Montaigne, *Essais*, II, 12.
Classification of Occupations, H.M.S.O., 1970.
Nancy Mitford, *The Pursuit of Love*, Popular Library, 1975.
Jonathan Gathorne-Hardy, *The Rise and Fall of the British Nanny*, published in the U.S. as *The Unnatural History of the Nanny*, Dial, 1973.

Chapter 1

Brian Masters, *The Dukes*, Blond and Briggs, 1975.
Shakespeare, *Henry V*, Act V, Scene 2.
Jane Austen, *Persuasion*.
Richard Hoggart, *The Uses of Literacy*, Essential Books, 1955, and Oxford University Press, 1970.

Chapter 2

Nancy Mitford, ed., *Noblesse Oblige*, Greenwood, 1974.
Harold Acton, *Nancy Mitford*, Harper & Row, 1976.
Geoffrey Gorer, *Exploring English Character*, Criterion Books, 1955.
Colin Bell, *Middle Class Families*, Humanities Press, 1969.
Althea, *A Baby in the Family*, Dinosaur.

Chapter 3

Jonathan Gathorne-Hardy, *The Rise and Fall of the British Nanny*, published in the U.S. as *The Unnatural History of the Nanny*, Dial, 1973.

Chapter 4

Jonathan Gathorne-Hardy, *The Public School Phenomenon*, published in the U.S. as *The Old School Tie: The Phenomenon of the English Public School*, Viking, 1978.
Douglas Sutherland, *The English Gentleman*, Debrett's, published in the U.S. by Viking Press, 1978.
Anthony Sampson, *The New Anatomy of Britain*, Stein & Day, 1973.
Ann Thwaite and Ronald Hayman, eds., *My Oxford, My Cambridge*, Taplinger, 1979.

Chapter 5

Ann Thwaite and Ronald Hayman, eds., *My Oxford, My Cambridge*, Taplinger, 1979.

Chapter 6

Peter Wilmott and Michael Young, *Family and Class in a London Suburb*, Humanities Press, 1961.
Jane Austen, *Emma*.
Nancy Mitford, ed., *Noblesse Oblige*, 1974.
Harold Acton, *Nancy Mitford*, Harper & Row, 1976.
W. H. Auden, *The Dyer's Hand and Other Essays*, Random House, 1968.
John Betjeman, *Collected Poems*, John Murray, 1970.

Ralf Dahrendorf, *Class and Class Conflict in Industrial Society,* Stanford University Press, 1959.
Colin Bell, *Middle Class Families,* Humanities Press, 1969.
J. M. and R. E. Pahl, *Managers and Their Wives,* Penguin, 1972.

Chapter 7

Nancy Mitford, *Love in a Cold Climate,* Popular Library, 1975.
Richard Buckle, ed., *U and Non U Revisited,* Debrett's.
Geoffrey Gorer, *Sex and Marriage in England Today,* Nelson, 1971.
Ivan Reid, *Social Class Differences in Britain,* Humanities Press, 1977.

Chapter 8

Geoffrey Gorer, *Sex and Marriage in England Today,* Nelson, 1971.

Chapter 9

Jane Deverson and Katherine Lindsay, *Voices from the Middle Class,* Hutchinson, 1975.
Lord David Cecil, *Looking Glass Library,* published in the U.S. as *Library Looking-Glass: A Personal Anthology,* Harper & Row, 1977.
V. Sackville-West, *English Country Houses,* William Collins.
Oscar Wilde, *The Importance of Being Earnest.*
John le Carré, *Call for the Dead,* Walker & Co., 1962; Popular Library, 1978.

Chapter 10

Percy Lubbock, *Earlham,* Greenwood, 1974 (reprint of 1922 ed.).

Chapter 11

Michael Nelson, *Nobs and Snobs,* Gordon-Cremonesi, 1976.
Harold Acton, *Nancy Mitford,* Harper & Row, 1976.

Chapter 12

Richard Buckle, ed., *U and Non U Revisited,* Debrett's.
Alan S. C. Ross, ed., *What are U?,* André Deutsch, 1969.
Mrs. Gaskell, *Wives and Daughters.*
Paul Jennings and John Gorham, eds., *The English Difference,* Aurelia Enterprises, 1974.

Chapter 13

George Bernard Shaw, *Pygmalion,* Preface.
Geoffrey Gorer, *Sex and Marriage in England Today,* Humanities Press, 1971.

Chapter 14

Samuel Rogers, *Recollections of the Table-Talk of Samuel Rogers,* Folcroft, 1975 (reprint of 1887 ed.).
Hogarth, *Autobiographical Sketch,* 1748.
Frank Muir, *The Frank Muir Book,* published in the U.S. as *An Irreverent and Thoroughly Incomplete Social History of Almost Everything,* Stein & Day, 1976.

Chapter 15

J. E. M. Ruffer, *The Big Shots,* Debrett's, 1977.
Robert Lacey, *Majesty,* Harcourt Brace Jovanovich, 1977.

Chapter 17

Douglas Sutherland, *The English Gentleman*, Debrett's, published in U.S. by Viking Press, 1978.

Chapter 18

Geoffrey Gorer, *Death, Grief and Mourning*, Arno Press, 1977 (reprint of 1965 ed.).

Additional Bibliography

Robert Bocock, *Ritual in Industrial Society*, Crane-Russak, 1974.

Burke's Peerage.

Patrick Montague-Smith, *Debrett's Peerage and Baronetage*, new ed., published by Viking Press, 1979.

D. V. Glass, ed., *Social Mobility in Britain*, Free Press, 1955.

Colin Rosser and Charles Harris, *The Family and Social Change*, Routledge & Kegan Paul, 1965.

A NOTE ABOUT THE AUTHOR

Jilly Cooper's mother describes her as being upper-middle class. Her socialist aunt disagrees. Jilly lives (Horrors!) "south of the river" in London, which is not only suburbia, but frequently social death. She and her husband (who both consider themselves to have married beneath them) are veterans of publishing. Jilly has written fourteen books and has become a national institution in her newspaper columns and on radio and TV. She has two children, two mongrels (one of which is a dog of such vulgarity that even its own daughter, Cooper Dog No. 2, is ashamed to be seen out with it), and five cats (four of which are very common, and one very smart).

A NOTE ON THE TYPE

This book was set via computer-driven cathode-ray tube in Avanta, a film version of Electra, a type face designed by W. A. Dwiggins. The Electra face is a simple and readable type suitable for printing books by present-day processes. It is not based on any historical model, and hence does not echo any particular time or fashion.

Composed, printed and bound by Haddon Craftsmen, Inc.,
Scranton, Pennsylvania

Typography and binding design by Virginia Tan